ABOUT THE THEORY

The Universal Grammar of Story is the mythopoetic structure common to all story forms regardless of genre. It is based on four core pillars of storytelling rooted in the teachings and creative ideas of our literary ancestors as discovered by Hazel Denhart during many years of scholarly research. This is the 5th printing of the original book published in 2019 and remains the same except for a revised introduction and simplified table of contents.

Two supporting books and a game are also available to add to your enjoyment of this extraordinary work:
Universal Grammar of Story: The Workbook
Universal Grammar of Story: The Game Book
Universal Grammar of Story: The Complete Game

A forthcoming new series titled *Writing for the Soul of the World* will expand on the ideas of this book beginning with the first volume, *The Call to Write*.

The Universal Grammar of Story®

*An Author's Guide to
Writing for the Soul of the World*

Hazel Denhart, Ed.D.

© 2019 Hazel Denhart.
Fifth Printing with revised introduction, 2023.
Published by The Invisible Press, Seattle.

Library of Congress Control Number: 2018905998
Denhart, Hazel
Creative writing—Fiction; authorship, study and teaching, theories of, how-to, methodology, philosophy of, mythology in, hero's journey, psychology of.
Drama—Authorship, playwriting.
First edition.
Total pages: 234
Includes bibliographical references and index.
ISBN 978-1-936262-01-4 (paperback)
eBook ISBN: 978-1-936262-02-1

1. Creative Writing. 2. Fiction—authorship
PN3355-3383 Technique. Authorship
PN45-57 Literary Theory: Philosophy

Annotation: A mythopoetic, Jungian approach to creative writing integrating storytelling, mythology, depth-psychology, philosophy, society and culture, linguistics, and emotional and intuitive forms of intelligence. Challenging theories are made accessible through entertaining vignettes from the author's most unusual life. This rich, thought-provoking, practical guide will support writers as a steadfast reference across their career.

Keywords: mythopoetic writing; Jung; storytelling; mythology; depth-psychology; philosophy; sociology; linguistics; culture; fiction writing; nonfiction writing; call to write; creative writing; writing technique; writer's block; playwriting; dramatic writing; drama; screenwriting; criticism and theory; writing philosophy

All Rights Reserved. No part of this book may be reproduced in any form or by any electronic or mechanical means, including information storage and retrieval systems without permission in writing from the author, except by reviewers, who may quote brief passages in a review.

Inquiries should be addressed to:
The Invisible Press
7001 Seaview Ave NW, Ste. 160-474
Seattle, WA 98117
universalgrammar@invisiblepress.com
www.invisiblepress.com
Permissions and acknowledgments appear on pages 217-218.
5 6 7 8 9 10 I 23

DEDICATION

For Rick,

Who gave voice to the disenfranchised,

Fed thousands in famine,

And vanquished terror's mask with an enchanting smile.

You are my champion,

My Kahn

مَا شَاءَ ٱللَّهُ

CONTENTS

INTRODUCTION iii
PART ONE: THE CALL TO WRITE 1
    Chapter One: The Personal Call 5
    Chapter Two: The Social Call 11
    Chapter Three: The Mythological Call 25
    Chapter Four: Thinking in Balance 29
PART TWO: THE POWER OF LANGUAGE 43
    Chapter Five: Awakening to Language 47
    Chapter Six: Delilah's Scissors 53
PART THREE: THE CORE NARRATIVE THEORIES 63
    Chapter Seven: The Plot Situation 67
    Chapter Eight: Opposition and Conflict 71
    Chapter Nine: Story Chemistry 91
    Chapter Ten: The Structure of Timing 113
PART FOUR: THE PHILOSOPHY AND
MYTHOLOGY OF STORYTELLING 127
    Chapter Eleven: Joseph Campbell's Hero's Journey 133
    Chapter Twelve: A Moment in Heaven with Aldous Huxley 147
CONCLUSION 165
APPENDICES: CORE STORY SUMMARIES 175
    Appendix One: Summary of Oedipus the King 177
    Appendix Two: Summary of Beowulf 193
    Appendix Three: Summary of Hamlet 209
ACKNOWLEDGMENTS 217
ART SERIES ABSTRACTIONS 219
BIBLIOGRAPHY 223
INDEX 229

INTRODUCTION

In all chaos there is a cosmos, and in all disorder a secret order.
C.G. Jung, 1959

Down through a labyrinth of darkening memory, into the infinite within, we journey toward the center of our creativity with every story we set to type. Word by word we feel our way along inky black walls of fear and doubt, deep into the boundless cavern of the unconscious. There, the ancient archetypes—perfect forms of mother, father, elder—greet and enfold us into a family of existential phantoms. They beckon, we follow, into the impossible, straight through granite walls of compressed heartache, unfulfilled wishes, and fossilized tantrums. Our egos refuse. Our souls insist. And a fiery battle ensues. Out of the crackling embers rises the one we seek to guide our writing, our authentic self.

This is a book about transforming the world through characters in stories. It begins with the metamorphosis of the writer. The characters we command to transform through the story arc we design for them, turn, and watch us awaken through the telling, as if the dreamed become aware of the dreamer.

Schooled in modern life to forget what we intuitively understand, very few writers still know the ancient "grammar of storytelling." This is not the detested lessons from elementary school, but a means to transform our mistakes, glories, shame, and indignities into something noble and nurturing for the greater world. You innately know this method and philosophy of writing but have forgotten. It comes to us quite naturally in an alchemical ritual of gathering story elements, aligning them into the ancient form, infusing them with perennial wisdom, and sparking them to life with emotion, both cherished and reviled, from our personal and the collective memory. Drawing from Western history as well as my own story (childhood marriage, illiteracy, discovery of intelligence, education, striking moments of enlightenment), I guide you back to the center of your storytelling power in the service of the greater world.

Society turns to stories as if to a form of "divination" where writers cast the runes of generational struggles in hopes of revealing a better path. Powerful stories move audiences to lift the world to places never felt before or rediscover ones tragically forgotten.

The Universal Grammar of Story (*The Grammar*) is mythopoetic writing, not a genre but a method and philosophy built on four pillars: (1) story structure and logic; (2) language, how some words empower while others weaken us; (3) unconscious drives of the writer and audience; and (4) how mythology and mystical philosophy naturally move through stories.

There are simple elements within these pillars that are easy to understand and can be immediately applied such as changes made in your everyday speech to radically alter your writing. Another simple element is the basic story structure distinguishing it from a report, diary entry, or newspaper article.

Other aspects of The Grammar are more challenging, such as the choosing of a seemingly simple word—the principal adjective driving a character's arc. Other difficulties, surprises, or perhaps "shocks," come when some minor character has fooled you into thinking they are the central character, thus derailing the movement and stealing the story's energy. This is a case of "character block" and is the point where we, like August Wilson, begin arguing out loud with characters no one else can see.

This book and the series to follow titled *Writing for the Soul of the World* is your literary inheritance. Destiny calls you with this ancient knowledge to guide society along the uncharted edges of the social frontier with stories worthy of carrying wisdom from generations past to those long yet to come.

The ancients built great societies on great stories. They respected and educated their storytellers, nurturing them with the crucial resources necessary for their craft. They also recognized that humanity's intellectual growth depended on wisdom earned through the struggle to understand. In ancient Greek academies "students of grammar" were taught to weave philosophy, language, culture, and spirituality into transformational stories with the power to shape and guide their people. They recognized that all things, be they physical, psychological, or intellectual move according to the same pattern: disequilibrium—calamity—upheaval—failure—reconfiguration—evolution. Survival, real or fictional, depends on recognizing and accepting initial "failure" to be reconfigured into success.

However, in our time, failure is seen as a dead end to be avoided. Yet, no writer can avoid it because as the axiom goes, *there is no writing, only rewriting*. A good story often fails at least eight or ten times (realistically, more like 15-20) until at last the final draft emerges far grander than what we originally imagined.

In the Middle Ages, the reverence for educating storytellers sharply declined with the beginning of universities when studying grammar meant grooming the elite rather than shaping philosophers into storytellers. Being conducted in Latin, not understood outside university walls, led to suspicion that students of grammar were practicing the forces of "dark arts" and "secret doctrines." However, by the 20th century, society had accepted scientific sensibilities dismissing mysticism as absurd.

The Universal Grammar of Story brings back your "magical," "secret doctrine." Storytelling literally is magic, the art of conjuring a spell. We "spell" words to write stories that in turn hold the listener spellbound. An important part of The Grammar is choosing which words to spell out. It is also most definitely "secret," not because of any effort to keep it so rather, because it takes effort to understand it—the struggle the ancient Greeks knew we needed. In 1840, Søren Kierkegaard warned that the average westerner was no longer willing to struggle to understand and instead turned to computational devices to think for them. But writers are not average. We are in fact willing to think, to struggle.

If you crave to write, you are a writer. It's that simple. There are no prerequisites. Writing is not a choice to be made. It is a destiny to be carried out. So, claim it. There are no timelines or milestones to achieve before declaring your love of the written word. It makes no difference whether you have been writing for years to critical acclaim or if in your elder years you are just now setting your first story to the blank page. Most writers secretly live the Secret Life of Walter Mitty, daydreaming story fragments and craving to weave those wispy fantasies into fables.

After decades of teaching thousands of students, I have learned to tell a native-born writer from a nonwriter well before they scribble their first story across the page. Writers will almost always ask,

"How do I know if I really am a writer?" And "When can I call myself a writer?" Nonwriters rarely get that far. When realizing that the average story demands ten revisions, meaning a 350-page novel requires 3,500 pages of typing, nonwriters will leverage their time and talent by hiring a ghost writer to suffer in proxy. Writers, on the other hand, are willing to endure years of creative loneliness until at last the Sisyphean spell is broken and a moment of creative triumph arrives with the completion of a manuscript. Euphoria momentarily overtakes the past suffering and mercifully prepares us for that yet to come with inevitable, constant rejections, often 100 for every tepid show of interest.

In the face of suffering we keep writing because we see what the world cannot yet understand and bring to life what is desperately needed. Writers are visionaries.

Yet, at some point, you, like me and most other native-born writers, have sworn off writing forever. Again and again. But always some tantalizing glimmer of a story comes seducing and without realizing it, there we are, typing away, caught in the spell of casting spells. Nonwriters do not go through that level of suffering.

Another mark of the born writer is a compulsion to daydream. A lot. I was the kid always staring out the window at school lost in imagination. Even now, in the middle of a conversation, I suddenly realize that I don't know what the other person has said over the past four or five minutes because of my drifting away in thought. Daydreaming is the single most important characteristic of a writer. Spontaneous daydreaming is necessary and healthy, for this is how the archetypes speak to us.

Money, a career, and fame are the occasional fringe benefits of a few writers, but they are not why we write. Come wealth or poverty, fame or obscurity, sickness and in health we write because destiny unsympathetically commands us to write. Even when an insistent coquettish tale refuses to cooperate in the telling.

Your struggle is half the potential of great stories. The world's suffering is the other half.

ORIGINS OF THE UNIVERSAL GRAMMAR OF STORY

The Grammar was born out of my research for a master's thesis in 1990s. It was to be a simple analysis and comparison of Joseph Campbell's work on the hero's journey through the lens of other an-

©Rick Denhart 2018

cient and modern works on storytelling. Like an archaeologist, I dug into stacks of dusty books, slowly unearthing fragments lost to time that when pieced together revealed an ancient codex on writing. But it did not come easily.

I came into university life embarrassed of knowing nothing of Western civilization or the classics. I was a late bloomer, having not achieved literacy until I was nearly 30. Before then, I yearned to visit libraries but feared if I did someone would know I couldn't read and throw me out. Yet, I wanted to be near those books, to touch them, to smell them. Then, after literacy, what had been a barrier—being born with a profound visual perceptual disability compounded by dyslexia—revealed itself as a gift. I could see things that others with a regular education could not. Everything in education was new to me. I couldn't wait to open books and be welcomed within their worlds. I treasured books that others were using for doorstops and coffee table levelers.

As I plowed into stacks of books on philosophy, creativity, storytelling, psychiatry, and even neuroscience, the authors seemed to be talking directly to me. I conversed with Heraclitus, Aristotle, Hegel, Kierkegaard, and Jung. They directed me to dig out works buried in obscurity, like that of Edward Price who opened the first playwrighting school in the United States in the 1800s. I moved into the next century to Price's protégé Bernard Grebanier along with his contemporary (and likely mortal enemy) Lajos Egri. Then, I leaned toward the millennium and found a new wave of writing books where the heavy philosophy and demanding thought of the past gave way to the delightfully easeful reading of Syd Field's *Screenplay*, Gabriele Lusser Rico's *Writing the Natural Way*, Natalie Goldberg's *Writing Down the Bones*, and Annie Lamont's *Bird by Bird*.

But what I needed was not in the modern world and so I returned to the distant past in search of more wisdom. I sought the firmament of Confucius, the Tao Te Ching, Bhagavad Gita, and Gnostic Gospels before moving forward again into the sparkle of Spinoza, the genius of Hegel, and the sharp wit of Kierkegaard. They are woven together in these pages along with Freud, a lover of writing and of writers. He knew the medicinal value of ancient Greek stories and drew on them, along with Jung, in developing the new field of psychiatry. It was in the pages of Jung where the fragments of my life and all I had ever read fused into a new form. As if I had been digging up stones in a forgotten ancestral village that reformed by themselves into a castle.

The formation of The Grammar took place in the remote desert of New Mexico where I took refuge from the Pacific Northwest rain to write. Two years later, I returned home and defended the work before my university thesis committee. Once approved and the degree conferred, the work had to be tested in the real world.

I taught The Grammar for several years at my home university while pursuing a doctorate. Then, I took it abroad and taught it to writers from starkly different cultures. My students were in Europe, the Middle East, and Central Asia. They were young and old, capitalists and communists, Hindus, Buddhists, Jews, Christians, Muslims, and those who confessed no belief. The Grammar worked across language, culture, and genre, in fiction and nonfiction, among screenwriters, novelists, biographers, short story writers, poets, lyricists, advertising copywriters, and even musical composers.

Now, it is ready for you.

You were born a writer. But like the athlete, your native talent requires discipline, dedication, and rigor to transform ordinary performance into extraordinary achievement. The Grammar serves as your mentor, coach, and trainer. It will not be an easy journey, but it will be a meaningful and powerful one transforming your writing. Like wild, unexpected love, a story will find its writer. The infatuation that follows is highly personal and resists even the most carefully engineered rules of order. There is no right way to approach the chaos and disorder of a story's messy and disorienting arrival. But once you feel its presence, as soon as it demands to be told, there is a right way to tell it.

Destiny has called you to be found by your story.

And so it begins...

PART ONE

THE CALL TO WRITE

The greatest sources of our suffering are the lies we tell ourselves.
Elvin Semrad[1]

WE LIVE IN a world singularly obsessed with logic. Starting in kindergarten, a catechism of rationalism molds us into computational beings. Throughout our education we are driven to gather ever more information so as to fit into a society that is already severely information-overloaded. Save for the odd course in actors' training or Jungian psychology, institutional learning does little to sharpen our emotional intelligence. And completely missing from formal education is any legitimate training to advance our intuitive capacity—which is not even acknowledged to exist.

Creativity does not come through logic. It comes through intuition. Powerful emotions then cast its raw material into a vessel for unresolved anguish and shape it into artistic form. Insofar as logic enters the process it arrives last, like the engineering firm tasked with determining the structural integrity of what it has been handed by nature.

It is through intuition that three primal forces call us to write—one personal, one social, and one from the realm of myth and mystery. To recognize these forces and harness their energy we must first understand what they are and why they call us.

The *personal call* to write lures us into a story to wrestle with unfinished business in our own psychology. Here a private inner force taunts us with secrets so tightly held that not even the writer knows exactly what they are or why they have come.

Yet we are also drawn to write by a *social call* which drafts us into the archetype of artist to spin a single thread of our generation's collective dream. Millions of artists each contribute their thread to the grand tapestry of our generational struggle by depicting our society in all its shame and glory.

The *mythological call* to write beckons us through a mysterious primal drive, carrying us beyond our private selves or even our sense of the collective. It compels us to reach for the unreachable in order to discover something far greater, nobler, and more meaningful than any identity we might claim.

These three primal forces call to us from out of the deep unconscious through the daydreams of stories. Like dreams by night, they carry symbols into the conscious mind to be encountered and deciphered through the labyrinth of myth.

The next three chapters sharpen our attention to the "call to write."

---

1. In van der Kolk 2015, p. 11.

©Rick Denhart 2018

Chapter One
The Personal Call

I WILL NEVER FORGET the moment when I first realized I had exposed myself to the world through a play.

Baikal was my second play, produced by a small theatre company in Portland, Oregon. A newspaper article about a sixteen-year-old girl inspired the story.

Nestled into Portland's surrounding farm country is a tight-knit Russian Orthodox community of Old Believers. Their ancestors had left Siberia one hundred years before, outrunning religious persecution by the czar. Even over the course of a century, the community had not integrated into American culture. They remain apart, speaking and dressing like Russians in the wilds of Siberia a century before. The girl in the article had become pregnant by an outsider and was ostracized.

My play takes place in 1973, during the Cold War between the US and the USSR. My main character, Katrina, is pregnant, tossed out of her community, and unable to function in modern-day America. Driven by desperation, she jumps onto a Russian grain freighter in Portland and asks for asylum. Her simple plan becomes horrifyingly complicated when an army of outraged diplomats descends on the ship to demand her return. The Russians refuse, and a media spectacle ensues. Since the Old Believers do not register their children's births, the Americans cannot prove her citizenship. Neither can the Russians prove her asylum status. The battle for possession of Katrina becomes a symbol of the bitterness between the US and the USSR and a wrenching emotional struggle about what it means to be a Russian or an American.

I never thought this could be *my* story. I'm of largely British Isles ancestry whose linage grants me membership in the Daughters of the American Revolution. I was not from a farming family and was well into my thirties before I wrote *Baikal*.

Yet as I heard the lines spoken by the actors, I felt the whole world was hearing my story. In the postproduction audience discussion,

I fought a torrent of tears, trying to conceal the truth of my shameful past.

Baikal is a play about someone dislocated from an Old-World community who is disoriented in the contemporary world. That is very much my story. I was part of the first generation of a Kentucky clan to be born outside Appalachia. Although I lived in a city on the West Coast, the world inside my home was pure Kentucky in its faith, language, food, customs, and dynamics. Just as my Russian protagonist was kept from mingling with outsiders, I too was discouraged from making friends of non-relatives, in the tradition of my clan back east. My protagonist became pregnant, then exiled at sixteen—the same age I was when my mother's mother led me into marriage to a man in his twenties. Katrina could not read or write English. Neither could I read the marriage license that my mother signed granting permission for the matrimony. In the moment she scribbled me away, I desperately wanted someone with diplomatic authority to descend upon the small party at the county clerk's desk inside the courthouse and object to the sale of me. No one came. And no one ever would.

© *Hazel Denhart*

Hazel and Grandmother on Wedding Day 1973.

As I wrote that play, the personal call to write taunted me with symbols masking real struggles. It was a deeply private attempt to resolve the agony of that ceremony buried long ago. Recognizing the psychological block triggering *Baikal* was challenging, since that experience was too painful to confront in the naked light of conscious reality. That, of course, is why stories come to us in dreamlike images, waiting patiently for the truth behind them to be discovered.

Not long after *Baikal* was produced, I recognized a similar personal call in the work of one of my students. Tevin (a pseudonym) set out to draft a screenplay about an unsympathetic man who abandons his wife and baby for life among his street gang. Tevin had once been a teenage gang member but left that life for higher moral ground after the birth of his own son.

Tevin's screenplay *Bloodlines* (also a pseudonym) seemingly wrote itself for about twenty-five pages before dragging and ultimately collapsing by page forty (a typical progression for screenwriters). Tevin was surprised when I asked him if his own father had abandoned him for a gang. Indeed, his father had. It grieved Tevin to learn that instead of adding vitality to his story, the villain he modeled after his father weighed the story down until it ground to a standstill in a puddle of lifeless melodrama. I challenged Tevin to see the villain as *himself*.

"I would *never* abandon my son!" he screamed.

"Then you can't write this story," I replied. In defiance of my prediction Tevin returned to his script. After several weeks of struggle he stopped coming to class.

But the story would not give up on him. It stalked him day and night. Tevin languished in the paralysis of writer's block, growing ever more desperate to tell the tale that would not reveal itself. Finally, he came back to class and sheepishly asked what to do. The answer was simple: He had to identify with his father.

"I can't," he said.

"What if your old gang's rival suddenly decided to menace you?" I asked. "What if your son was in danger because of your presence in the home?"

"I'd leave," he said. "But only to protect my son."

"You are one step closer."

"No closer!" he insisted. "My father didn't leave to protect me. He left because all he cared about was himself."

"But you can conceive of leaving," I said. Tevin did not appreciate my insight, nor did he appreciate his assignment for the next week—to contemplate what would make him leave his son.

On the following Saturday, in the space of a few seconds, Tevin's writer's block abruptly vanished when he was confronted with a devastating truth about himself. He was working in his front garden with his two-year-old son at his side when a passing car backfired. Mistaking the blast for a gunshot, Tevin dove under the porch. When he came to his senses he saw his son standing alone in the yard staring at him in confusion.

"He wasn't old enough to understand," Tevin said. "But I did. I left him alone in the worst possible circumstance. Now I know why my father left. He'd rather look bad than weak and stupid." Tevin had abandoned his son for only a few seconds while his own father had abandoned him for an entire childhood. Even so, those few seconds were enough to change Tevin's writing, and his life.

Now with a compassionate eye for the villainous father in the story, Tevin returned to his screenplay which again seemed to write itself, gushing from his fingertips so fast he could hardly keep up with the words streaming into his mind.

Tevin's first attempt at the story had offered him a safe distance to pursue and slaughter his personal villain. This left him with little more than a child's angry crayon drawing rather than the commanding story that was trying to surface.

Getty Images

After his epiphany, Tevin's story transformed into an entity of its own and became fully realized, belonging now to itself rather than to the hurting inner child of its author.

Early work typically fails to get finished, published, or produced because it tends to be blindly and notoriously autobiographical with distorted villains and angelic heroes. Veteran writers look back upon their early work with humor and embarrassment, knowing that the more horrible a villain is, the more the writer has exposed a personal story.

Realistic stories, however deeply fictional and fantastical they might be, are ultimately about the pain of shattered relationships. Of course, it is not necessary, wise, or advisable to attempt to repair a destroyed or dangerous relationship in order to write a story inspired by its pain. Writing a powerfully believable story only requires the writer to understand the truth of that relationship and what the story is asking of that truth. In other words, writers need to see both sides of the story with equanimity.

The creative act asks the writer to let go of logic, receive intuition, and deeply feel emotion. In the Western world, we are so out of touch with our own emotional being that we struggle to even identify which feelings are coursing through us. The American poet Robert Bly lamented that most Westerners are "unable to distinguish or even find the words to discriminate between despair and depression, irritation and anger or between sympathy and empathy." Human emotion is too complex and varied to comprehend through logic alone. Scientific study of emotion cannot teach us how to develop our emotional intelligence to live full emotional lives, let alone orchestrate them to develop powerful characters.

It took Tevin a while to sort through his anger, grief, despair, and humiliation. Finally, he recognized through personal experience that it was *shame* he shared with his father. The melodramatic and brutally fierce villain in Tevin's early draft gave way to a realistic and worthy villain crushed beneath masked shame. This element sparked the story to life and propelled it forward.

The dream images of story beckon us to untangle impossibly dense personal struggles. Because we are social creatures those struggles will inevitably involve others. To succeed in working through our inner turmoil we must be willing to see ourselves in all the good and bad characters in our story. Doing so will bring us the gift of doubt. Through doubt we grow weary of the stale narrative we have been projecting onto the world and open our minds to something truly new. In the *Practice of Zen*, C.C. Chang writes, "The greater the doubt, the greater the awakening; the smaller the doubt, the smaller the awakening. No doubt, no awakening." [1]

Although I saw myself in Katrina, the protagonist of *Baikal*, it took years before I could see myself in the play's powerful sea captain or the communist party officer whom I had tagged as the villain. Like Katrina, these characters held secret messages for me from my own self. The captain was a metaphor for my growing power to navigate the world of literacy that I was beginning to command at the time I wrote the play. It was also a warning about how that power threatened to overwhelm me and cause me to lose my place in my clan. Likewise, the evil communist party officer reflected my family's propaganda (which had followed me everywhere and infiltrated my every thought) with the mantra that my schooling was a waste of time and resources. In those moments when I succumbed to that way of thinking, I looked into a dark, horrifying future in which I foresaw that abandoning my education could cost me my life.

We write stories to send messages to ourselves. Sometimes they take years to reach us. We also write to awaken ourselves by using fictional villains to dispel the anguish of real ones. Yet, ultimately, a story is not a dream to be kept to oneself. The story uses our personal misery in the service of something greater. At some point we must release our personal villains so that the villain in the story can serve the world by becoming fully human.

So it is that Oedipus is no more a personal tirade of Sophocles than Hamlet is a pouting rant of Shakespeare. Whether they were aware of it or not, these great writers successfully addressed the personal call once they released the characters from their own ego-centered daydream to be born into the greater consciousness of society.

---

1. Chang 1970, p. 23.

©*Rick Denhart 2018*

Chapter Two
The Social Call

JUST AS THE personal call to write led Tevin and me to work through unfinished business deep in the primeval forest of our private unconscious, so the social call draws writers to work through unfinished business roiling in the collective unconscious of their generation. The social call urges writers to join in the grand collaborative struggle against stifling social forces.

In 1974, the Jungian psychologist Rollo May wrote, "If you wish to understand the psychological and spiritual temper of any historical period, you can do no better than to look long and searchingly at its art."[1]

From the personal perspective, Tevin and I wrote two very different pieces from quite different places in society. Nevertheless, we responded in unison to the social call. In *Baikal*, my Katrina jumps onto a Russian ship to reconnect to her ancestral community. Likewise, in *Bloodlines*, Tevin's hero faces down shame to reconnect a father and son. In both works these individuals reconcile with their tribes.

The social call of our postmodern era compels artists to join in the consciousness raising of our time by expressing "union" and "reunion" in their work. Audiences will ignore writers who ignore this call. In other words, just as writers refusing the personal call will trigger writer's block, those refusing the social call will trigger "audience block."

2.1: Being Ahead of Your Time

Almost by definition, artists tend to be ahead of their time. They are the scouts who guide us along the uncharted edges of social frontiers. Because creative individuals perceive and respond to ideas that the world is not yet ready to address, their work is often a long, lonely, and painful endeavor. Few of those struggling in their craft find recognition in their lifetime. Those who do must often wait.

©Rick Denhart 2018

In the mid-1990s, I wrote a play called *Bite Your Tongue*, a comedy about an exuberant, young white English teacher from a small, isolated Oregon cowboy community. Concerned that her all-white class was missing important lessons on diversity from the wider American experience, she sets out to educate her students about the African American struggle by producing August Wilson's Pulitzer Prize-winning play *Fences* for the school's spring theatrical production. The teacher begins rehearsals with serious instruction in the formal grammar of African American Vernacular English (AAVE) using a difficult text by a respected linguist of the day. Despite their struggle to learn it, the students feel great excitement for the new language and their use of it soon spreads beyond the confines of the school. Not surprisingly, all hell breaks loose in the small community.

Bite Your Tongue is about an all-white community struggling with issues of racism that its members think they have never been complicit in. It acts as a metaphor for a nation refusing to acknowledge its responsibility for creating and maintaining the horror of racism and the reality of how much white culture is shaped by black culture. While the overt message focuses on white fear of facing guilt, the fundamental underlying message belongs to the social call.

Certainly, I knew the play was edgy at a time when it was strictly unacceptable for white Americans to speak AAVE. Even so, since it was a comedy, focused on respectfully "embracing the other," and (I hoped) would be directed by an African American, I thought the world was ready.

In her abrupt rejection of the play, the artistic director of the Portland Black Repertory Theatre said, "No black director in the country will touch this." Ashamed, I put the script away.

Twenty years later, my husband quietly submitted *Bite Your Tongue* to the Berlin International Literary Festival in Germany during a season of play performances themed on racism. It was accepted for a staged reading and performed for a packed house.

The world had changed and what had been impossible to produce two decades before, was now graciously received by Americans, both black and white, in attendance.

Where the personal call to write changes as problems come and go in the writer's life, the *social call* fixes upon a single generational dilemma. Of course, to every rule there is an exception, and we happen to live on the cusp of an exception. The decades leading up to and moving away from the turn of the millennium mark a transition between two eras. It was in this time frame that I originally tried to produce *Bite Your Tongue* which was written for the emerging postmodern era but rejected by a community still solidly in the modern era.

The Industrial Age of modernity is reaching its end but has not fully closed as the Information Age of postmodernity has arrived but not fully taken over. Each era has its own social call, so we still see a response to modernity in the work of older artists, while younger ones are well attuned to postmodernity. Within the next few decades, the call of modernity will fade away.

To better understand these eras and how to recognize the call of one or the other, we need a good old-fashioned history lesson.

2.2: A Brief Review of Modernity

Modernity began somewhere in a smear of time between the late 1700s and the mid-1800s. Coined by the French poet Charles Baudelaire in his 1864 essay, "The Painter of Modern Life," the term *modernity* has since come to embody a generationally held fear that we were losing our humanity to the machines of industry.

Before modernity we lived in the mediaeval era where we conceived of ourselves as children of Heaven favored above all things by Almighty God. Then a coup d'état in the modern age toppled God and replaced him with the logically based, mechanically sound god of science.

Modernity marked the rise of individualism, where we set ourselves apart from tribe and clan in a new light of autonomy. We separated ourselves from the strict and harsh Heavenly Father of medievalism, who once governed us as inseparable members of an earthly serfdom. Modernity gave us the power to reframe ourselves, to stand apart and make our own destinies as individuals. This, however, left us vulnerable to the new god—science—whose dox-

The Echo: an interpretation of Munch's 1893 The Scream.

ology of strict logic relentlessly and methodically transformed us into extensions of its machines.

The stripping of our humanity was carried out with the legitimization and militarization of the systematic genocide of Native Americans. That went lock step with the implementation of the federally protected, market-mechanized enslavement of Africans and generation upon generation of their American children. Both groups were regarded as valuing intuitive knowledge, which was used to cast them as belonging to the animal realm in order to dehumanize and invalidate their intellect. Once stripped of their humanity, the mistreatment of them became acceptable to the mainstream. As brutalization was codified, normalized, and automatized, the remainder of the population took little notice when the machine of modernity turned to devour them next.

We had lost our humanity and art went berserk to get it back. The social call of modernity began gently enough in the politely unsettling pages of Mary Shelly's 1818 novel *Frankenstein*. Then came the disturbing strokes of Edward Munch's 1893 painting *The Scream*, followed by the logic-destroying, melting pocket watches of Salvador Dali's 1931 *The Persistence of Memory*. Even poetry, that ancient source of comfort and repose, went crazy—not just by losing its rhyme but also abandoning punctuation and leaving letters sliding all over the page with nothing to hold them together. And in the background, at the turn of the 1900s, could be heard Scott Joplin's premonition of jazz tapping out disorienting, high energy notes of pure emotional chaos.

The more the god of science drove us logically into the jaws of machines, the harder artists embraced the avant-garde, using the weird and the bizarre to pull us back toward our intuitive and emotional senses. Franz Kafka's horrifying stories in the 1910s, depicting machines merging with bureaucracy to torture us to death, was a serious bucket of ice water in the face trying to awaken us.

Out of this milieu came a new artistic medium: film, born of the paradoxical coupling of science and art. Film could only exist in the hard logic of technology but told stories generated from the ethereal realm of emotion and intuition.

Charlie Chaplin's 1936 film *Modern Times* evoked our struggle against the cold brutality of the heartless machine with the story of a beloved little tramp who literally becomes part of a machine yet triumphs in the face of its brutality by holding onto his humanity through humor, which defies all logic.

Modernity is now giving way to the next era: Postmodernity, or the Information Age.

© *Roy Export S.A.S.*

Charlie Chaplin in Modern Times, 1936.

The changing of eras is neither smooth nor precise. Modernity came to save the individual and break the iron grip of mediaeval superstition retarding humanity's intelligence. But it left us spiritual bastards in the custody of science, who turned out to be a merciless foster parent that nearly starved our souls to death.

Fortunately, postmodernity heard our cries and came to re-gather us into some form of tribal community.

2.3: A Brief Review of Postmodernity

While the shift between any two eras is messy, we can track the transition from modernism to postmodernism with a few symbolic dates. Some argue that the beginning of the end of modernity came at 3:32 in the afternoon of July 15, 1972, in St. Louis, Missouri, with the dynamiting of the Pruitt-Igoe housing structures.[2] Designed in the twentieth-century architectural style of *brutalism*,[3] the Pruitt-Igoe project consisted of thirty stark, eleven-story concrete slab buildings of pure utilitarian design, aimed at streamlining racial segregation in the face of laws mandating integration. The buildings were so unpleasant that even when new they never attained full occupancy.

U.S. Department of Housing and Urban Development.
Pruitt-Igoe Housing Development Demolition, 1972.

Interestingly, July 15 also marks another huge historical shift in eras. On that day in 1099 European crusaders breached Jerusalem's wall and took control of the sacred city. Once inside the conquerors proceeded to slaughter tens of thousands, including the city's Christians who had maintained a faithful unbroken presence there since the days of Jesus. So massive was the killing that after three days, "Men rode in blood up to their knees and bridle reins."[4] The ghost of that moment would revisit the West a millennium later for a grim milestone in postmodernity: terrorist attacks on the World Trade Center in New York City on 9/11/2001.

Scholars commonly hold that postmodernity officially arrived at 10:45 in the evening on November 9, 1989, in Berlin, Germany, with the opening of the Berlin Wall. For America, however, the first major event in the postmodern age came with the brutal murder of thousands of innocents amid the destruction of the twin towers in New York. Remarkably, the Pruitt-Igoe buildings and the twin towers were both designed by the same architect, Minoru Yamasaki.

Regardless of where the milestone falls for the official kickoff of postmodernity, it has not yet overtaken the world as of the publication of this book. Although our foothold in modernity is fast weakening, we continue to straddle two eras. Privileging "logic" above all else and rejecting knowledge coming from emotion or intuition, constitutes the hallmark of modernity. We will know that modernity has passed when we value emotion and intuition as equally legitimate ways of understanding. Such is already beginning in medicine, where increasing numbers of doctors are advising their patients to "listen to your body."

©Rick Denhart 2018

A Blob of Time: an interpretation of Salvador Dali's The Persistence of Memory.

The legitimization of intuition is becoming ever more a part of mainstream storytelling. For example, the importance of intuition in a technological world is the center piece of the 2016 film *Sully*,[5] based on the true story of the emergency landing of a fully loaded passenger jet on New York's Hudson River. The film centers on the official inquiry into the crash in which twenty different computer simulations held that without a doubt the pilot had made an error and could have successfully landed at a nearby airport. However, in the emotionally gripping climax, postmodernity triumphs when the pilot successfully argues that "the human element," stemming from the pilot's intuition and emotion, was missing from the computer simulations. Adjusted to account for the "human factor," the computer models calculated that trying for the airport would have killed all 155 people aboard the plane and countless others on the ground in the densely-populated city. In *Sully*, we see the limit of logic and the relevance of emotion and intuition in reasoning.

While we are grateful to science-driven-logic for having pulled us out of the Dark Ages, humanity's modernist emancipation from emotional superstition came at another devastating price that we are only just beginning to recognize.

That price is the basis of Norwegian writer Henrik Ibsen's 1879 play *A Doll's House*. Ibsen introduced realism to the theatre with the story of Nora, a misunderstood housewife who runs away from her family because she no longer likes her husband. Nora's story suggested that women could see themselves as autonomous beings capable of living without their husbands or children, an idea so horrifying that censors in Germany angrily forced Ibsen to rewrite the ending. Directors attempting to produce *A Doll's House* as it was originally written faced difficulty finding actors willing to take the uncensored roles. And those theaters daring to stage the unrevised play faced protests outside their doors.[6] Ibsen's play was decades ahead of its time and one of the first major artistic pieces to advance the social call of the next phase of modernity. It sounded an alarm foreshadowing an imminent crisis on a scale unlike anything in human history: *The family system was about to collapse.*

As the standard course of affairs with any visionary work, Ibsen's play was immediately rejected. Ibsen was not condoning the disintegration of the family; rather his play was warning its audience of that danger. Society responded by silencing him in hopes the problem would go away.

The denial was catastrophic.

Since the beginning of our species as Homo sapiens some 200,000 years ago, we have lived in a tribal world consisting of extended families. In the span of a single generation our tribal life cracked and shattered. Over a period of a mere thirty years, beginning around the First World War in the 1910s, Saint Technology persuaded young adults to abandon their elderly on the farms and scatter amid little brownstone apartments near factories in the new urban hub. From there they flocked into suburban matchbox houses. Child rearing, once shared by several members of a family, was quickly consolidated into the hands of Mom and Dad, and increasingly just Mom *or* Dad—or neither. Lixin's 2009 Chinese documentary film *The Last Train Home* beautifully captures the postmodern anguish of humanity's realization that we have lost our tribe to factories.

While technology made life much easier physically, it magnified our emotional workload which exponentially increased with the loss of each extended family member. The postmodern, post-elder, nuclear family did not have the resources, time, or energy to pass onto its children what had been passed on to previous generations over hundreds, even thousands, of years.

In my own home, I experienced an extreme version of the shift. My mother had been raised in the hill country of Kentucky, in a tight-knit clan where grandparents, aunties, uncles, and cousins (second, third, and fourth) saw to her learning. Walking volumes of poetry, music, history, folk science, civics, philosophy, and religion surrounded her. The formation of her identity and intellect amounted to a community effort. My experience was radically different in a little matchbox house in the suburbs thousands of miles away from Appalachia.

My newly-modern mother tossed my father to the curb in the mistaken belief that she could raise four children on her own. Inside the house we were Kentucky in speech, diet, and manner, but gone was the living library that would have guarded against my illiteracy. Gone were the philosophers who understood the importance of quarreling as a catalyst for relationship building, and that all relationships go through natural seasons of closeness and distance.

These days American families mistake the pain of emotional distance for total loss. Individuals walk away from spouses, parents, and grandparents without understanding that deeply authentic human relationships come about only through the maturing rite of discord. When people on the farms experienced discord they had to face down and deal with tough issues, effectively reinforcing old bonds while forging new ones with the young.

But when relationships hit rough times in the postmodern home, young adults leave. It has become the norm, even an absolute expectation, for kids to grow up and leave home: often fleeing the towns, states, or even countries where they were born. Within a century of Ibsen's play, if American adult children did not leave home they were suspected of being abnormal instead of part of a healthy, intact, extended family. As a society we have lost our ability to build long-term familial bonds. Indeed, by and large we no longer even realize we need such relationships.

In the postmodern age, a plague of disorienting loneliness manifests itself in overwork and anxiety. This has triggered the social call for artists of postmodernity: *how to recover the loss of our tribes.*

©*Rick Denhart 2018*

2.4: The Wire Mesh Momma

The hallmark of postmodernity is alienation, a phenomenon perfectly illustrated in the hellish mid-twentieth century primate study conducted by psychologist and researcher Harry Harlow. In a perverted quest to understand the nature of love, Harlow separated newborn rhesus monkeys from their mothers and placed the babies alone in cages where wire-mesh "surrogates" dispensed milk from bottles protruding out of their metal "chests."

Live-in-hell-Harry, whose experiment forever casts him as an example of a man who had lost his humanity to the god of science, watched these monkeys grow into antisocial, mentally ill adults unable to bond or even interact with other monkeys. This, even though they had all the logical necessities for healthy life: water, food, a secure environment, and plentiful rest. The wire-mesh "mamma" was even warm, as was the milk. Yet these babies could not project emotional warmth of their own because they had never encountered an authentic bond and thus never learned to offer one to others.

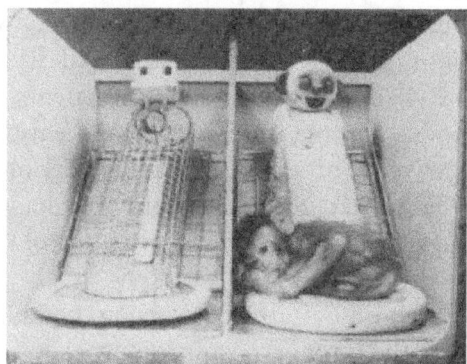

American Psychologist.
A Monkey in Harlow's Study, 1958.

Today, we have *wired relationships.* Social networking systems mimic extended families but deny us the warmth of face-to-face intergenerational interaction with its ethos-forming discipline and reassurance. These days, we prefer the text message to the phone call, and an actual visit is out of the question except with those who are highly desired.

As postmodernity spreads across the globe so does its signature phenomenon: alienation, marked by the breakup of family and clan. Elders around the world watch in bewilderment as their descendants avoid intergenerational bonding, preferring to direct their eyes toward glowing screens rather than into the eyes of other human beings.

In the west, the tradition of a family "ancestral home" is nearly extinct. What was once hallowed ground connecting the present generation to its forebears and unifying the living through a shared sense of place and identity, is now commonly reduced to the idea of a monetary "inheritance." These homes tend to be sold off quickly and the proceeds channeled to a narrow swath of descendants who have often given scant physical, emotional, or financial help to the elderly who had kept the legacy intact until now.

But we are not only losing physical ground. The ritual meaning of holiday gatherings as a sacred mechanism for family cohesion and survival is also dissipating. For instance, children born between the 1930s and the 1960s constitute the last generation who would find it unthinkable to have Thanksgiving dinner without including their grandparents.

In 2013, in the week leading up to Thanksgiving, I drove a ninety-year-old woman fifteen hundred miles across the US to attend "Grandparent's Day" at her great-grandchildren's school. The elder's granddaughter, born in the 1970s, had eagerly invited her grandmother to make the journey—with the caveat that her grandmother had to leave the day before Thanksgiving. Friends were flying in for the holiday to join the granddaughter and her family for a drive to a vacation spot in another town. The grandmother was hurt upon hearing that she was not invited for the feast. At first she chose not to make the trip at all. However, as Thanksgiving approached, two devastating losses befell her and her grieving brought about a deep need to be near her grandchildren and great-grandchildren.

To get there she had serious obstacles to overcome. For one, she insisted on driving and refused the easier route of flying. Riding in a car is not a passive act for the elderly. At the age of ninety it roughly equates to riding a bicycle at the age of twenty. Three or four hours of it is quite fatiguing. For the grandmother, the twenty-five hours of road time amounted to an excruciating marathon. She began training for the road by taking increasingly longer daily car rides with me. But she harbored doubts about doing it right up until five o'clock in the morning on launch day when she grabbed the handle of her bag with determination and said, "Let's roll."

She arrived a week later, exhausted and sore but jubilant.

Throughout the journey she held out hope that once her grandchildren saw what she had endured to reach them, they would make a place for her at the feast table. It was not to be. Although she won victory over the road, she did not win victory over postmodernity. Her tribe had so disintegrated that its oldest living member spent

Thanksgiving Day in a budget hotel room with me on the road home.

That the family of this grandmother could not make a place for her among their friends, even for the few hours of the meal, was particularly startling because the granddaughter was a Harvard educated, ordained minister of an American founding faith that is considered a stalwart of social justice. Here a person who is placed in a respected position, and who ostensibly provides moral leadership for the wider culture, affirmed a new meaning of Thanksgiving—one that by at

public domain

"Grandmother" 1926, welcomed for Thanksgiving as a baby in the arms of her mother.

least one way of looking at things is excruciatingly postmodern.

Our need for authentic human interaction includes an inherent need to be with the elderly. This primal, instinctive need makes us smile with delight as we greet an energetic "old timer" on a mountain trail or a centenarian stepping giddily into a restaurant. Just as we coo over babies, so we do for the vibrant elderly. The simple act of saying hello and shaking hands on the street provides us with a moment of comfort, while we fool ourselves into thinking the greeting was for the benefit of the elder. Yet in the postmodern age we ignore the elderly in our own families who connect us to our own vanishing past. Every day fewer remain to teach us from their fast-fading living memory about "us" in "our" tribal life. As they step steadily toward extinction, audiences seek stories of their experience, craving whatever fragments of knowledge about this vanishing tribal existence they can glean. Even the James Bond action-adventure thriller *Skyfall* uses as a centerpiece intergenerational encounters in which the spy "sons" of a maternal British Intelligence figure re-tribe, however violently.

While American television programs from the fading days of the modern era such as the popular 1990s shows *Friends* and *Seinfeld* modeled how to create "pseudo tribes," programs written after the millennium like *Arrested Development* or *Transparent* demonstrate how to survive the agony of discord and hold onto the family. Characters in the 2010s hunger so deeply for tribal experience that they endure what no character would have in the 1990s. In doing so, the characters of the 2010s discover

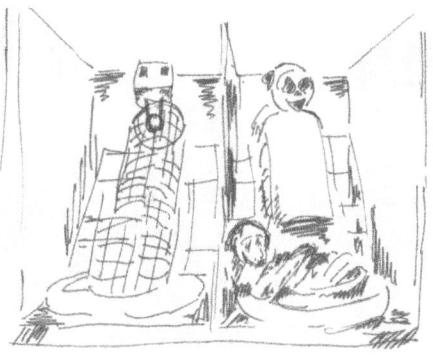
©Rick Denhart 2018

on their own what was once taught on the farm: Moving through discord requires respect, commitment, and sacrifice—the ingredients of authentic love.

My play *Baikal* responded to the social call of postmodernity with an ostracized American teenager from a Russian Old Believer colony jumping onto a Soviet freighter in search of her ancestral world. Likewise, Tevin's screenplay *Bloodlines* responded to the social call with a father and son navigating shame and loss to form again their marginal family.

While modern audiences seek stories about independent characters finding their humanity against the mechanized world, postmodern audiences by contrast turn to stories depicting intergenerational tribes struggling to hold onto their bonds.

The postmodern social call to write summons writers to grant their audience vicarious experience of tribal survival projected through an artistic creation where heroes use intergenerational wisdom to lead tribes/families through threatening discord. A story lacking this quality will feel sharply out of step in the present era.

With an understanding of the personal and social calls in place, we now turn to the more abstract and difficult *mythological call*.

---

1. May 1975, p. 53.
2. Jencks 2002.
3. Banham 1966.
4. Krey 1921, p. 266.
5. Eastwood 2016.
6. See, Ibsen and Harad 2005.
7. Mendes 2012.

Chapter Three
The Mythological Call

IKE A PUPPY wiggling into warmth at the middle of its pack, I nudged to the center of a dense crowd gathered against the biting chill in Portland's Pioneer Square for the last few moments of 1998. First, the countdown: "Three, two, one!" Then a great "Hurrah!" rattled through the square. Discordant but excited echoes of "Happy New Year!" followed. There came a pause for kisses and sweet murmurs of congratulations before a peculiar thing happened: We spontaneously stepped back to form an empty-circle stage. I stood along the "eye wall" of people waiting with expectation and excitement. But no one took the sacred space. We looked with embarrassed disappointment to one another, lingered a little longer, then closed the circle and returned to our shouts of "Happy New Year," now with weaker and hollower voices.

It would not have taken much to grant us an encounter with the intuitive aspect of ourselves that we long to feel but rarely find these days. We expected mystical grace to descend into a leader who would orchestrate the majesty of the moment. A story was needed to dispel past regrets and fill us with hope anchored in the innocence of unfolding time.

The ancient Greeks were masters of such public ritual. To attract the transformative power of stories they held festivals for their god Dionysus in a sacred theatre built in Athens just for this event. Like parishioners of the mediaeval church, Athenians came not for entertainment but as an act of worship. The plays were free of charge and all citizens were expected to attend.[1]

In today's theatre, bourgeois entertainments are driven by profit not enlightenment. We live in a time when going to a movie is considered an extravagance, to be enjoyed only after the important work of the day is finished. Not surprisingly, our mass market films appeal to escapism by stirring base excitements and sympathies, rather than appealing to reverence with grand and noble philosophies.

In our time we are experiencing philosophical as well as environ-

Ruins of the Theatre of Dionysus. *courtesy Jorge Lascar*

mental devastation. Like the evaporating Aral Sea, our tradition of generating sustaining and nourishing stories is also rapidly vanishing.

However, the modern voices of Carl Jung (1875-1961) and Joseph Campbell (1904-1987) remind us that the Ancient Greeks had something vital. We are no different in having the same inherent need for mythological encounter through veneration in drama. The work of Jung and Campbell has triggered a slow renaissance in story reverence among writers at the cusp of postmodernity. Jung, a psychiatrist whose work has touched nearly all the social disciplines, firmly believed that the plague of emotional illness endemic in modernity is an artifact of our loss of mythic encounter. Campbell, in his immensely popular 1949 book *The Hero with a Thousand Faces*, urged writers to take seriously their archetypal role of bringing the mystical into the world through great stories.

Even publishing icon Jason Epstein described a "religious-like" feeling in the act of shepherding a piece of literature from the early drafts of a writer's daydream, through the bloody red marks of an editor's pen, into the messy black ink of presses, and finally along the tidy shelves of bookstores where it falls into the hands of the world.

With the personal call, *writers* are directed to do something (like overcome bitterness). With the social call, *audiences* are directed to do something (pull the family back together). But, with the mythological call, *we are all* directed to *be* something.

Through stories the mythological call challenges us to humble our personal and social egos, gather together in collective reverence, and unite through the shared experience of something greater than ourselves. Stories are the catalyst allowing us to reframe painful memories into positive, forward-moving energy.

Like all human beings, I have turned to the transformative comfort of stories to remedy my miseries. My first deliberate use of stories as medicine began around the age of four, when my father left our home and the remaining collective began an accelerating descent into cold dark anarchy.

An early sign that order had been lost came when a mad dog entered our yard. In a panic, my older sister grabbed me off the swing and held me in front of her for a shield. As the dog lunged, I wrenched an arm free from her petrified grip and raised it to my throat. Fangs sunk into muscle and young bone. These were the days before rabies vaccines, and some time passed before we knew if I had been fatally infected or if the dog was just insane. I contemplated the possibility of death, while my sibling struggled with the newly imprinted mark of permanent guilt.

As the years passed, injuries sparked by distress mounted one upon the other, building into mountains of irreconcilable horror, guilt, and anguish that crushed us all. To comfort myself I created stories about God coming to visit me for long talks before taking me flying.

But in adulthood a child's fantasies were not enough to overcome deeply rooted anger and bitterness. Feeling abandoned by the Bible I turned to other sacred stories, pursuing a life of relative isolation to immerse myself in the holiness of the Pentateuch, Upanishads, Bhagavad Gita, Tao Te Ching, Nag Hammadi codices, and the writings of Socrates and Yogananda (it would be many years before I discovered the Qur'an). While I experienced moments of intense joy, I could not yet free myself from the chains of calcified despair.

Ironically, after years of monastic reading, fasting, and meditation, my freedom would come from watching a simple, secular story.

I had no plans to see the BBC documentary *The Race For Everest*, about Tenzing Norgay and Sir Edmund Hillary summiting the world's most infamous mountain, but my mountaineering loving husband sitting next to me was mesmerized by it. I thought I was ignoring it until the mythological call snared me with exactly the metaphor I needed. As Norgay and Hillary neared the top they were exhausted, cold, hungry, in pain, dangerously short of oxygen, and with absolutely no chance of rescue. Yet as they stepped onto the summit, they were not bitter, angry or disappointed by the brutality of the journey. Instead, they were euphoric at having survived. These climbers perceived their struggle as one of triumph over the greatest challenge of their lives. Once they realized they had reached the top, they fell into rapture. In the worst condition of their lives they were the happiest.

Their journey struck a deep, resonant chord in me. Suddenly I saw myself as a mountain climber instead of a trauma survivor. From this new perspective I looked back on my life and instead of seeing familiar horrors, I saw a magnificent path. Like Norgay and Hillary, I too had reached a summit and was euphoric. By reconceiving my suffering through the story of another I was emancipated from history and memory. From that vista came the grace to think of my relatives without bitterness.

To transform something painfully negative into anything positive requires an encounter with the mystical realm of being. While not all of us have experienced great tragedy, we all nonetheless live with some level of suffering and instinctively turn to stories for mystical encounter to help us deal with it.

Superficially, stories offer escape. More fundamentally, they provide the means for us to vicariously confront our personal demons, and in doing so transform our fears into primal joy.

To reach this apex requires us to orchestrate our differing modes of thought by developing skill with "thinking in balance."

1. Harrison 1913.

Chapter Four
Thinking in Balance

Eyes and ears are bad witnesses if the soul is without understanding. The senses show a different world to each man.
Heraclitus[1]

EVEN THOUGH EDUCATION in the Western world traffics exclusively in logic, there are points of tolerance within institutions of higher learning at the undergraduate and early graduate levels for a modicum of emotional learning, generally to accommodate the arts. But in the pursuit of research at the terminal level, there is no place for the researcher's show of emotion or intuition in any form. So it was that my path to becoming a scientist eventually brought me to a painful choice: my education or my artistic ability.

At the time, I was an established local playwright and had done some print and television journalism for the military. I was also a comic writer whose work (similar to Erma Bombeck) brought an offer for me to write a weekly kitchen-comedy column for a small-town paper. As an artist, I depended on emotion and intuition for my work. But to continue in education, to earn the prized title of "doctor" before my name, required "rewiring" my brain to a logic-only mode that would exile the artist within me.

This experience gave me a clear understanding of what happens to creativity when logic, emotion, and intuition get out of balance.

4.1: Thinking in a Logical Frame

My first full-time semester at the university ended in devastating failure. I read day and night until my eyes could no longer focus and my head ached, but I still failed to progress. I changed to part-time study but still had not earned the bachelor's degree after ten years.

Finally, a wise counselor advised me to be tested for a "learning disability." This required my taking an intelligence test. The idea frightened me. I had been treated as intellectually inferior my whole life and now faced the prospect of a test that might officially prove that. If I did not have the intelligence to learn to read before, how could I possibly possess it now? I feared being found out as a fraud and dismissed from the university.

My dread proved well founded. After a miserable eight-hour examination and a stressful week of waiting for results, I was told I had a reading IQ in the subnormal range. In days gone by, I would have been labeled "retarded" in that area. Yet in many other tested areas, including my verbal reasoning, my IQ ranked in the top one percentile and even maxed out some of the subtests' ability to measure it. The psychiatrist who reviewed the results explained that reading with my eyes blocked powerfully gifted areas of my intelligence. I was labeled "dyslexic" and given all my books in an audio format. *My intelligence began to soar.* I finished the bachelors and then completed a masters with honors, on time with my cohort.

Then, I faced another challenge when I entered the doctoral program. My developing mind would be harshly confined to one path: logic. A mentor guiding me on how to succeed in academia advised that I abandon all habits of relying on emotional or intuitive thinking. "You can be a scientist," he said, "or you can be an artist. You can't be both." He was still lamenting the death of his own inner artist for a Stanford Ph.D.

At first, I had no reservations about giving myself over to logic. My mind was starving for knowledge, and I eagerly dove into the beautiful and bountiful world of logic like a hungry pauper having just inherited a diner. Still, I held fast to the fantasy that I could also be an artist.

My grip on imaginative writing did not last long under the sledgehammer of academia where my doctoral committee mercilessly drove creativity and feeling from my work. Fearful that the kitchen comedy reflected my bygone days of ignorance, I passed on the column and gave up comedy writing altogether.

Another problem rose from a need to prove myself. My university did not yet possess the self-esteem to withstand the potential blow to its reputation by letting someone with a "learning disability" into the higher ranks of its pride. Some professors were skeptical of my accommodations, considered them cheating, and openly doubted my ability to succeed. A few peers refused to cooperate with me in group-work. And at my first oral defense, the former dean of the school publicly stated that it was his duty to keep people like me out of academia. To survive, I had to prove again and again that my intelligence was worthy of development.

I became obsessed with logic, grasping the world ever more mathematically. I categorized, ranked, and labeled everything tangible. For the intangibles I used statistics, to calculate the probability for everything from when my daughters would call to when flour would go on sale.

It worked, but it came at a price. By the end of my third year it was clear that my creative ability had withered. I could no longer cook, play music, write a single lyric, or line of dialogue. I was between worlds, unable to return to my previous life, yet seeing no prospect of a career after graduation. I had wagered my family life and artistic soul on a wild bid to prove my intelligence in a world where people were set on defeating me.

In the end, in some respects the environment of constant threat at the university turned out to be a powerful gift. By driving me to overachieve it made my research particularly strong. At the end of the five-year program, my logical mind rejoiced at my achievement, while my intuitive mind grieved that not so much as a spark of artistic creativity was left within me. Along with my ability to cook, play music, and write stories, I had also lost my sense of humor. Not even the best comedians or most popular comedies could make me laugh.

In order to regain emotional agility, I would have to mount a rescue mission in search of the artist within me. It was not a journey I relished for it meant facing down another dragon that kept my intellect in a dungeon of ignorance: emotion.

©Rick Denhart 2018

4.2: Thinking in an Emotional Frame

Of the hundreds of research articles that I devoured in graduate school, the ones on emotion would stand above the stacks to form a makeshift compass for me to find my way back to my senses. While emotion is not logic, it certainly is a form of intelligence.[2]

I was most intrigued by Lloyd Sandelands' reasoning in 1995 that all knowledge—even hard science—first comes to us as feeling. Our decision to avoid, attack, accept, like, or analyze something depends first on how we *feel* about it. In a logical frame of mind, we work very hard to deny this fundamental aspect of ourselves by accepting as valid only those ideas proven by the scientific method—a process that can take years.

By contrast, understanding something emotionally takes less than a second. In an *emotional frame of mind* we use our gut-instinct to assimilate data in a given situation. In less than one-tenth of a second we use emotion to "know" if we are going to like a stranger we have just met[3] and within a few minutes we understand whether the new person will be a future friend or foe.[4] Emotion is exponentially faster than logic but lacks reliability when driven by the ego.

I was particularly delighted to discover reports amid the research literature that dyslexics tend to have unusually strong emotional sensitivity as well as heightened receptivity in all five senses.[5] Perhaps like my verbal reasoning, my emotions were also a gift. Maybe I could increase my emotional capacity as I had increased my logical capacity. I thought of the genius of Avicenna, da Vinci, and Einstein who all attained the highest level of logic while retaining the sensitivity of artists and philosophers. Just as there exists a fallacy that people are either right-brained or left-brained (both sides are always working),[6] so I began to think my mentor had been mistaken about my needing to embrace logic at the expense of emotion.

But moving back into my feelings meant dealing with a lot of anguish I had shelved.

Before achieving literacy I spent most of my mental energy on emotional survival. From time to time that top one-percent of intelligence (suggested on the IQ test) would slip out and disquiet those family members around me whose self-esteem depended on my inferiority. They easily squelched my emerging thoughts by casting them as ignorant, wrong, or ungodly. The intensity of shame and anxiety triggered by their words felled my thoughts and paralyzed my ability to think at all.

Even after I earned the doctorate my family still wielded the capacity to close down my intellect with simple emotional attacks. To conquer this, I had to dive into a tidal wave of chaotic feeling, embrace the discomfort flooding over me, and consciously map the landscape. In quick order I saw that whenever I challenged someone's intellectual superiority, they countered by seeking moral superiority over me through a form of shame or fear warfare.

Someone's aggression against me would send adrenalin pumping through my system. It began in my legs, raced to my heart, and smothered my thoughts. As a child, this prevented me from escalating the violence by sending me into a cocoon of intellectual and emotional paralysis to wait for the ordeal to be over. As I grew older, I transferred the avoidance of fear and shame outside of my family to the wider world. When a teacher called on me in my undergraduate years, fear of revealing the dyslexia and being thrown out of school paralyzed my thinking. I could not answer even the most fundamental question. The only way to topple the tyranny of fear and shame was stay conscious in the face of it.

I chose the martial arts strategy of turning into the attack. When accused of being wrong, I apologized for the error, confessed regret, and experienced the shame without defending myself. My ego did not like this at all and soon stormed out in defiance. As I became more skilled at consciously recognizing and accepting shame, it weakened. Eventually, humility took its place.

But that did not yet solve my problem. My new sense of humility threatened the self-righteousness of others and they could still use fear to shut down my thinking.

Shame is an artifact of ego, making it easier to overcome than fear which exists for physical survival. Facing fear meant I had to triumph over misconstrued biological forces. Intellectually, for instance, I knew no one would again use me for a dog shield. But on a primal level my body still trembled at the dog-shield-holder's metaphorical acts of violence.

It took years of self-observation to recognize what was happening. Eventually, I realized that I could never dispel the strongly held emotion *but I could discipline it* by summoning deep logic to work in concert with it.

Once I brought them into balance, I could begin once again to play music, write poetry, and chef delightful food. Now what remained was to tap into the mysterious power of intuition.

4.3: Thinking in an Intuitive Frame

As I was getting a grip on literacy near the end of the 1980s, I wrote a novel. *To Walk in the Sun* is the story of a Soviet scientist, Sergey, who is close to completing a revolutionary new mining technology that will unlock Siberia's vast treasures and secure Russia's economy for another century. But he is running out of time. The imminent collapse of the Soviet Union threatens to close his research installation, and he is dying of a disease born of his experimenting. In a desperate bid to complete the project, Sergey convinces two other scientists to secretly travel with him to America to steal the last few technological components he needs. Just as they manage to slip through into the West at the Hungarian border, the Iron Curtain falls behind them. Sergey's team abandons him amid the chaos of a new world order.

©Rick Denhart 2018

I asked my Soviet Studies teacher what he thought about the premise.

"That is not even remotely realistic," he said. "The Soviet Union is not going to collapse without warning any time soon and definitely not beginning in Hungary."

Months later, newspapers around the world published photos of Hungary's prime minister with bolt cutters in hand cutting away the barbed wires of the old Soviet fence. The Soviet Union had abruptly disintegrated beginning at the Hungarian border.

In my story, the scientist comes to Seattle to steal what he needs from a research lab at the University of Washington. Then another catastrophe befalls him when a plane crashes into the terminal at Sea-Tac Airport injuring his American contact who was sipping coffee in the café where the plane landed. I wrestled with feeling this was too melodramatic, but I kept it. A week later I watched news footage of a small plane that had crashed into a café at Sea-Tac Airport.

I drafted another story, a comedy called *The Ghost of Popayan*, about a young Columbian-American man who travels to his ancestral home of Popayan to find a way to be rid of a ghost that is plaguing him. Before I finished the story, a news article appeared in the Popayan paper reporting of a ghost in the town.

Carl Jung coined the term *synchronicity* to characterize the meaningful coincidence of two or more events having no causal connection and eluding explanation by the mathematical probability of chance.[7] The idea of synchronicity came to Jung amid a series of dinner conversations he had with Albert Einstein in Zurich from 1909 to 1913.[8] These two extraordinary individuals engaged in fruitful interdisciplinary discourse through which Jung gained an understanding of Einstein's vision of time as a dimension. According to Einstein, if we could perceive the temporal dimension we would be able to see all of time at once and understand synchronicity differently. With our limited consciousness we can only experience the *movement* of time in one direction.

We might have a better understanding of what another dimension means by taking the viewpoint of Edward Abbott's characters in his 1885 novel *Flatland*. Abbott's Flatlanders are two-dimensional beings living in a two-dimensional world. Like life on a flat sheet of paper they can only see the edge of what touches the paper. If a pencil is pushed through the paper, it would appear to the Flatlanders as small, black, round graphite "when born," that becomes surrounded by bare wood growing increasingly wider as it moves toward "adulthood." In full maturity the pencil changes to a thin yellow hexagon that surrounds the wood and graphite. At old age it turns to wrinkled round metal. Finally, it becomes soft, round pink rubber just before it dies.[9] If the residents of Flatland could rise above the paper into the third-dimension, they would be able to see the entire pencil all at once instead of just the two-dimensional cross section as it moved through their world. So it is with the time dimension: if we could rise off our third-dimension and move into the time dimension we could see all of time all at once.

Jung knew that synchronicity could not be understood in a scientific world still doggedly focused on cause and effect—an idea rooted in linear time. Jung and Einstein discussed that

©*Rick Denhart 2018*

synchronicity needed to be studied by our turning away from focusing how one thing *causes* another, to look instead at the *attraction* of one thing to another in time. From Einstein, Jung came to realize that phenomena are linked to one another in ways we are not even prepared to begin to understand.

For me, synchronicity means *thinking in an intuitive frame.* I experienced many synchronistic phenomena while deep in the throes of writing. But they stopped cold when I donated my brain to science for the doctorate.

Yet another aspect of intuitive thinking continued for me: sudden insight. It would generally happen just as I was waking or sometimes while swimming. The answer to a complex problem that had been dogging me for days or weeks would become suddenly clear. This was no step-by-step syllogistic sequence, but the entire package arriving all at once and infinitely faster than I could capture in words. The existential psychologist Rollo May wrote about this phenomenon with particular regard to creative artists in his 1975 book *The Courage to Create*. May observed that sudden insight occurs most often in the transition moments between work and play. Forty years on, a few brain researchers began validating May's ideas with hard science. Yet little is empirically known about this phenomenon. The largest body of knowledge regarding it remains in the intuitive domains of the mystical traditions.

I believe sudden insight is part of the same experience people characterize as "having visions" or "epiphanies." Clearly it is another channel of dream-like thought in which the unconscious speaks to the conscious. Brain researchers tell us that a dream lasts only a few seconds, yet to the dreamer it can seem very long in unfolding and even longer translating into language to share with someone else.

Whereas logic can be shared through language, by contrast, intuitive thinking exists outside of language where it manifests only through direct experience. With language we can teach each other how to develop logic to solve complex problems but not how to develop sudden insight to do so. We cannot even adequately describe sudden insight. Aldous Huxley used the metaphor of maps to explain the difference between logical and intuitive modes of thinking. He reasoned that no amount of time spent poring over two-dimensional maps on a table can ever equate to the direct experience of traveling to that place and experiencing it first hand in the three-dimensional world.

Advancing my capacity to think in an intuitive frame required my setting aside any doubt of its existence and fully open myself to the experience. For me, it was enough that intuition allowed me to stumble onto astonishing ideas. Whether the experience was crazy or not, real or not, acceptable or not: *it worked*.

My academic and tribal troubles actually benefited my development of sudden insight by driving me to seek peace in meditation. The more skilled I became at putting my mind into the direct experience of joyful repose, the more I received intuitively derived ideas. While we cannot consciously train intuition (because it does not emanate from the conscious-willful mind), research in psychology indicates that sudden insight does come more often for those who meditate.[10] We need to make an inviting place for insight by quieting down, becoming receptive, and listening respectfully through the practice of mindful meditation.

©Rick Denhart 2018

It takes courage to openly explore intuition and emotion when we live in an era so dominated by logic. While our scientific and technological achievements will be remembered for time immemorial, our achievements in the arts will hardly compare. The magnanimity of our mediocrity in this era is held in the contemporary belief that artistic expression is still an extravagance rather than an absolute necessity.

4.4: Logical, Emotional, and Intuitive Frames on a Societal Level

The present era demands that we validate ideas through objective, scientific study. For example, our present day understanding of human emotion comes not from our experience of them, but from the *logical* study of them in the scientific field of psychology. This gives us an odd understanding of ourselves but at least we have something. When it comes to intuition we really have nothing. Because it cannot be scientifically studied or even logically grasped, intuition has largely gone unrecognized. It used to be considered some vague extension of emotion, which might explain why it is beginning to attract slight attention in psychology (albeit more cognitive) with studies in sudden insight. Regardless of whether science validates it or not we nonetheless intuitively know that intuition is as much an equal part of our tripartite system of thinking as logic and emotion.

A brief summary of the three modes of thought helps to clarify them.

Logical thinking is tidy, if not well-behaved, and respectfully observant of time. We are in a logical frame of thought in business meetings, classes, or religious services when we check the time to mark how much of the event has passed and how much is left. At these events we like to have ready guides such as agendas, syllabi, or orders of service so that we can better organize and mark the time. We see the world in terms of sequences of action.

Intuitive thought by contrast is impulsive, messy, and oblivious to the clock. We are in the intuitive realm when we lose ourselves in a story or a compelling conversation that we loathe to end. It is also the mode granting us sudden insight. Time seems meaningless where hours can pass without our knowing and where incredibly complex ideas can come to us in an instant.

The emotional mode is not particularly characterized by time. We might be keenly aware of the clock or not. What matters in this domain is how we feel about things. Knowledge comes to us instantly just as it does with sudden insight in the intuitive frame, but with value-laden emotion driving us to instantly judge it as good or bad, right or wrong.

When we hit a sweet spot and achieve a balance between the logical, emotional, and intuitive frames of mind it can feel as if our writing is happening to us—as if we are taking dictation from another realm.

When an entire civilization manages to hold these three forms of thought in balance it experiences a "golden age." Such was the case with classical Greece around the sixth century BCE, an era that produced the delightful comedy of Aristophanes, the transformative philosophy of Socrates, the mythological tragedies of Sophocles, and the irrefutable logic of Euclid's mathematics along with spectacular art and architecture. These all came bursting forth with such power that they remain part of our everyday lives even now.

The tribes of the Abrahamic world have experienced two notable golden ages. First came the Islamic Golden Age which lasted about 500 years beginning with the establishment of the House of Wisdom in Baghdad in the ninth century. There, Muslim, Jewish, and Christian scholars along with those from the advanced societies of India and China received extraordinarily high wages to build the world's largest library in pursuit of as much knowledge as possible.[11] Great books of previous golden ages (Egyptian, Greek, Indian, and Chinese) were translated into Arabic, the common language of study. Thus, after reading the ancient mathematics of Diophantus, al-Khwarizmi discovered algebra as well as making serious advances in optics and in the understanding of the nature of light. The medical arts also dramatically evolved through the development of the systematic training and licensing of physicians and in the development of surgery. Innovations in architecture altered the face of cities with stunning beauty. In the language arts came Rumi's enchanting poetry which still ranks among bestsellers today. Perhaps most significant for the present era, Ibn al-Haytham developed the scientific method which remains the principal test of scientific validity today.

The second Abrahamic golden age began to emerge just as the last vestiges of Jewish and Islamic intellectualism were vanishing from Spain.[12] From 1400 to 1700, the Renaissance spread like flood waters across Europe giving rise to such spectacular geniuses as Leonardo da Vinci in whom advanced science and high art balanced on the fulcrum of a single mind. In the seventeenth century came the calculus of Newton and Leibnitz, the philosophical wonders of Spinoza, Descartes and Hegel, and diamonds dripping from the pen of Shakespeare.

But by the middle of the 1800s, our golden era had collapsed into a black, sooty monotony, driven by the single-mindedness of profit in an industrial revolution that turned logic into its strongman. Science rose in stature while philosophy and art plummeted to the bottom of the social hierarchy. Like table legs or boxes of baking soda, literature went into mass production by the 1840s churning out thrilling pulp fiction. The genre started with the caliber of Poe but went steadily down from there.

Søren Kierkegaard (1813-1855), in his 1846 publication *The Present Age*, warned of our intellectual decline. He argued that the West had become lazy by being too logical. Instead of thinking for ourselves, Kierkegaard argued that we were using well-illustrated rules of conduct and "ready reckoners" or "calculators" to do our thinking for us. We were no longer engaging in the healthy struggle over making our own judgments. Instead, we were turning to clever thinking devices to direct our decisions. Kierkegaard saw the era as obsessed with understanding facts but without the passionate desire to pursue knowledge.

The idea that we were mechanizing our thinking was new but the notion that we failed to think for ourselves was ancient. Two thousand years before Kierkegaard, Heraclitus (535-475 BCE) warned us that too much effort went into collecting information and not enough into understanding the meaning of it.[13] Our struggle to understand the meaning of information in this era of mechanization is further clouded by the perennial human struggle to distinguish reality from illusion.

Kierkegaard was gravely concerned that we had moved into an age of advertisement, of style without substance when nothing of significance happens and yet immediate publicity of "nonevents" flourishes. He takes the example of an advertisement for an event where a man is to daringly skate over the thin ice in the middle of a lake. But in fact the man skates only close to the shore on the safe ice—yet the audience deludes itself into thinking something exciting and dangerous really did happen. So it goes today with super-hyped publicity pushing opening night ticket sales for mediocre films that audiences quickly forget.

In the early twentieth century, Carl Jung appeared on the scene to redirect our concept of stories. His revolutionary insight suggested that we are born with mythic archetypes already imprinted in our psyches and that we turn to stories seeking to follow after them.

Joseph Campbell built on Jung's work a generation later and earned widespread recognition for his monumental scholarship which aimed to guide writers back toward the conscious integration of mythology in stories. By the fin de siècle, the marketplace had watered down Campbell's work causing it to degenerate into trendy concepts peddling "helpful templates" (think Kierkegaard's handy reckoners) and generic "hero's journey" themes. Story writing was left to continue its downward spiral into moneymaking literary pabulum.

Artists, scientists, engineers, and philosophers who defy the mediocrity of rationalism will herald the coming of the next golden age of civilization. They will find the courage to put rationalism in its proper place, develop great skill with their emotions, and open our minds to the audacity of intuitive encounter.

1. Guthrie 1968, pp. 43-44, Fragment DK22B40.
2. Gardner 1983.
3. Willis and Todorov 2006.
4. Sunnafrank and Rameriz 2004.
5. Rodis, et al. 2001; West 2000; and Lafrance 1997.
6. Tokuhama-Espinosa 2010.
7. Jung 1976.
8. Jung 1973.
9. Jenson, 2004. See note in bibliography.
10. Ostafin and Kassman 2012.
11. Al Khalili 2011.
12. Some 500-years later, the Spanish government granted citizenship to the descendants of the banished Sephardic Jews. See Associated-Press 2016, and Al-Jazeera 2015.
13. Graham 2015.

©Rick Denhart 2018

PART TWO

THE POWER OF LANGUAGE

The difference between the right word and the almost right word is the difference between lightning and a lightning bug.
Mark Twain

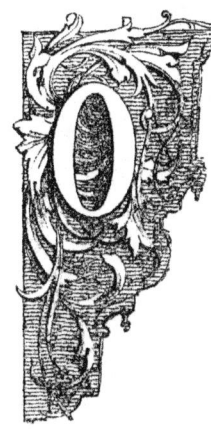LYMPIC CHAMPIONS ARE born with natural athletic talent but this potential remains unmanifested until it is transformed into specifically directed power through the ordeal of training. An athlete wins an Olympic medallion through discipline, sacrifice, and endurance. Likewise, for writers, attaining a Pulitzer Prize comes by embodying those same qualities. The writer must prepare just as the athlete: through constant vigil in all walks of life. The mastery of a given language in its written, spoken, and nonverbal forms is attained through constant practice in everyday encounters.

The next two chapters explore the nature of language and how the mindful artistry of it forms the writer's fundamental training ground. The success and longevity of our stories are tied to the language we use when taking out the trash.

Chapter Five
Awakening to Language

5.1: Written English As a Foreign Language

HAD THE UNUSUAL experience of reaching adulthood in America without literacy. Toward the end of my twenties I ventured to the threshold of education and from there took two decades to go the distance to a doctorate. Along the way I climbed word by word from the lower rungs of rural life to the lofty reaches of the academy largely through a shift in my vocabulary from mostly Anglo-Saxon to more Greek and Latin-based words.

I inadvertently mapped my journey by circling words I did not understand in my textbooks. In the margins near those circles I wrote the meaning of the word, underscored the root and noted the etymology. As my knowledge of words expanded I could more easily decipher other strange words built from the same roots. It was a long and tedious process. In the early years of my studies those notes filled the margins of nearly every page of my textbooks, disturbing relatives who thought books were too important to write in.

These scribbles were the claw marks of my climb out of ignorance leaving a record of my intellectual evolution as I struggled to keep newly learned vocabulary from slipping away.

In time I noticed that I never circled words of Anglo-Saxon origin—the everyday words of rural America. It was the Greek and Latin that I did not understand—the words of printed language, professional elites, and academic wizards. Such words felt stuffy to me and required much cracking before I could learn to read.

Eventually, I realized that the written form of English was actually a different language from the spoken. Written English sounded familiar to me but used differing vocabulary and differing rules of grammar to paste its words together.

As I struggled with the new language, a compassionate English teacher took pity on me by suggesting I audio-record my thoughts for a paper and submit it for critique before attempting to write. After listening to a few of my recordings the teacher commented that

I had "very strong insight" and advised me to write for the school newspaper. I was terrified at the prospect until assured that I could audio-record the stories and then type them out. The strategy proved a major breakthrough for me by freeing my deeper intellect from the tedium of translating thought into word into letters onto a page.

Then came a brief tangent. That same English teacher suggested I write a play for the community college's drama festival by using the same method of recording and transcribing. Nothing could have made me happier. In childhood I had spent many days tumbling across empty velvet seats in a community theatre where my mother and her fellow actors rehearsed long hours in the evenings. There, I had developed an ear for dialogue while eavesdropping at the margins of literacy.

The community college gave a full production of my play *The Frailling*. Then the school's literary journal published one of my poems. I felt as if I had achieved the height of success being recognized as a writer in three distinct areas—even though I had not yet made much headway into real-world literacy.

But my path took a dramatic downturn when I graduated from community college and transferred to the university. I struggled for years to succeed. The effort was so intensely exhausting that I frequently had to take a term off from school to rest. It would not be until my tenth year of attempting the bachelor's degree, that I would undergo testing for a "learning disability." Until then I'd been plunking along trying to decode print with my eyes using a process badly constrained by dyslexia and complicated by a visual-perceptual disability which makes the world look like a Jackson Pollock painting to me. I see a mass of shapes and colors that go unrecognized until I focus on something with sustained concentration. The experience of vision for me is like the experience of reading for fully-sighted people. It is not something one can do from the minute they open their eyes in the morning until they close them at the end of the day. Vision is so exhausting for me that I only work to make sense of what is directly in front of me and leave the rest of the world as a blob. To me, Jackson Pollock was a realist rather than an abstract impressionist.

With these two challenges learning to read was brutal. Once I managed to understand what the letters on the page were, the dyslexia prevented me from understanding what they meant. All that radically changed when I began to receive the crucial accommodation of audio-recordings of printed material.

Suddenly, my eyes gave way to my ears, which set my intelligence free.

5.2: Getting into the Conversation

One of the most profound moments of my life came with the mail. The Library of Congress sent me a large box marked "for the Blind and Physically Handicapped." Packed inside was a heavy but portable LP record player with a speaker in the lid, like a child's toy upon which I expected "Disneyland" to be printed. A thin, plastic LP record about the size of a sheet of paper came in the mail the next day. I slipped the disk onto the machine and lowered the stylus into the grooves of the spinning record. Like Spinoza lighting Europe's way out of the Dark Ages, the audio recording of the *New York Times Large Print Weekly* carried me into the contemporary world with the beautiful voices of professional actors reading me news stories by the world's best journalists. I could hardly believe that I was "reading" the *New York Times* and that I understood it. Deep in my core I believed that if I could have the *New York Times*, I could have the world! It meant that I was going to succeed in education irrespective of whatever failures I had to weather. When the recording was over I washed my tear-soaked face and played it again and again until the next disk arrived a week later.

Next came a large cassette player followed by daily deliveries of packages of cassette tapes on which entire books were recorded. I played those books night and day loading as much as I could into myself like a glutton at a smörgåsbord. I hoped somehow the words would fall into me like an intravenous drip while I slept and fill my entire being with everything I had missed in life.

After several months something frightening happened. I turned off the machine and the room fell silent but the voices kept speaking. I could not silence my mind. For months neurons had been firing down new pathways in my brain and there was no "off" switch to put the fire out. The voices chattered on incessantly.

While I was in the grocery store contemplating the wisdom of feeding a sudden hot dog craving, Hegel commented in my head about the food as thesis, my hunger as antithesis, and eating as synthesis creating a new perspective, however small, from the nourishment. Marx joined in scoffing at Hegel for using Fichte's terms and shifting the argument into one of dialectical materialism on the changing economic and moral order of capitalist meat production and the resultant impact on worker exploitation and alienation from the product of their labor. They were both quelled by the melodic voice of Carl Sandburg opening his poem *Chicago,* only to have Paulo Freire stop the recitation by pointing out that the hot dog I was reaching for was vegan. Sandburg apologized. Marx did not and continued his argument that even if it was a vegan hot dog, separating the worker from a soybean was still worker exploitation. Freire agreed but insisted that the food, whatever it was, would still provide the nutrients I needed to give me the strength to pack more knowledge into my head which was the only way to emancipate plebeians like me from the socio-economic oppression of the capitalist machine.

I was pretty sure I was going mad—and for a while I did—until I realized that the genius of these great thinkers had saturated my mind. They were not possessing me, they were becoming part of my thoughts. I was not hearing them in my head, rather I was *thinking like them*—which is the point of education.

After months of reading by listening, my writing began to improve. I was gaining fluency in the new language of written English. I was also beginning to realize that books were a slow-moving conversation between writers both past and present. The more I read, the more I wanted to write a response and join the conversation.

However, reading is not the same as writing. Just as learning to read a foreign language does not make one able to speak without practice, so reading helps with understanding but not with creative expression. Written English would remain a foreign language for me until I could write it with ease. Then came some comforting discomfort. My playwrighting teacher at the university told me that I had natural talent but needed to write about 750,000 words before it would be disciplined and developed enough for the world to value it. It was comforting to know that all I needed was practice. But what a long, lonely, painful journey getting there would be. That was the Olympic-level discipline I needed.

Whether I loved or hated the words pouring out of my mind onto the page, I had to write. I wrote into the void. I wrote into isolation. I wrote into failure. I tried to write at least as many hours a day as I read.

On the journey to the 750,000-word milestone, I took up the systematic study of language to understand it the way a cabinet-maker understands woodworking. A skilled craftsman knows the difference between maple and myrtle, whether to use the band saw or chop saw, and when to use wood pegs or brass hinges to fasten the pieces together.

At first, I failed miserably at learning the tools of my trade in my native language. For dyslexics, abstract concepts do not stick easily in the mind, making it nearly impossible for me to remember which words were adjectives, adverbs, or participles.

That all changed when I entered first year Russian. This, one of the most difficult languages of the world, turned out to be a breeze for a dyslexic to learn the parts of speech. In Russian, words jump off the page screaming their identity at the reader. Adjectives decline in consistently recognizable patterns never to be confused with adverbs or nouns. Seeing a word in Russian, I immediately knew what part of speech it was and recognized its English counterpart. In this way, I learned English grammar through my study of Russian.

5.3: Brain Waves Literature

I use the word "playwrighting" rather than "playwriting" to convey the notion that plays are "wrought," like iron from a forge. Ultimately, all words are connotative because no sterile denotative meaning escapes contamination by the macrocosm of emotional, social, and political influence surrounding any language.

This, I learned when advancing from Russian grammar to Russian literature. The words of Tolstoy, Pushkin, and Chekov set my language on fire. The vibrancy of their glowing poetry and the rhythm of their symphonic sound made English seem like two-dimensional, black and white next to the three-dimensional, full-color Russian. I began trying to infuse my own art with that energy. Although my efforts were awkward, in time little sparkles of Russian beauty came through here and there. Then, to my surprise I found this vibrancy in my own native tongue in the work of Joseph Conrad, a Polish novelist who wrote in English. I assumed this beauty must be an artifact of Slavic thought. Then, when my English reading improved enough for me to take on Shakespeare,[1] I found it there. I saw it again in Walt Whitman and then on and on into the lines of endless others. At last I had been brought to the bounty of beauty in my own language.

When I entered the Russian sphere I had been given their finest literature from which to learn. By contrast, when I began my education in English I was given simple and quite often mediocre texts to study before working my way into the challenge of masterpieces. When I finally penetrated the world of great literature in English my mind filled with the melody of literary enlightenment in two languages.

Years later, I learned that phonological processing (decoding letters into sounds) can alter the neurological firing of the brain similarly to how music does. Neuroscientists have long been interested in how music alters our brainwaves and their findings were seized upon by the music industry which wisely exploited them to sell albums geared toward consumers' particular mental needs. For example, listening to Holst's "Venus, Bringer of Peace" has been demonstrated to put the listener into an alpha-wave pattern bringing on drowsiness and sleep. Alberti's *Sonata in D for 2 Trumpets* is thought to stimulate beta waves for lifting energy and focusing on tasks. And Vaughan Williams's *Fantasia on a Theme* is marketed as a creativity stimulant. However, we do not need science to tell us that Mother's lullabies put us to sleep or that a great song can compel us off our chair and onto the dance floor, even without a partner. The lay world has known for millennia that music influences mood.

While science has not yet definitively mapped how reading great works of literature makes us better writers, we nonetheless know it to be true. I have experienced it in my own life, witnessed it in my students, and am confident that one day researchers will empirically validate this intuitive knowledge with full-color, functional magnetic resonance imaging enhanced with glowing proton echo planar spectroscopic imaging correlates.

The science is not here yet but it is coming. Before long, neuroscientists will mark the "great art" brainwave pattern that we manifest when we are exposed to profound work—and when we create it.

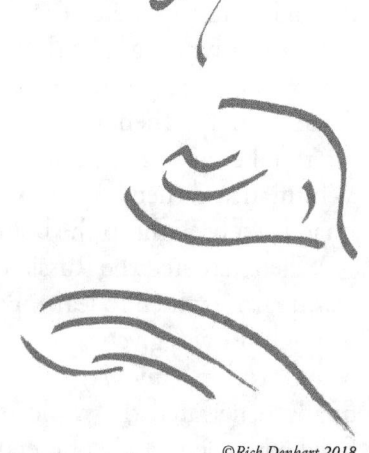

©Rick Denhart 2018

---

1. I read Tolstoy and Shakespeare in Russian before I could read either in English.

Chapter Six
Delilah's Scissors

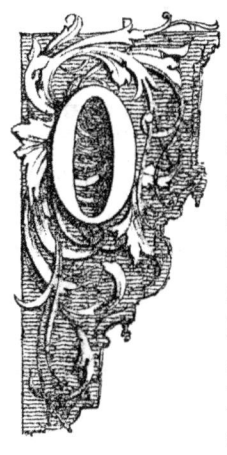

ONE MORNING, SOMETIME around the cusp of the millennium, my eighty-year-old mother decided to take out the trash while visiting me in a small Oregon mill town. At the curb she pulled the garbage barrel lid aside and found a mass of maggots wiggling across the tops of the rotting bags. In a seizure of anger she pushed the can over sending the bags tumbling onto the street. Mother, a beloved Sunday school teacher and columnist for a Baptist church, stormed back toward the house swearing loudly enough to rattle the curiosity of my neighbors along the block. Inside, she snatched up a bottle of bleach and demanded a bucket for hot water.

Cautiously, I peeled the bleach from her boney, threatening grip, gently put my arms around her and asked why bugs in a trash can were so upsetting. Mother's vicious scowl melted into a bewildered frown. After a long pause she told me the story of Christmas Eve, 1933, in the hill country of Kentucky.

She was eight years-old at the worst point in the Great Depression, in one of America's poorest regions. A generous relative had kindly invited her sharecropping family to come collect a smoked ham for the next day's feast. During the long journey home in the wagon, the fragrant meat rested on her lap and she ran her stinging-cold fingers across the sackcloth, fumbling with the tightly tied twine. Her mouth watered at the thought of putting sweet mustard on the salty meat. Sadly, upon arriving home, when the heavy cloth was pulled from the meat, she found it infested by a colony of maggots. The horrid creatures left her hungry that most important day.

The memory was still strong enough to overwhelm an elderly lady on a neighborhood street seventy years later and thousands of miles away.

The profanity that overtook her came before thought, expressing pure emotion through meaningless words. Certainly, Mother was not actually calling for the Almighty to reign down damnation on the mill-town maggots.

Profanity releases the pressure of emotions that we fail to identify or control. We hear that effect in daily traffic when an angry driver screams, "M-----f----r," at another for having been abruptly cut-off in traffic. The screamer is not seriously accusing the offender of maternal incest. This rude but common cry on American roads is code for, "I feel disrespected by you!"

Strangely, it is more acceptable in America to use unacceptable language than it is to say what we really feel with acceptable words because people in Western culture have difficulty translating strong emotion into words. If we were good at it we would not curse so much. Nor would so many of us be willing to spend more than a full day's wage for a single hour with a psychologist to figure out what we feel.

It takes effort and discipline to understand the thicket of emotions strangling our thoughts. We can take a big step in that direction by abstaining from language and paralanguage that has no direct or literal meaning. Words such as "wow," "awesome," "um," "really," and "you know," as well as all the clichés and all the profanity constitute *filler words* which we use to emphasize emotion at the expense of understanding that emotion. Filler words have a place and even poetic beauty when used rightly but they weaken us when used mindlessly.

As a practice, in place of filler words, I direct my writers to develop their emotional expertise with meaningful words. I am not seeking permanent change here. This is just an exercise to empower their writing.

Of all the filler words, profanity is arguably the most important to discipline. Commanding profanity is about *control* not propriety. Language is the only stock-in-trade writers have and command of one's own everyday communication is crucial in the pursuit of literary mastery. Taking control of profanity requires us to fully understand the emotion behind it, rather than caving into the overwhelming desire to inarticulately spew feelings all around us. Before we can understand those feelings we need to be able to recognize them.

Controlling profanity has been a clumsy venture for me. While giving birth to my children, even though the first involved forty-eight hours of labor and the second, thirty-six, I refused to utter a single forbidden word even at the urging of nurses. Contemplating the sanctity of my newborn children I made a vow not to tarnish their innocence with curse words. In their toddler years I held fast to that vow. Then they got older. When the pre-teen years came they would not listen to me. Ever. It was then that I discovered the power of profanity in interpersonal interaction. The first time a "goddammit!" burst from my mouth, they stopped fighting, dropped their jaws, dropped the coveted item they were wrestling over and *listened*. It was sheer magic. Until, with repetition the magic vanished and left me the fool.

Profanity signals communication failure, yet it has purpose and value when understood and used consciously. A look into the rumors of its past helps us understand our naughty little words better.

It is difficult to track the origins of English profanity because for centuries it almost never appeared in print. Some academics fancy the tantalizing theory that perfectly good Anglo-Saxon words began turning bad on October 14, 1066 when William the Conqueror (first known as William the Bastard) crossed the English Channel from France and defeated England's forces under King Harold at the Battle of Hastings. William is known for having brought the soft beauty of French into everyday English while at the same time seeing to its slow bastardization. Perfectly nice Old English words such as "shit," became "sh**," having turned unutterably dirty under William's influence. He created the new normal (or shall we say "Norman?") by relegating Anglo-Saxon to inferior status and casting some of it as outright disgusting. Social climbing in William's society required one to speak the "superior" language of the new king—a rule remaining with us today where in polite company we can use the Latin-based "fornicate" but not the Anglo-Saxon-based "f***." The etymology of our profanity tells of a conquered people whose language was trashed by their conquerors.

Recently, an idea has been advanced in popular culture that swearing is supposed to be "good for us." The argument extrapolates on limited medical research demonstrating that profanity seems to have an analgesic effect on pain (or at least on the pain of plunging one's hand into a bucket of ice water).[1] However, we lack research comparing the effect of what happens when a subject can authentically articulate what fuels the profanity.

Profanity projects power by impairing logic in favor of raw

emotion carried forth in meaningless words. To harness this energy and use it to our benefit we need skill in identifying and articulating the wild emotion driving it—be it our own or that of our characters.

It might take weeks or even months of awkward false starts but sooner or later writers who fast from filler language and struggle to articulate (at least to themselves privately) what they actually feel, eventually discover that the "powerful profanity" they have been putting into the mouths of characters turns out to be but a lazy try at adding excitement to a dulling story. Writers able to articulate the emotional interior of their characters develop vibrant believable characters with a distinct presence.

Junk words, like junk food, offer us a momentary jolt of excitement—but always at the expense of long-term vitality. The Russians characterize filler words more harshly—or perhaps more accurately—calling them, "слова паразиты," which translates as "parasite words."

Purging parasite words includes the goody-two-shoes substitutes for profanity. This means no "rats," "gosh," or "darn," either. Likewise follows eschewing its nonverbal/paralanguage counterparts including facial expressions, gestures, and the uses of space. In other words, I suggest my writers practice avoiding scowling, giving anybody the middle finger, or moving to another chair in a huff.

Instead, my students commit to six months without filler language while keeping a journal about the experience. The journals typically begin with humor that in time gives way to an exploration of their growing personal power, especially in regard to their strategic use of eloquent silence.

At the beginning of the filler-word fast, many of my writers use silence to squelch the profanity trying to roll off their tongues. Bluntly telling those around you what you are feeling is not the goal of this exercise. Writers need to write about what they are experiencing. In time, my students begin to notice that their change in language and paralanguage bewilders some people while altering formerly entrenched power relations with others. Silence is a marker of power and measure of status. Those at the top of the hierarchy are afforded the comfortable and unlimited use of it while subordinates feel disturbed by it and are expected to babble away, dispelling the quiet with meaningless filler words.[2]

In the Western world, people in close proximity looking into each other's eyes cannot tolerate more than three to five seconds of silence between them. In the Asian world, it extends to a generous seven to nine seconds.³ Westerners, especially subordinates, feel unbearably awkward after five seconds and will fill the silence. When the boss waits next to the mail clerk for an elevator, the mail clerk starts making insignificant comments, perhaps about the weather or some accessory the boss wears. The words lack any real significance but they do serve very specific purposes. The babbling subordinate reinforces the boss's power while the boss's reaction to the comments gives the subordinate important information about the superior's state of mind. Among my students, the journals of youngest sons invariably include stories of their eldest brothers accusing them of impudence when the younger fails to fill the silence.

So it was that my climb up the social ladder from the bottom of a family hierarchy, that in turn was situated at the bottom of a social hierarchy, required more than changing my language from country talk to academic rhetoric. I also had to develop confidence in strategically using silence.

After my students complete their six-month filler language fast, most of them return to using it but they do so deliberately and skillfully by choosing less of it to more powerful effect.

Mastery of language takes effort, sacrifice, and discipline. With it comes an incantation of magnificent words improving not just stories but also the life of the writer.

Caution should be observed in changing our use of language and paralanguage. Abstaining from curse words can lead to blunt speech wreaking havoc in one's life. The writer needs to be advancing diplomacy with such an exercise rather than deteriorating it. Coordinating this exercise with classes in interpersonal and/or nonverbal communication (or seeking an advisor for guidance) can help avoid difficulties while expanding one's growing understanding of their own communication practices.

6.1: Bonsai Language

In addition to being good storytellers, writers are also the stewards of language who shape and manage its organic change. We are the gatekeepers for what passes into the official standard, to no longer be targeted by the English teacher's red pen. Indeed, the grand Oxford English Dictionary, that official repository of the language, turns to writers for quotes to validate the inclusion of new words or new uses of existing pieces of language. Language evolves from the ground up, unofficially on the street and then officially through publication.

I witnessed such a change near the turn of the millennium. In the 1980s, as I was gaining literacy, my father, a devotee of English grammar, held a widespread mistaken belief that it was forbidden to end sentences with prepositions. He helped me remember this rule with a joke about a little boy who ends a sentence with five prepositions in a row by asking his father, "why did you bring the book, I don't like to be read to, out of, up for?" Apparently, the little boy grew up to write for *The New York Times* because by the end of the millennium a new generation of writers were ending sentences with prepositions on its front page. Of course, these writers would have been well versed in Andrew Lloyd's 1938 text on English usage which corrects this misconception and grants his wholehearted blessing for the terminal use of prepositions. The point being, that the social psyche held a rule that did not exist. Yet, many older writing teachers, themselves confused, still mark incorrect the use of a preposition to end a sentence with. And, the use of "and" to begin them. The are no rules against ending with prepositions or starting with "and" or "but." Nevertheless, these persistent nonexistent rules are fading as writers refuse to obey them.

Another change is on the horizon just now with a chorus of writers evolving the way we use pronouns. It began in the 1980s with a serious attempt to balance gender inequity. Until that time the pronoun "he" was the default. For example:

> "The hero, having reached the point of All Hope is Lost, at last witnesses the disintegration of his ego."

After about 1985, the "split pronoun" was preferred:

> "The hero, having reached the point of All Hope is Lost, at last witnesses the fall of his/her ego."

But lately, we are questioning the need for gender in pronoun use. In spoken English, the plural pronoun "they" is more frequently used regardless of subject plurality in the sentence. Ever more writers are supporting that shift. For example:

> "The hero, having reached the point of All Hope is Lost, at last witnesses the fall of their ego."

For many this shift feels awkward, and certainly grammar checkers and writing teachers will mark it incorrect. Nonetheless, it is gaining traction. While I enjoy using "they," for singular subjects, I also try to avoid pronouns altogether when possible so as to escape the awkwardness. For example:

> "The hero, having reached the point of All Hope is Lost, at last witnesses the ego's fall."

Should enough writers persist in publishing the plural "they" for singular subjects for a long enough period of time, it will become the new rule and a comfortable standard—as it is in many other languages.

The point here is that writers shape more than just stories. We have a responsibility to the care and maintenance of our language in a way that others do not.

6.2: Listening into the Deep Beginning

Learning the rules of language advances our logical skill. Gaining command of filler words and profanity advances our emotional skill. What remains is to develop our intuitive capacity.

Every language has its elders. The elders of English are Anglo-Saxon, Middle English and Elizabethan English. Listening to the elders of English and its modern-day cousins can help us advance our intuitive capacity with the language.

I challenge my writers to begin with *Beowulf* in the original Old English by passively listening to audio recordings or observing its sound waves converted to sine waves. The point is to make no effort to understand the words but to let the sound fall over them like acoustical music or snowfall. The goal is to feel the sound and melody without meaning or structure. Those approaching the language visually can embellish the sine waves with color or patterns of light. This needs to be a playful approach to the language without work or effort.

Next, is the move to Middle English with some delightful Geoffrey Chaucer or stuffy William Langland. The familiarity of these works tempts understanding but the goal is to hold onto feeling over meaning.

Then comes Elizabethan, or Early Modern English, through the bountiful compositions of William Shakespeare, Christopher Marlowe, and their contemporaries. As the words become more clear it becomes more difficult to resist understanding. Still, resistance is a must.

Next, is a turn to modern languages related to English but which the listener does not understand. Possibilities are: Frisian, Dutch, Afrikaans, Swedish, and Scotts or Irish Gaelic. Here one gets to savor the modern sound through melody, beat and rhythm without the distraction of understanding.

On the way back to modern standard English, I ask my writers to find another variety of modern English that is incomprehensible to them. For example, as a Pacific-Northwestern-American speaker of English, I cannot understand a Hebridean Scott and must rely on writing to communicate our shared language. Many varieties of English are incomprehensible to one another and finding one to enjoy can be enlightening.

There remains a few more steps before returning to standard English. Next is to listen to a story in a variety of English that is understood but rarely heard. For example, I do not often hear South African English as spoken by native speakers of Afrikaans, although it is perfectly understandable to me. Listening to Athol Fugard read by a South African Afrikaans speaker of English gives me new feeling for the rhythm of my everyday language.

If the writer is a non-native English speaker, then now is the time to return to standard English. However, native speakers have one more step; to thoughtfully revisit their home variety of the language. For example, my home language is Oregon English, where one says, "Jeet'yit?" when asking, "Did you eat yet?" or "puddem ear," for "put them here."

This exercise in shifting through the different manifestations of English is a way of calibrating the language that we are about to cast forth into a story.

Throughout my writing life, I pause every now and again to revisit the music of my language as it transforms from Old English to Modern English with a few tangential visits to neighboring forms. Doing so awakens the primal form preceding meaning.

This is the drumbeat in the forest drawing us together.

Now our passive enjoyment must turn to the heavy intellectual work of the Core Theories of Universal Grammar of Story. These dense and multifaceted ideas hold the keys to the kingdom of phenomenal writing.

A warning now: the going will not be easy. And so, here begins the Olympic training.

1. Stephens, et al. 2009.
2. Baker 1955.
3. Jaworski 1993.

©Rick Denhart 2018

PART THREE

THE CORE NARRATIVE THEORIES

OTHING EXISTS WITHOUT some kind of structure. The structure of human DNA brings us into existence and differentiates us from other things with DNA, like chimpanzees and butterflies. Stories also have a unique structure distinguishing them from other types of compositions such as recipes, technical reports, or impassioned diary entries.

Emerging writers sometimes resist lessons on structure, fearing it will stifle their creativity by forcing them into a mechanistic, paint-by-numbers formula. However, the core narrative theories are no more a stifling formula than our own genetic code. We differ from the chimpanzee and bonobo by only one-percent of our DNA,[1] and precision in story structure is just as critical. Altering the configuration may well yield an interesting artistic expression, but without the exact base elements in the right sequence, it will not be a story.

Story structure remains the same regardless of whether the tale is a simple farce consisting of a single character on a park bench or an epic saga wherein a cast of thousands blow up entire galaxies in high-tech, graphically driven, nonlinear time sequences.

The universal rhythms of movement and proportions of timing in stories have one fundamental aim; for the villain to reveal the hero's true self which is hidden behind a tightly held façade. This revelation leads to the transformation of the hero—and the villain—and it grants vicarious catharsis for the audience. Universal Grammar of Story is a metaphor for our evolution into authentic maturity.

The next four chapters take up the core narrative theories of dramatic structure and character development.

Chapter Seven reviews the ideas of French writer Georges Polti, who carries forth from the Enlightenment the startling claim that only thirty-six possible plot situations exist for all the conflicts of the world.

Chapter Eight discusses the work of Lajos Egri with his mid-twentieth-century adaptation of Heraclitus's theory of the *Unity of Opposites*, holding that all characters move toward their opposing personality—just as we do in lived reality.

Chapter Nine builds on Egri by further detailing an exciting "chemical structure" for stories developed in the late nineteenth-century by William Price and revised in the mid-twentieth-century by Bernard Grebanier.

Finally, Chapter Ten finishes the section beginning with Syd Field's theory of screenplay timing from the 1970s which reveals a grander literary theory providing a slide rule of sorts for all story forms.

The theories described in the coming chapters can be complicated, dense, and challenging for even the most seasoned writer or literary critic. They are best understood within the practical construct of stories rather than in abstraction. I have chosen five stories to illustrate them: *Oedipus, Beowulf, Hamlet, The Miracle Worker,* and *Rainman*.

Three of these stories, *Oedipus, Beowulf,* and *Hamlet,* have withstood the test of time following humanity across hundreds, even thousands of years. While most contemporary people have heard the titles, few have actually read them or seen them produced, and far fewer have studied them deeply. Because these stories are distantly removed from the context of our daily lives and are no longer easily grasped, they can feel foreign in their complexity. Nevertheless, their value remains undiminished and they are worth reclaiming. To aid the reader, simplified summaries of *Oedipus, Beowulf,* and *Hamlet,* are provided in the appendices. My aim with these summaries is to make these stories familiar and comfortable again. However, the serious writer need brave reading the full-text translations of *Oedipus* and *Beowulf* in their proper form and *Hamlet* in the original.

The remaining two stories, *The Miracle Worker* and *Rainman,* are simple and transparent films that are easily understood by watching them or reading their scripts.

Some students question why I place such simplistic, fuddy-duddy stories as *The Miracle Worker* and *Rainman* alongside near-sacred historical ones of rich complexity. I chose these two stories *because* of their simplicity and transparency. They are also modern yet already refer to bygone days. That makes them familiar enough for us to identify with yet allow us to study them with the objectivity of temporal distance. Finally, they were popular enough in their time to continue to be held in most library collections and are therefore easy to access and likely to remain so.

---

1. Wong 2014.

Chapter Seven
The Plot Situation

WE BEGIN OUR exploration of the core narrative theories with Georges Polti (1867-1946) who published *The 36 Dramatic Situations*[1] in 1921. According to Polti, the original manuscript was composed in the 1700s by Italian playwright Count Carlo Gozzi (1720-1806) who analyzed the plots of hundreds of great plays, epic poems, stories from scripture, and even real-life legal proceedings. Gozzi is said to have discovered that only thirty-six possible plots exist among all the world's stories. Polti tells us that the manuscript next went to Friedrich Schiller (1759-1805) who painstakingly scrutinized its soundness, before it traveled to Johann Wolfgang von Goethe (1749-1832) who also validated its usefulness.

I have not yet located other sources in support of Polti's provenance for the origin and evolution of "Gozzi's manuscript." However, even while its origins might remain clouded historically, this text nonetheless constitutes an exceptional contribution to literary theory and criticism. I agree with Polti that it stands as a testament to its author's fine insight. Polti's in-depth 1921 text is a must read for the serious writer. Here follows a thimble sized review of the thirty-six plot situations, dangerously simplified and reordered alphabetically.

The 36 Dramatic Situations:

1. Abduction.
2. Adultery.
3. All Ruined for Passion.
4. Ambition.
5. An Enemy Loved.
6. Bold Adventure/Enterprise.
7. Conflict with God.
8. Crime of Love.
9. Crime of Vengeance.
10. Deliverance.

11. Disaster.
12. Discovering Dishonor of a Loved One.
13. Fatal Misjudgment.
14. Hatred of a Relative.
15. Humble Appeal for Aid.
16. Killing of Unrecognized Relative.
17. Loss of Loved Ones.
18. Madness.
19. Mistaken Jealousy.
20. Mistaken Judgment.
21. Murderous Adultery.
22. Needful Sacrifice of a Loved One.
23. Object to be Gained.
24. Obstacles to Love.
25. Pursuit.
26. Recovery of a Lost One.
27. Remorse.
28. Revolt.
29. Rivalry between Superior and Inferior.
30. Rivalry of a Relative.
31. Self-sacrifice for a Relative.
32. Self-sacrifice for an Ideal.
33. Solve the Riddle.
34. Unintended Crimes of Love.
35. Vengeance for Family.
36. Victim of Misfortune.

These thirty-six plot situations are not of themselves plots rather, they provide the structure for the world that we as writers are about to conjure.

Some plot situations such as Abduction, Deliverance, Loss of a Loved One, or Disaster, are imposed on the hero by outside forces. Others, such as Conflict with God, Remorse, Crime of Vengeance, Fatal Misjudgment, or Hatred of a Relative, arise from within the ego of the hero.

Regardless of how the plot situation comes into being, it must be strong enough to hold the hero and antihero together while driving them relentlessly into one another until their egos shatter. This happens quite naturally when perfect opposites are forced into unity.

When two opposing characters are placed into one of these situations, the grand plot of the drama will materialize. For example, when a ruthless warrior is juxtaposed with a coward in plot situation thirty-five—Vengeance for Family—we have *Hamlet*. When a scheming manipulator is juxtaposed with someone pathologically honest who cannot be manipulated, and then placed into plot situation twenty-six—Recovery of a Lost One—we have the film *Rainman*. When a disciplinarian meets a badly spoiled, unruly child in plot situation ten—Deliverance—we have the play *The Miracle Worker*. And when a pompous warrior pledges to save a dignified king in plot situation thirteen—Fatal Misjudgment—we have the ancient Anglo-Saxon saga *Beowulf*.

The plot sparks to life when opposition and conflict settle into one of these plot situations.

©*Rick Denhart 2018*

---

1. Available free in the public domain at:
   https://archive.org/details/thirtysixdramati00polt.

Chapter Eight
Opposition and Conflict

The sad truth is that man's real life consists of a complex of inexorable opposites—day and night, birth and death, happiness and misery, good and evil. We are not even sure that one will prevail over the other, that good will overcome evil, or joy defeat pain. Life is a battleground. It always has been, and always will be; and if it were not so, existence would come to an end.

Carl Jung[1]

BOTH OF MY early plays, *Baikal* and *Bite Your Tongue,* stopped writing themselves at the end of the first act. Though I knew they were destined to be full-length plays not one new word would stick to their pages. Eventually, I acquiesced to their brutal apathy and sent them into production as one-acts. Yet, they kept hounding me to finish them even as they refused to cooperate. I finally gave up, tossed them into a box and onto a shelf in the attic to gather dust. As the dust-fall grew higher, those plays continued to haunt me.

One night, an ancient Greek philosopher bravely crossed a distance of twenty-five centuries to explain the problem. I had fallen asleep with an audio recording of a philosophy textbook playing. The book unraveled itself into a dream in which I was trying to claw my way out of a paper plaster sarcophagus built of pulped textbooks, research journals, Shakespearean plays, and the *New York Times*. I remember hearing a muffled man's voice emanating from the gooey mess. Then, quite suddenly, Heraclitus spoke with crystal clarity that some: "men are unaware of what they do when they are awake just as they are forgetful of what they do when they are asleep."[2] Most people, he argued, sleepwalk through life—an idea I awakened to while sleeping. Heraclitus would have liked that.

I fumbled in the dark for the "stop" switch on the Library of

Congress book reader and opened my eyes. It was a rare night in western Oregon when the full moon coincided with a clear sky. Moonlight glistened on the stationary wheels of my mammoth cassette player, but even in the good light I confused the multi-colored keys with thick braille letters and selected the fast-forward instead of rewind. "Many do not understand such things as they encounter, nor do they learn by their experience, but they think they do."[3] Pause. Rewind. Fast-forward. Knock the player off the nightstand. Cassette falls out. I jam it back in, wrong side up. "Present, they are absent."[4] What came next was an intellectual stretch for two o'clock in the morning.

According to Heraclitus, people need to struggle intellectually in order to deeply understand. This is the reason, he argues, that Heaven presents messages obliquely: "The Lord whose oracle is at Delphi neither reveals nor conceals, but gives a sign."[5] And so, Heraclitus also imbedded his brilliant ideas in clues, puzzles, and riddles demanding hard thought to crack open.

He was particularly fond of paradoxes. His most famous argument reasons that we cannot step into the same river twice. Upon stepping in the second time, the water swirling around our ankles is entirely different. Heraclitus observed that a river stays the same only because it constantly changes. And so it goes for all of life—Heraclitus argued that everything in existence is in flux and that *nothing stagnates*.

©Rick Denhart 2018

Crying for the Soul of the World: an Interpretation of Moreelse's Heraclitus.

That was a bit much for Plato and Aristotle who commented that, "Heraclitus violates the principles of logic and makes knowledge impossible."[6] To them he was illogical, incoherent and extreme. Certainly, "Heraclitus made every effort to break out of the mold of contemporary thought."[7] Indeed, he was a visionary who rattled the settled sensibilities of the day.

He rattles them still.

It is wonderfully ironic that Heraclitus was credited with coining the term *logos,* which he used to denote *the word* or *the ordering of the world.* We derive our term *logic* from logos but Heraclitus applied logos to quintessentially non-logical ideas. He could not have enjoyed the beauty of his illogical logic because formal logic had not yet been conceived of in his lifetime. Yet he was not aiming his message to the likes of logical thinkers whom he would have accused of sleepwalking anyway. His thoughts were aimed at awakened souls capable of scaling the barricades of logic to reach the wisdom beyond.

After establishing his argument of flux, Heraclitus turned his attention to the *direction* of the change. According to his brilliant theory the *Unity of Opposites,* everything moves toward its opposite in time. Heraclitus explains,

> As the same thing in us are living and dead, waking and sleeping, young and old. For these things having changed around are those, and those in turn having changed around are these.[8]

Heraclitus believed that everything encounters opposition and that opposition is the very basis, the vital energy, of life itself. In the ancient world, opposition was seen as a resource to be harnessed rather than a problem to be resolved. The ancient Greeks believed that the highest form of knowledge came from the clash of opposing speakers where one speaker sets forth an idea that is negated by the "anti-idea" of another.[9] Out of the clash of thesis and antithesis comes an entirely new view of an issue in the synthesis of the two distinct viewpoints.[10] The term *dialectics* derives from the different "dialects" spoken by debaters coming from across the ancient world to debate. Dialectics has since come to mean the transformation of thought that happens when we see an issue through the perspective of another.

I paused the book reader as it dawned on me, in the still of the night, why I could not finish those two plays: They had no dialectic. Heraclitus reasoned that there is no life without "life-giving struggle—" which my characters lacked.

I hit the play button again. Heraclitus declared, "War is the father of all."[11]

He was right. We are what we are today through the cumulative impact of relentless life-and-death struggle since the beginning of time. Be it petty or catastrophic, everything with DNA must take the life of something else with DNA and merge the taken life into its own for food. There is no getting out of it no matter how hard we try. Even the pious monk who in his spiritual quest refuses to take plant or animal life for sustenance, dies himself from starvation and is thus guilty of killing.

To this, Heraclitus added that the more we struggle, the more we become like that which we struggle against. Like quicksand pulling us down we merge into the very thing we oppose. All things move toward their opposites in time: day becomes night, sleeping becomes waking, wet becomes dry, hot becomes cold, and young becomes old. Heraclitus saw life as existing through a series of transformative struggles without which life would be impossible and through which we evolve to ever more extraordinary life.

Heraclitus upped the ante on his radical reputation by further suggesting that things appearing to be opposites are actually the same. For example, he argued that *good* and *evil* exist as different points along the same continuum. He used the term *strife* (ἔρις) to describe situations that we perceive as out of balance or in opposition to us, and the term *justice* (δίκη) to describe the very same thing when we view it as in balance or in harmony with us. For Heraclitus, justice comes only through opposition which causes us to shift the balance on the continuum of strife back to what we perceive as harmony.[12] But because the correction is never evenly distributed, what is "just" for one person will not be so for another. Victory in battle does not yield justice from the perspective of the losing side.

Perhaps because his argument appeals to intuition more than it does to reason, my sleepy brain that night succeeded in its struggle to understand Heraclitus. As I lay in the moonlight, I began to visualize how I could finish those two plays. The solution was remarkably easy: the characters must become like each other. In *Baikal,* my dedicated, savvy, Soviet sea captain would need to transform to become like his exact opposite: a rebellious, backward, runaway Russian American farm girl. In *Bite Your Tongue,* a conservative, controlling, small town European American principal would become like a flamboyant, sophisticated, urban, African American transgender showgirl.

Though excited, I yawned. After all, it was the middle of the night. I set the book reader with a new cassette and the next philosopher began. I drifted into the Dark Ages of dream with a Heraclitan lullaby in my mind.

When I woke, the moon had become the sun, it was time for coffee, and the book reader was advancing Georg Wilhelm Friedrich Hegel (1770-1831), who was in turn advancing Heraclitus' Unity of Opposites:

> Contradiction is the root of all movement and vitality. It is only in so far as something has a contradiction within it that it moves, has an urge and activity…Something is alive, therefore, only to the extent that it contains contradiction within itself.[13]

Heraclitus used the Unity of Opposites to examine the natural world as well as that of human affairs. Hegel took the idea a step further by applying it to abstract notions such as decision-making.

Hegel argued that the moment a decision is made, forces are set in motion to counter it. A decision is an attempt to cast our will into stable form through an idea. In a world where nothing remains constant, not even thoughts, the idea soon becomes limiting and in need of revision. As one revision leads to another, eventually we no longer recognize why we settled on the original idea without having better thought it through. Down the road we find ourselves in the complete opposite frame of mind. The point, according to Hegel, is not to value the stability of an idea but to value its evolution in the process of life. In other words, it is the *movement* of an idea along a continuum that matters rather than the fixed idea itself.

Everything contains its own contradiction, and the very existence of this contradiction is the essence of life.

In the mid-twentieth century, Lajos Egri stepped into the stream of thought flowing from Heraclitus to Hegel and directed it to storytelling.

8.1: Egri Takes Heraclitus and Hegel to the Theatre

In 1942, Lajos Egri (1888–1967) published *How to Write a Play* while he was teaching at his influential playwriting school in New York. Four years later, he revised the book and published it again as *The Art of Dramatic Writing*. Over time, the second publication grew into a sensation among writers of all genres and remains a bestseller today.[14]

The core of Egri's work revolves around *character transformation* which he considered the defining feature distinguishing stories from other forms of prose. While Egri does not follow the thread of his ideas the full distance back to the great philosopher, he nonetheless fervently advances Heraclitus' thesis that "war is the father of all."

Egri demonstrates how any writer can master the art of bringing life-giving warfare into a story. All one needs do is juxtapose two perfectly opposite personalities together with no means of escape. The key here is *no means of escape*. The situation must be such that characters whose opposing personalities might not otherwise collide are placed into an intolerable situation where conflict is inevitable.

©*Rick Denhart 2018*
Lajos Egri

Let us pause for a moment to discuss a few terms. The *hero* of a story is known by many labels including the protagonist, primary character, principal character, and main character. Conversely, the *antihero* is synonymous with the villain, antagonist, and secondary character. For this part of the discussion of the Unity of Opposites, we will narrow the use to the terms *hero* and *antihero*. The term *villain* connotes "bad," which is not relevant to this moment in the discussion. We are concerned only with the forward movement of the hero which the antihero sets out to block at all costs. Antiheroes might fall anywhere along a continuum from frighteningly evil to blissfully innocent, even angelic.

For example, in Neil Simon's lighthearted comedy play *The Odd Couple*, the antihero is Felix, a polite and tidy man who moves in with his best friend Oscar, the hero, who is a slob. They had always gotten along splendidly until being forced to live together where Felix's neurotic cleaning overwhelmingly destroys Oscar's sense of peace in comfortable chaos. The relationship between these otherwise mundane characters so powerfully embodies the Unity of Opposites that the spark between them generated a hit play that became a hit movie and then a long running television series.

In *Oedipus*, the Unity of Opposites expresses itself in the relationship between a narcissistic king and his humble brother-in-law with whom he quietly shares equal rule. In *Beowulf*, it expresses itself in the relationship between a bombastic, egotistical strongman and a wise and dignified king who needs his help. In

Hamlet, we see the Unity of Opposites in the antagonism between a coward and a ruthless killer. In *The Miracle Worker*, it comes when a badly spoiled child is forced into the care of a strict disciplinarian. And in *Rainman*, we see the Unity of Opposites in the relationship between a manipulative businessman and his gentle, un-manipulatable brother.

As the first step in creating a Unity of Opposites between two characters, Egri directs us to juxtapose opposing adjectives. Table One offers examples of some opposing adjectives with the potential for a strong Unity of Opposites.

Table 1: Examples of Pairs of Adjectives for Unity of Opposites

- Kind/Cruel
- Quiet/Noisy
- Introvert/Extrovert
- Ethical/Immoral
- Diplomatic/Insensitive
- Compassionate/Ruthless
- Lazy/Hardworking
- Meticulous/Sloppy
- Dedicated/Apathetic
- Liberal/Conservative
- Strict/Lenient
- Respectful/Disrespectful

My play *Baikal* had nothing like this. Not even close. The hero, Captain Karanov, is a dedicated Soviet sea captain on his final voyage before retirement to a country dacha. The antihero, Katrina, is a frightened, misunderstood teenage runaway. Instinctively, I had generated opposites: *runaway/dedicated, naïve/hardened, young/old* and *rural/urban*. However, these traits depict opposing *outer* worlds not *inner* ones and thus were too weak, making for little more than a colorful backdrop waiting for a story to take up residence. A strong Unity of Opposites demands fundamentally different personalities, which is to say, internal states, regardless of the outer world. *Baikal* made it into production because it was short, funny, and flew in the face of media accounts that only Russians defected to America and never the other way around. Nevertheless, without a compelling dynamic to propel the action, it was little more than a skit.

With *Bite Your Tongue,* I had misidentified the hero by confusing him with the antihero, which was still wrong because I also mistook the antihero. It turns out my beloved teenage cowboy, Jodi, although central to the action is not even the antihero but holds the lowly rank of the third character. I had mistakenly reasoned that having a naïve high school boy going up against the hardened principal would provide enough opposition. Just as I had in *Baikal,* I juxtaposed external traits of naïve/hardened and young/old rather than internal personality identifiers. Much to my surprise (and disappointment because I did not like him) Mr. Saturn, a caustic, blunt, tyrannical principal turns out to be the hero. The production worked only because the play was short, comic, and offered a controversial challenge to the prohibition against European Americans speaking African American Vernacular English in the 1990s.

For a story to be worthy of an audience, the hero and antihero must be locked in diametrically opposed psychological positions without hope of escape from the confines of an intolerable story space. Their opposing psychological traits must be inborn and recognized from infancy. While it might seem that naïve and hardened are opposites, in fact, they are temporal states that change with experience. Whereas as a inborn trait reveals how we react to the states of naïveté or to becoming hardened. For example, after decades of being wrongly imprisoned, Nelson Mandela used his hardening experience to bring peace, unify his nation, and offer dignity to those who imprisoned him. Throughout history we have seen others in similar situations who have instead extracted brutal revenge.

According to Egri, the Unity of Opposites builds on frustration as the antihero tugs at the hero's façade until it finally gives way to reveal, and free, the hero's authentic soul long lost behind it.

Through a series of carefully executed, escalating conflicts, the antihero negates the hero's façade until it loses all flexibility, cracks, and shatters allowing the authentic hero to emerge from the broken shell and enter the world as if for the first time. Egri reminds us that no one can keep a façade in place in the heat of battle. Therefore, "A character stands revealed through conflict."[15] Since all stories are battles, they are fundamentally journeys of self-discovery. The removal of the hero's façade and revelation of the devastating truth behind it acts as the catalyst for the hero's emancipation from suffering. It takes a great deal of suffering before the hero can get out from under the original cause.

This journey to self-discovery always begins with a single descriptive adjective. While this seems easy enough in theory, it can be baffling in practice even for veteran writers. First, we must identify who among a shifting milieu of intriguing characters actually is the hero. In theory it seems obvious, but as I learned writing my play *Bite Your Tongue*, this is not always the case. Fortunately, the Unity of Opposites provides a surefire litmus test to identify both the hero and antihero.

The hero is that character who experiences the greatest psychological transformation by the end of the story. Audiences think of a "hero" as a "champion" or otherwise good guy. But within Universal Grammar of Story, the hero can be any kind of character from innocent and sweet to jaded and violent. Heroes can even appear less often in a story than other more flamboyant characters. Steven Spielberg's 1998 film *Saving Private Ryan* offers a good example of an obscured hero hidden amid a cast of more colorful figures. Most audience members mistake Captain John Miller (played by Tom Hanks) for the hero. The actual hero is disguised in the character of the translator, Corporal Timothy Upham (Jeremy Davies), who experiences the greatest transformation as he changes from a gentle pacifist to a cold-blooded killer. He is a difficult hero to spot because he does not appear on the screen as often as the other characters do, is listed seventh on the cast, and does not even appear in story summaries or posters for the film.

The very purpose of drama is to transform the hero through the fire of conflict. Without a Unity of Opposites driving the conflict between hero and antihero, a writer might well have generated 300 pages of beautiful prose, but it will not be a story. Character transformation can be subtle such as that of Oscar in *The Odd Couple,* or horrifying such as the grotesque transformation of Oedipus.

Creating transformation requires nothing more than selecting a single adjective describing the hero's dominant personality trait. For example, the hero might be cowardly, vicious, compassionate, greedy, controlling, gentle, or ethical. Importantly, this must be a *personality trait* and not a physical attribute. In *Rainman* the hero is Charlie, who is manipulative. The antihero is Raymond, who is un-manipulatable. While most descriptions of Raymond identify him as autistic, that has nothing to do with the Unity of Opposites. Autism is not a personality trait. Rather, it is a physical manifestation in the world, a quality like being tall or short. Autistic and non-autistic people alike have wide-ranging personality types. When it comes to the Unity of Opposites, what matters for Raymond is that he cannot be manipulated.

Once the adjective for the hero is fixed it instantaneously produces another for the antihero. In great drama the antihero will always be described by the antonym of the hero's adjective. Therefore, Charlie being manipulative means Raymond must be un-manipulable.

Choosing the hero's adjective typically begins with brainstorming a list of possibilities and narrowing to one. The problem arises in trying to choose that single one when so many feel right. Charlie and Raymond each offer a generous list of possible traits. Consider the dramatic situation; a story of two brothers who do not know about each other until their father dies. The story opens with Charlie trying to aggressively manipulate his business out of imminent bankruptcy. When his estranged father dies, he learns that the family fortune has been left to a heretofore-unknown brother, Raymond, who lives such a quiet and disconnected life that he has no concept of money. Charlie tries to get his fair share of the inheritance by kidnapping Raymond.

Aligning Charlie's adjectives with Raymond's helps pinpoint the necessary one for a perfect opposition. We can describe Charlie as insensitive, demanding, aggressive, rule breaking, egotistical, materialistic, money-driven, extroverted, cruel, manipulative, and bullying. Raymond is also insensitive and demanding. Raymond can be further characterized as: rule following, self-focused, controlling of material things on a small scale, oblivious to money, introverted, apathetic, un-manipulable, and gentle. However, we need only one adjective for the hero—and its opposite for the antihero.

Since the brothers share the traits of being insensitive and demanding, we can eliminate these first. Charlie is aggressive, but Raymond is not passive because his persistence manifests in iron-willed, exacting demands to get what he wants—not exactly an opposition, either. Where Charlie is a rule-breaker, Raymond is a rule-follower, but this does not generate tension enough to drive the story because the rules Charlie breaks (kidnapping his brother, cheating at gambling) do not bother Raymond. Likewise, Charlie is not interested in breaking Raymond's rules. He only does so out of need; otherwise, he tries to respect them. While Charlie is egotistical, Raymond is extremely self-focused—not an opposition but, in fact, something of a similarity. Also, Charlie is materialistic in his aggressive money-driven business practices, but Raymond, although he has no grasp of money, demands certain material things in particular order. For example, he must have exactly eight fish sticks for lunch on Wednesday with green lime Jell-O for dessert. Both brothers are equally obsessed with the material world wherein the fish sticks are just as emotionally important to Raymond as the exotic car business is to Charlie. The introvert/extrovert opposition is not a cause of conflict either because Charlie insists on leading while Raymond willingly follows.

We are left with three hard adjectival pairs: bullying/gentle, cruel/apathetic, and manipulative/un-manipulatable. Charlie's bullying causes conflict (i.e., Raymond has a breakdown when Charlie tries to force him to fly), but it only appears in moments and does not drive the emotional underbelly of the film. Two pairs remain: cruel/apathetic and manipulative/un-manipulatable. Charlie is certainly cruel, but not always. While he makes fun of Raymond, he also tries to protect him from touching dirty things on the floor or being hurt by others (i.e., the angry driver screaming at Raymond in the crosswalk). More importantly, Charlie's cruelty has no impact on Raymond who is gifted with an incredible degree of apathy. Not one insult gets under Raymond's skin.

We are left with manipulative/un-manipulatable. Above all, Charlie is a born manipulator. No one in his world is safe from his natural gift to get people to do what he wants them to do. No one that is except Raymond with whom Charlie is defenseless. Without any intentional effort, by simply being un-manipulatable, Raymond pulls off Charlie's masque[16] of the "strong bad boy," revealing the vulnerable character underneath and forcing Charlie to experience a profound transformation.

Like Charlie, Helen, the hero in *The Miracle Worker*, shares many traits with the antihero Anne. Both are brilliant, disabled, stubborn, and unwanted by society. The irrefutable Unity of Opposites arises from their difference in the matter of discipline. While Helen refuses it, Anne insists on it. Helen's deliverance from animal barbarity to intelligent being therefore begins with the perfect opposition: undisciplined/disciplined.

One half of the adjectival pair determines the other: the inverse of the hero's adjective yields the antihero's, and vice versa.

There will always and ever be only one hero and one antihero in a great story. All other characters (with the exception of "the third character," to be discussed later) are but support, and/or backdrop for entertainment. Emerging writers sometimes make the mistake of choosing two or more villains, arguing, for example, that "the government" is the villain and therefore, all characters representing the government are antiheroes. Regardless of how strong or brilliantly crafted many characters appear to be, only one can rise to the status of hero—and only one to that of antihero. A story with more than one hero or antihero loses its continuity and becomes a collection of short stories.

This is the case for Michael Mann's 2001 film *Ali,* the life story of the great boxer Muhammad Ali. The tale begins with Ali's wife as the antihero, but long before the film ends the love story gives way to a new story: Ali's struggle against the US government. *Ali* is an interesting film and one of historical significance, but it loses strength by breaking in half to become two shorter stories.[17]

Antiheros exist to block heroes from using their natural strengths, aptitudes, and abilities that until the opening of the story have worked well for them. We see this in *Rainman* with Charlie's ability to manipulate other people, and in *The Miracle Worker* with Helen's ability to get her own way by throwing temper tantrums. Once these heroes encounter their antiheroes, they are plunged into a bewildering environment where their strengths no longer work and they grow increasingly weak. Just as Charlie cannot manipulate Raymond, Helen's temper tantrums have no currency with Anne. We see this symbolically in *Beowulf* when the mighty sword, Hrunting, which has never before failed, cannot so much as cut the air in Grendel's lair.

And so, things must change.

8.2: Transformation; The Hero-Villain Theory of Convergence

Just as the ancient Greeks sought new perspectives through opposition, so the dramatist tries to transform characters in a story through conflict. In *Rainman*, Charlie changes when he no longer sees Raymond as an idiot and a source of money but instead recognizes him as a long-lost brother worthy of loving and cherishing. In *The Miracle Worker*, Helen transforms by ending her battle with Anne by coming to love her as an angel of deliverance.

In strong stories the direction of the hero's transformation is always the same. Without exception heroes transform into the opposite of their defining adjectives at the beginning of the story. In other words, *the hero becomes like the antihero.*

Long ago, Heraclitus observed that the Unity of Opposites is not a matter of the fixed identity of one thing or another. Rather, it describes the realization that opposites "replace each other in a series of transformations: they are interchangeable or transformationally equivalent."[18]

The hero's journey to salvation comes through villainy—which they will soon discover is their own.

We see this in the transformation of self-righteous King Oedipus from the all-magnificent and revered savior of Thebes into a powerless blind pariah who is banished forever. We see it as Beowulf's bloated confidence gives way to depressive self-doubt. It comes when: spineless Hamlet evolves into a brave avenger, barbaric Helen becomes teachable, and, when ruthless Charlie breaks and kneels at his brother's feet in compassion.

Writers who have not yet gotten beyond the personal call to write (in order to take up the impersonal demands of the dramatic form) will hit their first serious writers' block by refusing to allow their heroes to transform into shadowy less honorable persons. At least for a moment, the natural progression of the dialectic requires that the writer place the hero in the shoes of the villain. Without the hero careening toward the mindset of the antihero, the Unity of Opposites will collapse and take the story with it.

Of course, Heraclitus reminds us to balance the transformation. Just as the hero moves toward the villain psychologically, so an authentic dialectic will drive the villain toward the hero. Little by little, the hero and antihero become like each other on their journeys toward the opposing adjectives on the continuum of opposition. In Universal Grammar of Story this movement is called the *Hero-Villain Theory of Convergence.*

Writers using their stories to take metaphorical vengeance on real-life enemies will find the desire to continue writing abruptly stifled at this point. The physics of drama, the incontrovertible law of story demands recognition on some level in the conscious mind, or unconscious intuition of the writer, that the villain is the salvation of the hero. The writer's personal call might get the story going and provide a nourishing place for it to gestate, but the writer must now do away with personal motives and release the story. Without doubt this is one of the most painful moments in a writer's life. It can feel like watching one's child leave home as a new adult who no longer needs, wants, or respects the parent's intensive oversight that has brought the child this far.

The more rigid the villain, the more difficult it will be for the writer to release the hero into that villainy. Early career writers sometimes try to protect themselves from their villains by depicting them with one-sided stereotypes. This inevitably results in the work developing into little more than a poorly veiled diary. Even purely invented, single dimensional characters bear the mark of their creator on some level. Seasoned writers learn to cast personal motives aside and free their characters to grow into entities of their own—full of all the good and bad traits of real people. In doing so, writers will experience a transformation of perspective along with their characters. While such moments can be unsettling, the new understanding serves not just the writer but the wider world as well.

The heroes and the antiheroes in *Oedipus, Beowulf, Hamlet, The Miracle Worker,* and *Rainman* embody a full spectrum of good and bad elements and are thus granted autonomous being.

The transformation of characters must be slow yet recognizable over time. Little by little in the heat of conflict their façades slip away revealing vulnerabilities through which their transformation will happen.

But not without the blessing of villainy.

8.3: The Sacred Role of Villainy

We must now dispatch with the term "antihero" to fully embrace the morally laden, evil-seeming, shadow energy of villainy. Villainy, like gravity, cannot be seen. We know it only by observing its effects which we perceive most clearly in people we do not like.

The complicated dynamic energy of villainy dwells in all of us. In a strong story it moves covertly through every character—and most especially the hero. Stories where good and evil never mingle are melodramas at best or cartoons at worst where super-good heroes can never experience transformation and thus remain locked forever in secret villainy.

The element of evil is not to be loathed, trivialized, or idealized. Rather, it needs to be understood and balanced in the service of life. In *The Miracle Worker*, none of the characters appear to be villainous, yet the evil threatening to take Helen's life is very real as it shifts throughout all the good people in the story.

Villainy appears in many forms, but its core essence is unrestrained ego bringing misery to the world. Paradoxically, the true mission of villains is to drive heroes to triumph over personal ego in pursuit of transcendence. This comes about spontaneously in a moment of sacred humility arising when the hero feels a measure of compassion for the villain.

While the villain's outward role is to block the hero's pursuit of a goal, ironically the villain's "evil" turns out to be the very thing the hero needs to achieve salvation. The hero's defining adjective will turn out to be a weak point through which the villain enters and makes way for reformation—but not before the hero falls from grace at the hands of the villain.

Because we are the heroes of our own life stories, anyone with whom we have conflict will become a momentary villain. In conflict our masques of goodness and self-righteousness slip shamefully, exposing gluttonous egos—to us and everyone else. Only when we see our own ego do we begin to dismantle it.

The meticulous Greek scholar Guthrie (1906-1981) relates Socrates' thoughts on this:

> Virtue, like colour, was in the eye of the beholder, it did not exist 'by nature'... 'No man does wrong willingly'. [Socrates'] point was that if anyone understood the true nature of goodness its appeal would be irresistible, and failure to comply with its standards could only be due to a lack of full understanding. ...He [Socrates] conceived it his mission to convince men of their ignorance of the nature of goodness and so persuade them to seek, with him, to remedy it. In carrying out this task, he developed the dialectical and elenctic [Socratic] methods of argument to which later philosophers owed so much.[19]

No one believes themselves to be a villain. We see ourselves as forces of good. Nevertheless, there is a role for *healthy* personal villainy which when successfully confronted reveals a more worthy and beautiful true self—the one hiding behind the masque of the hero.

As the masque of the hero shifts incrementally during transformation, the audience makes allowances. Early glimpses of villainy in a goodly hero are ignored with Machiavellian justifications. We dismiss little white lies and moments of seemingly benign personal evil with the belief that a little bad is acceptable in the greater service of good. It is not until combat escalates and the hero's naked ego stands revealed to the dismay of all—save for the villain who saw it all along—that the hero and the audience both feel deeply conflicted.

Like the rest of us, fictional heroes and villains sooner or later begin to doubt the self-projected goodness of the stifling, heavy masques they carry. As Lao-Tze (c. 400 BC) teaches in the Tao Te Ching, *those who believe they are good are not good, while those who believe they are not good are good.* Genuinely good people never claim to be good but strive instead to be so. Heroes inevitably begin stories believing they are fundamentally good until the point known as *All Hope Is Lost* (Chapter 10.5) where they discover they are not so good after all. If only for a fleeting second, this moment of disequilibrium permits heroes to recognize pieces of themselves in the faces of the villains. Critically, heroes cannot deny the specter of their own ego once they see it in their villain. Those who can see the masque of goodness for what it really is will cast it off and transform into true heroes. Those denying what they see will replace the masque and in doing so cross a shadowy threshold to become the next villain.[20]

Up to this point, in every frame of every scene, we see the hero devoting all energy to keeping the ego's masque in place as the villain struggles to pull it away. Rare is the friend or kin who will tell us the truth about ourselves—and rare is the enemy who will not. Villainy's sacred role is to reveal the hero's deep inner truths. Once the masque is off the transcended hero seeks to be free of the filthy thing. Replacing it would be like slipping into someone else's dirty clothes after a bath.

For all heroes the *direction* of the arc of internal movement never varies as they careen toward the standpoints of their villains. However, the *method* of that travel will vary considerably. In other words, everyone is going to the same place but how they get there differs.

For example, a *coward-hero* is one without self-love, trust, or confidence. This hero's insecurity hides behind the ego-protecting masque of the gentle, sweet-but-righteous person who is so passive and kind that conflict is avoided, and the ego of the coward remains hidden. In every scene, regardless of the degree of conflict, this hero will become sweet to avoid a fight but in the heat of battle will become disrespectful and cold. We know this story will be about gaining courage to face battle without running from it. This hero makes the journey to self-love, confidence, and trust, demonstrated by ultimately maintaining self-control and self-respect. The villain of this coward-hero will be a bully, pushing conflict on this panic-stricken hero in every scene. In response the hero's own acts of disrespect will escape more and more until finally, the masque of gentle sweetness completely crumbles. This hero will become humble and then strong. This is the story of Nora in Henrik Ibsen's *A Doll's House* and Timothy Upham in *Saving Private Ryan*. Hamlet is also a coward-hero, although with a masque of madness for escape rather than Nora's sweetness or Timothy's passiveness. The end result is the same: avoiding conflict at all costs.

By contrast, the *rebel-hero* is not sweet and gentle at all but wild and disorganized, having the potential for power, without the knowledge to use it. The villain of this hero's story will be calm, cool, calculating, and conservative. The hero will slowly develop these same traits while the villain will lose ever more control, slipping bit by bit into the wild chaos that the hero embodies at the beginning of the tale. This is the story of *The Miracle Worker*.

In the world's great stories, heroes and villains are equally matched and often confused for one another. In *The Miracle Worker* Helen could easily seem the villain with her willful, barbaric, unacceptable behavior. But alas, Helen is the hero for she undergoes the most fundamental change. Anne acts as villain by blocking Helen's status quo.

Anne's villainy is clear in her lack of love for Helen, which she openly admits. Helen's villainy is even clearer in her violent temper tantrums. Yet while all the characters in *The Miracle Worker* share the host for the shifting ghost of villainy, there remains one clear antihero, Anne, juxtaposed against one clear hero, Helen.

The beauty of *The Miracle Worker* lies not just in the story having a solid hero and villain but also in the spirit of villainy set loose to shift through all the characters. Outside of Helen that spirit is most destructive in the otherwise kind and gentle mother, Kate, who clings to Helen with such force that she keeps her child imprisoned in ignorance. The good-hearted mother calls for Anne to help but repeatedly blocks Anne's efforts to discipline Helen. If Kate's indulgence is not destroyed it will lead to a horrible death for Helen. Here, the villainy comes from a mother who cannot bear to see her child in distress. Even so, this child needs to feel distress in order to grow. Kate's need to protect Helen repeatedly sabotages Helen's hope for life. This villainy is difficult to spot because it is not situated in overt cruelty. The mother is no sadist but in love with and dedicated to her child. Still, Kate's appeasing Helen only soothes herself to avoid the ugly face of her own agony.

Sometimes writers try to dodge the struggle of creating authentic villains by using detrimental stereotypes to project evil. Such a tactic guarantees weak stories. Race, ethnicity, culture, or any other physical attribute cannot be used in lieu of a descriptive adjective in the Unity of Opposites. They have no antonyms. One race is not the opposite of another. They might be positioned in opposition to one another, but that does not make them inherently opposites. Their situation is temporary not universal and the present significance will be meaningless to future generations. A few hundred years from now no one will recognize a German in a 1940s American film as being inherently villainous because of ethnicity. Nor will a Russian from the 1960s or a Middle Easterner from the turn of the millennium have relevance as stereotypical American villains because the context of the culture wars will be lost, just as it has been lost to us in the works of antiquity. When time destroys temporal context, the use of stereotypes will reveal a writer to be embarrassingly ignorant.

Because they contain universally villainous characters based on ego not cultural stereotypes, powerful stories are race-proof, culture-proof, and any other physical-description-proof. *Oedipus, Beowulf, Hamlet, The Miracle Worker,* or *Rainman* could be set in the glory of an Aztec metropolis or an ancient Mesopotamian village and still have the same power because the villainy and heroism are unchained from race and place.

---

1. Jung and von Franz 1964, p. 85.
2. In Graham 2015, Fragment DK22B1.
3. Ibid., DK22B17.
4. Ibid., DK22B34.
5. Ibid., DK22B93.
6. Graham 2015, sec. 3, para 1.
7. Ibid., sec. 2, para 1.
8. In Graham 2015, Fragment DK22B88.
9. Guthrie 1962-1982.
10. Plato, et al. 1894.
11. In Graham 2017, Fragment DK22B53.

12. Burnet 1914.
13. Hegel 2010, p. 382.
14. One of Egri's most famous students, filmmaker Woody Allen, commmented in 2000 that Egri's book was still the best book on writing he had ever seen. See Lax 2000.
15. Egri 1960, p. 63.
16. The French spelling *masque* takes root in drama and mysticism from the medieval Latin *masca* meaning "spectre." I choose this spelling because in drama, characters transform by conquering their indwelling evil spirits.
17. Having made that point, it should be noted that a collection of short stories can make an effective feature-length film or play if it begins, continuously returns to, and ends with one dominant story. Examples include films such as: Tarantino's 1994, *Pulp Fiction;* Girard's 1998, *The Red Violin;* and Curtis' 2003, *Love Actually.*
18. Graham 2017, sec. 3: The Doctrine of Flux and the Unity of Opposites.
19. Guthrie, vol. 1, p. 9.
20. Campbell 1949.

courtesy of Perkins School for the Blind
Helen Keller and Anne Sullivan, c. 1888.

Chapter Nine
Story Chemistry

ACCORDING TO THEATRE professor and scholar Bernard Grebanier[1] (1903-1977), the first playwrighting school in the United States was founded in the late 1800s by a Kentucky lawyer turned New York theatre critic, William T. Price (1846-1920). Price opened the doors of his school to some of the most influential writers, directors, and producers of the day, who sought their place in America's lucrative new theatre market.

Price's academy was founded on an idea he called "The Proposition," a logical three-step structure based on Aristotle's syllogism that Price adapted to analyze dramatic plots. Yet despite Price's popularity his ideas were nearly lost after his death. Even the name of his school is forgotten.

Two generations later, Grebanier—who believed Price's work to be the most significant contribution to theatrical writing since Aristotle's *Poetics*—revised it and returned it to the theatre world. Grebanier's 1961 book, *Playwriting: How to Write for the Theater*, was devoted to advancing Price's ideas. But alas, Grebanier's own effort nearly fell into obscurity in the decades after his death. Now, two generations later it returns anew.

©Rick Denhart 2018
Bernard Grebanier

Standing on Aristotle's shoulders, Price and Grebanier hoped the philosopher's syllogism would let them "calculate" the best (and hopefully only) course of action for a given story. The syllogism lets us deduce a single true conclusion from two correct and related statements. We see the basic structure of the syllogism in Table Two, followed by Aristotle's most famous syllogism in Table Three.

Table 2: The Structure of Aristotle's Syllogistic Reasoning

1. Major premise.
2. Minor premise.
3. Conclusion.

Table 3: Aristotle's Most Famous Syllogism

1. All men are mortal.
2. Socrates is a man.
3. Therefore, Socrates is mortal.

Aristotle
©Rick Denhart 2018

Because the first line of Aristotle's most famous syllogism, "all men are mortal," is true and because the second is a sub-statement of that truth, "Socrates is a man," it therefore follows that the conclusion, "Socrates is mortal," will also be true.

To this day the Western world still functions on the basis of syllogistic reasoning as our principle method of deducing truth. In Table Four, we see a common logical sequence for deducing that whales are warm blooded.

Table 4: Common Western World Logical Sequence

1. All mammals are warm-blooded.
2. Whales are mammals.
3. Therefore, whales are warm-blooded.

The major premise lays out the general category: mammals. The minor premise narrows the category to specific mammals: whales. As long as the major and minor premises are true, a true and logical conclusion follows: whales are warm-blooded.

Used correctly, the syllogism lends mathematical-level authority, precision, and validity to conclusions in nonmathematical domains. When used incorrectly, it advances illogical and false ideas, as in Table Five.

Table 5: False Syllogistic Reasoning

1. Organic foods are healthy.
2. This cup of sugary soda is organic.
3. Therefore, this cup of sugary soda is healthy.

The conclusion is false because the first statement, the major premise, is false. Not all organic foods are healthy. Still, millions of people unwittingly reason their way into heart disease and diabetes by using false syllogisms like the one above.

Price turned to the syllogism as a means of locating an internal logic for developing pitch perfect stories. In doing so he created "The Proposition," as depicted in Table Six.

Table 6: Structure of the Price-Grebanier Proposition [2]

1. The Condition of the Action.
2. The Cause of the Action.
3. The Resulting Action Question.

The first step, the Condition of the Action, provides the general context by describing the *active situation* in which we find the hero at the beginning of the story. Price identified the Condition of the Action for *Romeo and Juliet* as:

> Romeo and Juliet, members of the houses of Montague and Capulet, in a deadly strife, fall in love.[3]

Grebanier tells us that although Price knew he was on the right track, he was never quite satisfied with his work. In time, Grebanier realized Price's error—his first statement was incorrect which naturally led to an incorrect conclusion. Price had identified two heroes (both Romeo and Juliet) when only one is possible. Price's first step was too broad to successfully narrow to a second. Thus, Grebanier revised the statement:

> Romeo, scion of a family at feud with Juliet's family, falls in love with Juliet at first sight.[4]

With this Grebanier was able to narrow the Cause of the Action to a specific act taken by one hero that was rooted in the Condition of the Action:

Although their families are at feud, he marries her.[5]

This immediately triggers the third step, the Resulting Action Question:

Will he find happiness in this marriage with her?[6]

Answering this question is the principal work of the plot and the only reason an audience remains interested.

Table Seven depicts the nearly completed Price-Grebanier Proposition for *Romeo and Juliet*.

Table 7: Price-Grebanier Proposition for Romeo and Juliet, without The Climax

> 1. Condition of the Action: Romeo, scion of a family at feud with Juliet's family, falls in love with Juliet at first sight.
> 2. Cause of the Action: Although their families are at feud, he marries her.
> 3. Resulting Action Question: Will he find happiness in this marriage with her?

Just as Grebanier advanced Price's work, so we must further evolve Grebanier's. In doing so The Proposition takes on new dimension with the reformation of three of four parts which are known in Universal Grammar of Story as: *The State of Affairs, The Challenge,* and *The Dramatic Question*. As we shall see, Grebanier's original theory of *The Climax* (Chapter 9.4) is retained.

Table Eight provides a simple overview of Universal Grammar of Story Proposition.

Table 8: Four Base Elements of the Universal Grammar of Story Proposition

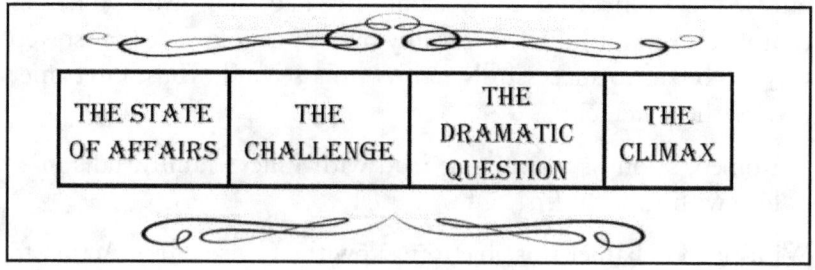

9.1: The State of Affairs

Let us take a moment to step away from the heady world of syllogistic reasoning to visit a delightfully common childhood experience in American education. I very clearly remember when my third-grade teacher integrated a popular art and science lesson. She directed our class to spend an afternoon at the art table making a papier–mâché mountain with a hollow center from green and brown painted strips of newspaper and wheat-flour plaster. The next day, after this messy paper-and-glue affair was dry, we moved it to the science table where, with a mischievous smile, our teacher set a bottle of vinegar next to a box of baking soda. The scene was set for an exciting explosion.

I like to use the metaphor of this lesson because of what happened to the real mountain outside our classroom window. Fifteen years after that science lesson, the perfectly coned Mt. St. Helens—a mere sixty-miles away—erupted in the opposite direction from us. Within moments, hundreds of square miles of pristine ancient forest vaporized leaving nothing but a grey moonscape.

Like the papier–mâché mountain and its miniature Mt. St. Helen's eruption, stories act as models for understanding real life. While the physical world of a story (such as inner earth or some distant galaxy) might not seem real, the psychological and emotional chemistry of the characters must exactly mimic human experience.

Using the metaphor of *story chemistry*, we can ramp up the explosive potential of the Price-Grebanier Proposition. It begins with identifying five elements necessary for the active setting of a strong story:

1. The hero's inner conflict.
2. The Unity of Opposites.
3. The destabilizing situation.
4. The stakes.
5. The potential resolution to the conflict.

These five elements condensed into the space of a single sentence make up the *State of Affairs,* the first step in the Universal Grammar of Story Proposition.

Long before any story begins its hero will have been menaced by two incompatible needs teetering side by side, waiting for a plot to force them into collision.

Shakespeare paints Hamlet with the heart of a loyal son conjoined with that of a coward. Hamlet's need to fight and need to run, struggle for the rule of his ego. He is a sensitive man who cannot tolerate the crush of relentless emotional shocks he endures. When the death of his father (the king) brings him home from school in Germany, he discovers his Uncle Claudius—Hamlet's father's brother—has seized the throne and already married Hamlet's mother. Hamlet then learns that Claudius murdered his father. In grave distress Hamlet breaks up with his girlfriend Ophelia. Then he tragically kills her father by mistake. Driven mad, Ophelia commits suicide. Things get worse. As an early forerunner of postmodernity, Hamlet has no tribe and no one to lean on for support. For a time he falls into madness ostensibly feigned but we are never sure. We do know that he is a sensitive man crippled by grief who is hesitant and indecisive. His ruthless uncle-come-stepfather, Claudius, attacks Hamlet's grief as "unmanly." The famed Shakespearean actor Sir John Gielgud explained that Hamlet was, "A simple man in an impossible predicament."[7]

Paralyzed by grief, haunted by indecision and with no one to trust, not even himself, Hamlet resides in the worst of miseries. He asks himself, "Am I a coward?"[8] He is by no means a scaredy-cat, after all, he follows after his father's ghost when even the guards are so afraid that they try to hold Hamlet back. But for the son of a king, and one who should be king, Hamlet's refusal to fight for the throne that is rightfully his makes him nothing short of a coward. Grief may sideline an ordinary man but not a king.

While the *external* conflict between hero and antihero must hold an absolute Unity of Opposites, the hero's *internal* conflict is less so. The terms "coward" and "loyal son" are not antonyms but they do successfully block one another.

Whether for good or bad the hero's transformation comes out of the battle between conflicting inner needs. If the nobler side wins, the hero triumphs to become a true hero. If the worse side prevails, as happens in many stories, then the hero is condemned to the shadow realm and the world gains a new villain.

Hamlet's cowardice has kept him alive by allowing him to avoid conflict. Now the rising power of the loyal son brings his two sides into struggle. If the loyal son wins, Hamlet will challenge Claudius, which means almost certain death. Out of this wrenching inner struggle comes Hamlet's most famous line: "To be, or not to be: that is the question."[9] The stakes cannot get any higher for Hamlet.

Building the five elements constituting the State of Affairs begins with the hero's inner conflict. For Hamlet, we have "loyal son vs. coward," as the first element.

The second element depicts the exterior conflict held in the Unity of Opposites. For Hamlet that gives us a coward pitted against a ruthless warrior.

The third element introduces the destabilizing situation when the ghost of Hamlet's father reveals that he was killed by Claudius for his throne and wife.

The fourth element lays out the stakes: a son's loyalty to his murdered father, the salvation of his mother, the leadership of the kingdom of Denmark, and his own life.

Finally, the fifth element points to a potential resolution: Hamlet is left to seek justice.

Table Nine depicts the complete State of Affairs for Hamlet.

Table 9: State of Affairs for Hamlet

> Hamlet, a <u>coward</u> but <u>loyal son</u>, learns from his father's ghost
> <small>Unity of Opposites for Hero + Inner Conflict</small>
> that his <u>ruthless</u> uncle-stepfather Claudius <u>killed his father,</u>
> <small>Unity of Opposites for Antihero</small>
> <u>married his mother, and stole the throne of Denmark</u> leaving
> <small>Destabilizing Situation + the Stakes</small>
> Hamlet <u>to seek justice</u>.
> <small>Potential Resolution</small>

If Shakespeare had created Hamlet differently, fashioning the play's hero perhaps as a brave warrior (like Fortinbras), then Hamlet would simply kill his ruthless stepfather or be killed by him and we would have no story, only a gory battle scene like we have at the play's end but without all the grandeur and the poetry between the first scene and the last. Alternatively, had Shakespeare created Hamlet as a bitter and disloyal son, then Hamlet would be satisfied with his father's death with no need to avenge it, and again we would have no story.

Now, let us turn to the State of Affairs for the film *Rainman*. This story belongs to Charlie, a manipulative bully whose business teeters on the verge of bankruptcy. In youth, his father's harsh abandonment has left him emotionally crippled, hardhearted, and incapable of love. Charlie's hurt intensifies when his father dies and he discovers that the entire family fortune has been left to a brother he never knew existed. The only solution for Charlie to avoid utter financial ruin is to use Raymond to get a share of the inheritance. To Charlie's dismay he quickly learns that Raymond cannot be manipulated.

Table Ten depicts the five elements for Charlie's State of Affairs.

Table 10: The Five Elements of Charlie's State of Affairs in Rainman

1. Hero's Inner Conflict	An emotionally crippled, manipulating bully needing love.
2. Unity of Opposites	Manipulating vs. un-manipulatable.
3. Destabilizing Situation	The death of Charlie's father and the discovery of Raymond, whom Charlie never knew existed, and who inherited the entire family fortune.
4. The Stakes	Financial Ruin.
5. Potential Resolution to the Conflict	Charlie will manipulate Raymond to get his rightful share of the inheritance.

Table Eleven details the State of Affairs for Charlie in *Rainman*.

Table 11: State of Affairs for Charlie in Rainman

> Charlie, an emotionally crippled, manipulative bully, without family, who was abandoned by his father in youth and left unable to love, and who is on the verge of bankruptcy, learns that his father has died and left the family fortune to an un-manipulatable, bully-proof, institutionalized brother, Raymond, whom Charlie never knew existed.
>
> (Inner Conflict + Unity of Opposites for Hero; the Stakes; Destabilizing Situation; Potential Resolution; Unity of Opposites for Antihero)

Table Twelve depicts the five elements for the State of Affairs for Helen in *The Miracle Worker*.

Table 12: The Five Elements of Helen's State of Affairs in The Miracle Worker

1. Hero's Inner Conflict	A strong-willed, undisciplined tyrant who is desperate for human communication.
2. Unity of Opposites	Undisciplined vs. disciplined.
3. Destabilizing Situation	Anne comes to teach Helen.

4. The Stakes	Helen will die if she does not learn to communicate.
5. Potential Resolution to the Conflict	Helen gaining the discipline from Anne to learn to communicate.

Table Thirteen shows us the completed State of Affairs for Helen in *The Miracle Worker*.

Table 13: State of Affairs for Helen in The Miracle Worker

Helen, an intelligent but brutally ignorant, strong-willed, undis-
_{Inner Conflict}
ciplined, and badly spoiled deaf-blind child, who desperately
_{Unity of Opposites for Hero}
wants to communicate and who will die if she cannot learn how,
_{Inner Conflict}   _{the Stakes}
becomes the student of Anne, a severe disciplinarian, who is
_{Destabilizing Situation/Potential Resolution}   _{Unity of Opposites for Antihero}
charged with teaching Helen language.

A separate State of Affairs can be written for each character in a story. Table Fourteen provides the State of Affairs for Anne.

Table 14: State of Affairs for Anne in The Miracle Worker

Anne, a tough, strong-willed, unrefined, severe disciplinarian teacher, who is incapable of love, accepts her last hope of a job by teaching Helen, the badly spoiled and violently undisciplined, deaf-blind daughter of a wealthy and refined Southern family.

Anne's inner strength of discipline expressed in her pitiless governance of Helen conflicts with her need to be vulnerable in order to receive love. Anne believes her tough discipline is what kept her from dying in an institution as a child, and she knows that without the same discipline Helen will die in such an institution. Yet, it is this same toughness keeping Anne from getting a job to ensure her survival. Helen constitutes Anne's last hope for work, without which she will likely starve as a partially blind, rough, vulgar, orphaned Irish immigrant in 1880s America. Anne's future hangs by a thread perilously dangling in the righteous brutality of her own hands.

With the State of Affairs we have all the ingredients for an explosive volcano set out on the science table. Nothing has happened yet but we can feel the anticipation and inevitability. The first sentence of the State of Affairs acts as the "once upon a time" opening the story with the status quo of the everyday world.

Now we must challenge the status quo.

9.2: The Challenge

The State of Affairs is of itself static, providing only potential conflict. *The Challenge* ignites the conflict. It mixes those chemicals on the science table.

In The Challenge the hero takes an act toward the antihero in a way that forever alters the status quo of both. This must be an act of such finality that it cannot be undone—once the vinegar is poured over the baking soda neither can be restored to its previous state. The Challenge forces the characters across a threshold into a new realm from which return is impossible.

In *Rainman*, The Challenge comes when Charlie kidnaps Raymond and holds him hostage for his inheritance. Now his life can never be the same. The old world is gone forever and a new landscape is at hand. Table Fifteen depicts the State of Affairs and The Challenge for Charlie in *Rainman*.

Table 15: The Challenge for Charlie in Rainman

State of Affairs	Charlie, an emotionally crippled, manipulative bully, without family, abandoned by his father in youth and left unable to love, and who is on the verge of bankruptcy, learns that his father died and left the family fortune to an un-manipulatable, bully-proof, institutionalized brother, Raymond, whom Charlie never knew existed.
The Challenge	Charlie kidnaps Raymond.

Many writers miss a crucial point: The Challenge must be an action *willingly and intentionally taken by the hero*. No act of fate done *to* the hero or *for* the hero by nature, the gods, or someone else will suffice. The character swept up by a tornado or shipwrecked has not yet reached the point of The Challenge. It must be an act of absolute free will in which the hero's ego gambles everything in order to preserve itself. To this, Aristotle adds that the act should be one "…of a man who is not eminently good and just, yet whose misfortune is brought about not by vice or depravity, but by some error or frailty."[10] The point here is that *the act is startling in exceptionality, unexpectedness, and daring*. This is more than just another simple, everyday act of habit that is easily explained away: This is a momentary lapse with permanent consequences.

In *The Miracle Worker*, Helen takes The Challenge by getting angry at Anne (for trying to make her learn a word), flying into a rage, knocking out Anne's tooth, locking her in the guest room, and throwing the key down the well. While this might seem an act of depravity, this is no act of personal evil. Rather, this is an error in Helen's thinking that leads to her great misfortune. Whatever power Helen might have had with Anne up to this point is now radically undermined and life will never be the same. Table Sixteen depicts the State of Affairs and The Challenge for Helen.

Table 16: The Challenge for Helen in The Miracle Worker

State of Affairs	Helen, an intelligent but brutally ignorant, strong-willed, undisciplined and badly spoiled, deaf-blind child, who desperately wants to communicate, and who will die if she cannot learn to, becomes the student of Anne, a severe disciplinarian, who is charged with teaching Helen language.
The Challenge	Helen knocks out Anne's tooth, locks her in the guest room, and throws the key down the well.

Looking at Anne's Proposition, The Challenge comes when Anne orders the family out of the dining room during supper, locks herself in with Helen, commences a knockdown drag-out fight destroying the room and refusing to give Helen a single bite of food until the child responds to a first lesson in discipline: using a spoon. All order in the house is lost and no one will be the same after this traumatic event. Table Seventeen illustrates the State of Affairs and Challenge for Anne.

Table 17: The Challenge for Anne in The Miracle Worker

State of Affairs	Anne, a tough, unrefined, severe-disciplinarian teacher, who is incapable of love, accepts her last hope of a job by teaching Helen, the badly spoiled and violently undisciplined deaf-blind daughter of a wealthy and refined Southern family.

The Challenge	Anne locks Helen with her in the dining room and commences a knockdown, drag-out fight, forcing Helen to eat with a spoon.

Turning to Oedipus, we find the story of an arrogant and egotistical king who had come to the throne through sheer luck when he solved a riddle that freed the city of Thebes from a terrorizing Sphinx. His reward was marriage to the widowed Queen Jocasta and an equal share of the tripartite rule of Thebes alongside Jocasta and her brother Creon. Oedipus, however, succumbs to the gluttony of pride at seeing himself in the role of savior and king, and exaggerates his glory and status by acting as if he is the sole ruler. Angered at Oedipus, the god Apollo casts a brutal plague over Thebes, threatening total annihilation. Not knowing why Apollo is upset, Oedipus sends Creon to Apollo's Oracle for guidance. Creon learns that the murderer of King Laius (Jocasta's late husband) goes unpunished and freely roams the city. Oedipus loudly and enthusiastically jumps on the chance to be a great savior again. To help, humble Creon brings forth an old blind prophet who is said to know the killer's identity. When the prophet refuses to speak, Oedipus flies into a rage and brutally forces the elderly man to tell all he knows. The prophet reluctantly says that Oedipus is the killer of Laius. This is the moment where Oedipus takes The Challenge by publicly accusing Creon of plotting against him with the old prophet. In doing so, Oedipus irrevocably destroys his relationship with Creon and there is no going back to the way things were.

Beowulf, like Oedipus, is also burdened with a morbidly obese ego. When he hears that the Danes have suffered twelve years of terror at the hands of the ogre Grendel, he charges to Denmark to save the day. Boldly, Beowulf strides up to King Hrothgar and tries to demonstrate his strength by yelling as loudly and fiercely as he can, "I am Beowulf!" Then, even before hearing what the king has to say, he starts bragging to an embarrassing degree about his being the brave and righteous warrior who has come to save the Danes. Beowulf then impulsively takes The Challenge by announcing to Hrothgar that he will fight Grendel barehanded. Grendel can take thirty men with one arm, but so Beowulf claims to have the strength of thirty men. So, he will fight Grendel as an equal, hand to hand. Hrothgar has listened silently, letting Beowulf rattle on until running out of steam and becoming quiet. Then to Beowulf's disappointment, Hrothgar greets him not as a savior but as a young man coming to pay the debt of his foolish father. Beowulf's bragging and his bold claim to fight Grendel barehanded were attempts to bolster his ego ahead of the disappointing story that Hrothgar begins to recount. Years before, Beowulf's father had rashly killed a man in a rival kingdom and nearly triggered war. King Hrothgar stepped in, gave Beowulf's father shelter and paid blood money to the offended kingdom to avert war. Only then could Beowulf's father return home in peace. By declaring that he will fight Grendel barehanded, Beowulf seeks to bring some dignity back to his family's name. But his plan proves even more foolish than his father's mistake. Fighting barehanded, Beowulf is unable to kill Grendel cleanly—causing even more misery for Hrothgar.

Hamlet takes The Challenge when he makes a highly inappropriate visit to Ophelia in her room, which in turn places him squarely in the crosshairs of Claudius' suspicions. Before this moment, Hamlet could have waffled forever between cowardice and loyalty. Now that Claudius has taken notice of him, a fight to the death is inevitable.

Getting the hero to the point of The Challenge is the easiest and often most exciting part of crafting a story. Just past this milestone begins the hard work.

Seeing what we need to change in life is easy. Implementing that change is difficult. At The Challenge our heroes commit to the perilous journey of self-discovery. In truth, they do not go it alone because *the writer also commits to a journey of self-discovery*. No writer gets through a story unscathed any more than a parent gets through childrearing unchanged. Creation—whether of children or characters—brings consequences.

I learned this long after writing my plays *Baikal* and *Bite Your Tongue*. Both pieces crashed hard into writer's block right after I reached The Challenge. In playwrighting, The Challenge always falls at the end of the first act, which let me pass them off as one-act plays. They were, however, failed full length plays whose life energy withdrew because I was not yet ready to face the demons waiting for me behind the ones about to pounce on my characters.

9.3: The Dramatic Question

As my third-grade teacher took the cap from the vinegar bottle and began to pour the pungent liquid into the handmade mountain full of baking soda, not one child turned away. We were riveted, waiting for the answer to the question, "Will the volcano erupt?"

In a story, the moment the hero takes The Challenge, a question springs into the mind of the audience. This question forms the next step in The Proposition with *The Dramatic Question* which asks if the hero will overcome the inner conflict to transform the relationship with the antihero. Where the State of Affairs focuses more on the inner struggle of the hero, the Dramatic Question by contrast addresses the relationship between the hero and antihero.

The desire for its answer keeps the story moving and the audience invested in it.

At The Challenge, the hero takes a foolish risk in the face of vulnerability, and in seriously underestimating the antihero. Once that vulnerability is exposed, the antihero relentlessly blocks the hero's remaining strengths until the only path left is directly through that vulnerability. What the hero prized as strength before The Challenge now becomes liability. And, by the same measure, what was once weakness will soon become a powerful path to salvation.

Here we find echoes of the perennial philosophy (Chapter 12). Across time and place, the world's sacred scriptures have reminded us that: "our weakness is our greatest strength." Indeed, the hero's vulnerability opens the door through which the hero moves from one pole of the Unity of Opposites to the other. The Dramatic Question essentially asks if the hero will make the shift on that continuum.

In *Rainman*, we see the beginning of that movement in the series of events leading up to the Dramatic Question. The hard-hearted schemer Charlie visits Raymond in the institution to plot how he can manipulate his inheritance. There, Charlie finds that instead of feeling empowered by capturing this "inferior being," he feels intense heartache. Charlie learns that while their father abandoned him, the father remained close to Raymond—even letting Raymond regularly drive the same prized car for which the father had Charlie jailed when he once dared to drive it as a teenager. Charlie will use that same car to kidnap Raymond, uprooting him from the safety of his institutional life and holding him for "his rightful inheritance." What Charlie fails to understand is that his "rightful inheritance" also includes Raymond and his autism. Raymond easily manages to block Charlie's strength of bullying-through-manipulation by being utterly bully-proof and un-manipulatable. This leaves Charlie helpless. Yet unlike Raymond's autism, Charlie's emotional crippling is no artifact of nature. Charlie has imposed this disabling situation upon himself out of bitterness.

The Dramatic Question in *Rainman* asks whether Charlie will face his vulnerability, find the emotional courage to remove his armor of aggression forged against emotional pain, and build an authentic relationship with Raymond.

Table Eighteen illustrates the nearly completed Proposition with the Dramatic Question for *Rainman*:

Table 18: The Dramatic Question for Charlie in Rainman

State of Affairs	Charlie, an emotionally crippled, manipulative bully, without family, abandoned by his father in youth and left unable to love, and who is on the verge of bankruptcy, learns that his father has died and left the family fortune to an un-manipulatable, bully-proof, institutionalized brother, Raymond, whom Charlie never knew existed.
The Challenge	Charlie kidnaps Raymond.
The Dramatic Question	Will Charlie overcome his emotional crippling and build a relationship with Raymond?

In *The Miracle Worker*, the Dramatic Question springs forth when Helen physically assaults Anne. In doing so, Helen encounters real battle for the first time in her life, only to come out the loser. Table Nineteen illustrates the nearly completed Proposition with the Dramatic Question for Helen in *The Miracle Worker*.

Table 19: The Dramatic Question for Helen in *The Miracle Worker*

State of Affairs	Helen, an intelligent but brutally ignorant, strong-willed, undisciplined and badly spoiled, deaf-blind child, who desperately wants to communicate, and who will die if she cannot learn to, becomes the student of Anne, a severe disciplinarian, who is charged with teaching Helen language.
The Challenge	Helen knocks out Anne's tooth, locks her in the guest room, and throws the key down the well.

The Dramatic Question	Will Helen overcome her strong-willed, undisciplined brutality, yield to Anne's discipline, and develop a relationship with her teacher in order to learn human language?

Finally, Table Twenty depicts the Dramatic Question for Hamlet.

Table 20: The Dramatic Question for Hamlet

State of Affairs	Hamlet, a coward but loyal son, discovers that his ruthless uncle-stepfather Claudius, killed his father, married his mother, and stole the throne of Denmark leaving Hamlet to seek justice.
The Challenge	Hamlet arouses Claudius's suspicions when, disheveled and acting like a madman, he inappropriately visits Ophelia in her room.
The Dramatic Question	Will Hamlet overcome his cowardice to do his duty as a loyal son by killing Claudius to bring justice?

The Dramatic Question will not be answered until near the end of the story. Before then, at a point known as *The Climax,* we get a hint as to how the question will likely be answered.

9.4: The Climax

In general, audiences think of a story's climax as the culminating rush of action peaking in a crescendo of excitement. However, in Universal Grammar of Story the literary turning point known as *The Climax* tends to pass unnoticed by the audience—which senses that something has happened without recognizing its significance.

The Climax, Grebanier explains, signals a shift in the relationship between the hero and antihero. This marks a change in dynamics and the place where the audience stops wondering *what will happen* next and instead wonders *how the hero will react* to the events. More importantly, this is the moment the audience gets a sense for how the Dramatic Question will likely be answered. The answer is not assured, but we have a premonition about it.

Grebanier tells us that The Climax is signaled by an action the hero takes *toward a third character.* Throughout the drama, the dynamic has been centered on the relationship between the hero and antihero. The entry of a third character grants the hero a new perspective on that relationship. This reflects French theatre where the entry of any new character into a scene constitutes a new scene. By contrast, in American and British theatre scenes are divided by the conclusion of a series of actions around a theme. The French concept of marking a new scene with a new person conveys the more natural and intuitive change of energy we experience in our social reality. For example, when we are deep in conversation with a friend and someone else enters the room—even another close friend—the conversational dynamic changes. The dyad ceases to exist and the triad begins. It is a different interaction which is why the French cast it as a new scene.

In real relationships the impact of a third person has serious consequences. The interaction between two people in an exclusive relationship typically stays locked in a given dynamic until a third person enters into it. The third person acts as a witness giving the couple new eyes through which to see themselves. Bring a new friend into a relationship with someone else and the original relationship is altered because the new person acts as a mirror to the other two people. Glancing into that mirror makes change inevitable. It is exactly the driving change ignited by the third character that is so devastatingly depicted in Edward Albee's classic play *Who's Afraid of Virginia Wolf*?

In *Hamlet*, The Climax comes when Hamlet kills Ophelia's father, Polonius, by mistake. In doing so, he recognizes his capacity to kill and we sense his relationship to the king will take a sudden, lethal turn.

In *Rainman*, The Climax comes when Charlie calls his girlfriend and speaks gently to her. Never before have we seen him calm and compassionate. This suggests an answer to the Dramatic Question as to whether Charlie will overcome his aggressive bullying to find a loving relationship with Raymond.

In *The Miracle Worker*, The Climax comes when Helen and Anne are living isolated from the family in a small cabin along with Percy, a child servant. Anne is spelling signed words into Percy's hand when Helen pushes Percy out of the way and demands Anne sign into her hand. For the first time, we see Helen wanting Anne to touch her, and seeking to learn.

It is crucial to remember that The Climax never happens between the hero and the antihero, rather it must happen between the hero and the third character.

Grebanier explains that in a story with only two characters, the third character will be represented by an object. For example, Edward Albee's one-act play *Zoo Story* takes place between a shy milquetoast and a psychotic who come to fisticuffs over a bench in New York's Central Park. The park bench acts as the third character when the meek man gets angry enough to boldly stake a claim to it, and for the first time in his life demonstrate the willingness to fight for something.

At The Climax, the inner conflict within the hero resolves itself with the sacrifice of strength on the altar of weakness. In *Rainman*, Charlie gives over his strength of aggressive manipulation for his exceedingly vulnerable new capacity to love. Likewise, Helen sacrifices the power of her temper tantrums for the utterly foreign landscape of language. For Hamlet, The Climax comes when he offers up his cowardice for bravery the moment he runs his sword through the unknown form behind the curtain, who turns out to be Polonius.

Table Twenty-one offers the completed Universal Grammar of Story Proposition for Hamlet.

Table 21: The Completed Proposition for Hamlet

State of Affairs	Hamlet, a coward but loyal son, discovers that his ruthless uncle-stepfather Claudius, killed his father, married his mother, and stole the throne of Denmark, leaving Hamlet to seek justice.
The Challenge	Hamlet arouses Claudius's suspicions when, disheveled and acting like a madman, he inappropriately visits Ophelia in her room.
The Dramatic Question	Will Hamlet overcome his cowardice to do his duty as a loyal son by killing Claudius to bring justice?
The Climax	Hamlet kills Polonius.

Table Twenty-Two offers the completed Universal Grammar of Story Proposition for Charlie in *Rainman*.

Table 22: The Completed Proposition for Charlie in *Rainman*

State of Affairs	Charlie, an emotionally crippled, manipulative bully, without family, abandoned by his father in youth and left unable to love, and who is on the verge of bankruptcy, learns that his father died and left the family fortune to an un-manipulatable, bully-proof, institutionalized brother, Raymond, whom Charlie never knew existed.
The Challenge	Charlie kidnaps Raymond.
The Dramatic Question	Will Charlie overcome his emotional crippling and build a relationship with Raymond?
The Climax	Charlie speaks gently to his girlfriend on the phone.

Table Twenty-three offers the completed Universal Grammar of Story Proposition for Helen in *The Miracle Worker*.

Table 23: The Completed Proposition for Helen in *The Miracle Worker*

State of Affairs	Helen, an intelligent but brutally ignorant, strong-willed, undisciplined and badly spoiled deaf-blind child, who desperately wants to communicate, and who will die if she cannot learn how, becomes the student of Anne, a severe disciplinarian, who is charged with teaching Helen language.
The Challenge	Helen knocks out Anne's tooth, locks her in the guest room, and throws the key down the well.
The Dramatic Question	Will Helen yield to Anne's discipline and develop a relationship with her in order to learn?
The Climax	Helen pushes Percy away and demands Anne teach her.

Table Twenty-four illustrates the completed Universal Grammar of Story Proposition for the antihero, Anne, in *The Miracle Worker*.

Table 24: The Completed Proposition for Anne in *The Miracle Worker*

State of Affairs	Anne, a tough, unrefined, disciplinarian teacher, who is incapable of love, accepts her last hope of a job by teaching Helen, the badly spoiled and violently undisciplined deaf-blind daughter of a wealthy and refined Southern family.
The Challenge	Anne locks Helen with her in the dining room and commences a knockdown, drag-out fight, forcing Helen to eat with a spoon.
The Dramatic Question	Will Anne overcome her inability to love, soften, and teach Helen to be human?
The Climax	Anne expresses regret to Kate that she does not love Helen.

With the DNA of the story solidly built upon the Unity of Opposites, the sacred role of villainy, and the Universal Grammar of Story Proposition, we now carry the story forward into the field of time.

Table Twenty-five provides a detailed graphic of the completed structure of the Universal Grammar of Story Proposition.

---

1. Grebanier 1961.
2. Ibid., p. 89.
3. Price 1908, p. 50.
4. Grebanier, p. 93.
5. Ibid.
6. Ibid., p. 94.
7. BBC 1954.
8. Shakespeare, Hamlet, 1866, act III, scene II, line 545.
9. Ibid., scene I, line 56.
10. In Butcher 1951, p. 45.

Table 25: Detailed Graphic of the structure
of the Universal Grammar of Story Proposition

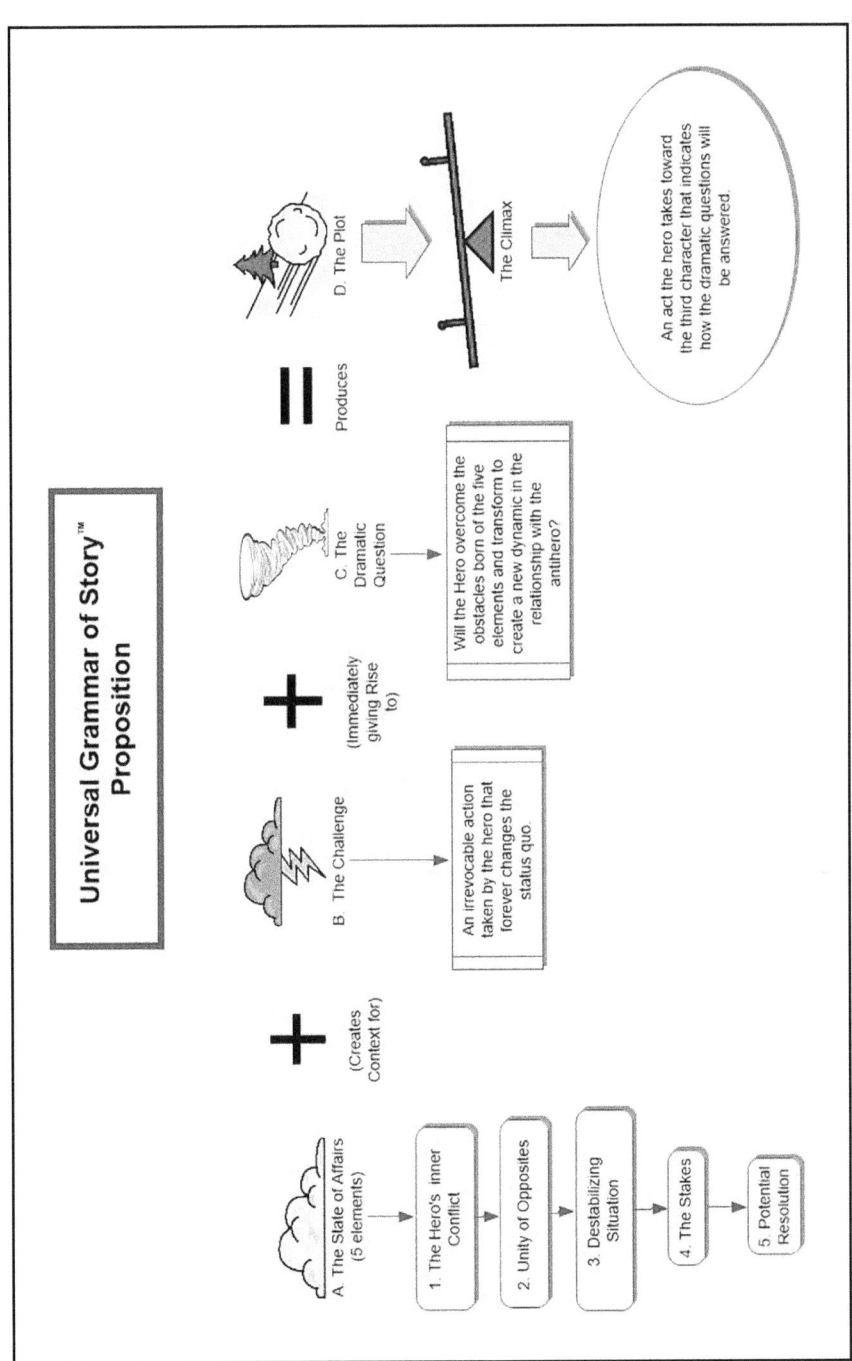

Chapter Ten
The Structure of Timing

JUST AS MUSICAL composers use metronomes to keep time in their symphonies, so writers need a steady beat to keep their stories rolling out with a mesmerizing cadence. The structure of timing is the writer's metronome.

Syd Field (1935-2013) earned his place in film-writing history with his observations about the uniform structure of timing in film. Field observed that within the typical 120-page script, near pages twelve, twenty-four, and eighty-five, "something" happens to "spin the story in a new direction." In his early work, Field did not specify the nature of these events nor did he contemplate their existential meaning; rather, he simply noticed them and wrote a wildly popular book *Screenplay*. Field describes three story milestones: "Setup," "Plot Point I," and "Plot Point II."

Whether he realized it or not, Field had stumbled onto something much larger than screenplay timing. He was describing the ancient cadence of storytelling wherein regardless of form, genre, or length, stories have universal proportions and their beat falls to a similar rhythm. An ancient play, medieval poem, modern epic novel, two-hour film, or one-page short story all share a universality of proportion.

And it all begins with a setup.

10.1: The Introduction

Field referred to the introduction of a film story as the *setup*. More specifically he saw that in the average 120-page script, all the major characters are introduced by page twelve. Since one page of a screenplay translates into one minute of running time we can use minutes and page numbers interchangeably in the discussion of timing.

Field also observed that film stories always begin with an "introductory event." Like iron filings to a magnet, the introductory event pulls characters into the story allowing the audience to "happen into" an already unfolding story. The audience discovers "who's who" and what kind of people they are as they react to this event. Field noted that when key characters are not physically present at the beginning of the film they would nonetheless be introduced metaphorically or symbolically in the first twelve minutes through a photograph or possession, or by being mentioned in conversation. Sometimes significant characters never physically appear in the film but their invisible presence is nonetheless powerful. For example, in *Rainman*, Raymond and Charlie's father dies before the film begins, yet he remains a force in the movie symbolized by the car that triggered Charlie's alienation from him. Therefore, he is introduced in the first twelve minutes.

Twelve minutes into a 120-minute film lands us at the ten-percent mark of the story. Moving beyond Field's work with movies we can see that the ten-percent mark is important in other forms of stories as well.

For example, in *Oedipus* the key characters are introduced by line 173 of the 1,729-line epic poem—exactly at the ten-percent mark. This, however, is no mere milestone of character introductions. Much more is happening. With this line Oedipus shifts the movement of the story:

> Come, children, take your supplicant boughs and go; up from the altars now. Call the assembly and let it meet upon the understanding that I'll do everything.[1]

On the surface, at least, Oedipus seems to be committing to action. While he might not yet have reached the point of The Challenge (Chapter 9.2), he is moving in that direction. The change in momentum comes from Sophocles having laid out four of the five elements of the *State of Affairs* (Chapter 9.1). We now have the Unity of Opposites (narcissistic/humble), the destabilizing situation (a plague), the stakes (all life in Thebes), and a potential resolution (Oedipus will save the day like he did before). Still missing is the inner conflict.

Beowulf is essentially two separate stories tacked together under one cover (see appendix B). The first completed story consists of 2200 lines, putting the ten-percent mark at line 220: the exact timing of Beowulf's arrival:[2]

> On the following day, at the due hour (line 220),
>   those seafarers sighted land,

...it was the end of their voyage and the Geats vaulted over the side, out on to the sand.³

Again, we have the first four of the five elements of the State of Affairs: the Unity of Opposites (bombastic/dignified), the destabilizing situation (Grendel menaces the humans), the stakes (monster will be superior to humans), and a potential resolution (Beowulf will kill Grendel.) Again, as with Oedipus, the inner conflict is not yet formed.

Field noticed that the momentum of the introduction continues for another twelve minutes, up to the twenty-four-minute mark. This same point is where the State of Affairs is completed just before The Challenge takes place.

Certainly, at the ten-percent mark we feel like we have arrived at something, having come to understand the *who, what, when, where,* and *why* of the story. Even so, neither the hero nor the audience is really committed to the journey until we reach the twenty-percent-mark when the vulnerability of the hero is fully exposed with the explication of the inner conflict.

In the first ten-percent of *Oedipus* we learn that the city of Thebes is threatened with annihilation because Apollo has cast down a plague. Not until the second ten-percent, however, do we see that Oedipus might not be such a righteous person after all. When Oedipus brags about his greatness as a king his internal conflict reveals itself. The boasting poorly hides his self-doubt and insecurity. Truly good people never brag. Rather, not-so-good people brag to convince themselves that they are good. Oedipus sees himself as a good king but inwardly he knows he is not. The life and death stakes of his internal conflict stem from his growing recognition of an awful paradox: To be a truly good king he will have to courageously do the very thing proving he is not a good king.

Hamlet's internal conflict is quite the opposite. He already knows he is not a good person and strives to change. The introductory event for *Hamlet* comes with the appearance of the ghost of Hamlet's father. At the ten-percent mark, (Act I, scene 2, line 255), Hamlet has hope for the first time, saying, "would that night would come!" At this point the major characters have been introduced and the energy of the play sharply pivots: Hamlet is no longer morose but now excited for the arrival of the ghost. Yet, the introductory event continues. Hamlet's inner turmoil has not yet fully manifested. This happens in the second ten-percent of the play where he learns from the ghost that he will have to overcome his cowardice and act as a loyal son. At exactly the twenty-percent mark of the play (Act I, scene 4, line 119), Hamlet is no longer passively overtaken by depression. Instead, he suddenly knows what to do. This is the moment where he exclaims, "O, Wonderful!"

The audience is on edge with him at this moment because this excitement stands in sharp contrast to the pouting boy, morose with "unmanly grief," that we have witnessed throughout the play so far. Hamlet's inner conflict is now fully manifested as we see both his certainty about what he must do and the staggering doubt he feels about being able to do it. The five core elements of the State of Affairs are now in place and the story proper is ready to begin.

The first ten-percent of the story lets us discover who the characters are. At twenty-percent of the story we know what kind of people they are as they struggle to regain their balance after being knocked aside by a destabilizing event.

The timing of the State of Affairs concludes at the twenty-percent mark where the hero—torn by doubt, standing on shifting ground, and facing life and death stakes—steps across a threshold by taking The Challenge at the Point of No Return.

10.2: The Point of No Return

According to Field, the second major timing marker in most films comes at the twenty-percent mark, or twenty-four minutes into a film. Field calls this "Plot Point One" and describes it as a change pivoting the story in a new direction.

Writers naturally sense that something must happen at this point, as do audiences, who will grow restless and abandon the story if the precise and necessary event does not happen. Emerging writers without a clear understanding of what is required will often throw a haphazard, exciting action into the story: a comet hits Earth or a war is launched. Regardless of the most exciting scene ever written or one using the most advanced whizzbang special effects, nothing will save a story that misses this crucial step.

For that, we evolve Field's work to develop a more specific concept known in Universal Grammar of Story as *The Point of No Return*.

This is the moment where the hero must commit irrevocably to an action. Once the hero crosses this line there is no going back. Sound familiar? Yes, the Point of No Return is the same as The Challenge. Twenty-percent of the way into the story, the hero willingly gambles everything and drastically raises the stakes by crossing the threshold with such significant force that return to life as it was before is impossible. If that does not happen at this exact point the story will weaken and ultimately collapse by the forthcoming one-third mark.

Again, the necessary event should not be confused with big external happenings. Certainly, after the comet hits the planet or a war starts, return to the old life will be physically impossible, but in this case the hero enters the new landscape with the same old psychological mindset, and thus, nothing has really changed.

At the Point of No Return, the balance of the psychological landscape radically shifts when the hero takes up The Challenge and triggers the Dramatic Question (Chapter 9.3)—which is what keeps the audience in its seats or the reader turning the pages.

Remember, the Point of No Return must be crossed of the hero's *own free will.* Nothing can be done *for* the hero or *to* the hero by another character, outside force, or act of God. A character swept into a new world is but an innocent bystander and therefore cannot be held accountable for the consequences of what is to come when all hope is lost.

10.3: The Doldrums

The first serious test of a writer's artistic placement of elements in a story comes at the one-third mark, known in Universal Grammar of Story as the *Doldrums.* The term comes from maritime language used to describe a band spanning five-degrees north and south of the Earth's equator where the northern trade winds moving southwest meet the southern trade winds blowing northeast. This belt, properly called the Inter-Tropical Convergence Zone, can at times be marked by completely stagnant air that leaves sailing ships stranded for days or weeks. Samuel Taylor Coleridge wrote of the misery of the Doldrums in *The Rime of the Ancient Mariner.*

If writers have not carefully calibrated the story compass to direct character development and plot movement at the outset of the journey (in the State of Affairs), then the story will most likely drift into the lifeless winds of the Doldrums and stall. This most commonly happens when the writer has not freed the story from the personal call (Chapter One), thus freezing the plot's rudder. But even if the writer has succeeded in the struggle of dispensing with the personal call, no amount of effort can steer the story back into the lofty trade winds if the sacred moments of the benchmark timing are not respected.

Inexperienced writers, who feel constrained by timing and consider it to be too formulaic, often attempt alternative ways around this without realizing that the structure of timing in a story is what makes a story a story—and what makes people want to hear it.

The stagnant Doldrums at the one-third mark of a story typically hits about forty minutes into the average two-hour movie. As we sit in the audience at the Cineplex this is where we begin checking our messages, thinking of what else should go on the grocery list, or about what we will do next which might include sneaking into the neighboring theater. I have not yet met a screenwriter or playwright who has avoided suffering the misery of the first draft of their script slogging or collapsing near the Doldrums.

Paradoxically, while the Doldrums are known for the stagnant air that killed many a sailor in the days of wind propulsion, this very same place can also produce persistent violent thunderstorms when precisely aligned.

The one-third mark of the story tends to be the place where plots either die or surge to life with utter genius. At this point in *Hamlet* Shakespeare writes one of the most famous lines in all of English literature: "To be, or not to be: that is the question."

Oedipus arrives at the Doldrums when Creon tells the people that Oedipus has wrongly accused him of plotting to overthrow Oedipus and take the crown. Up to this moment Creon has been loyal, gentle, and helpful to Oedipus. Now Oedipus has made an adversary of his ruling partner and caused a breach in the family that will lead to Oedipus's damnation.

In *Beowulf*, the Doldrums bring horrible upheaval when Grendel tears the doors of Hart from their hinges, gobbles down a man, and straddles Beowulf, poised to bite him. There follows the most difficult fight of Beowulf's life.

When a story is carefully brought to the coordinates of the Doldrums, writers can tap into a natural energy system that will carry the plot with hurricane force to a powerful conclusion. When the timing is blindly ignored and the winds missed, the plot will drift lifelessly and leave the writer fruitlessly paddling. No exciting scene or special effects can save a story that has not caught the violent energy of the Doldrums. A forced stopgap scene might keep a few audience members in their seats but most will soon abandon the story that has abandoned them.

10.4: The Midpoint Reversal of Fortunes

The next major point in story timing arrives on the heels of the Doldrums. At the fifty-percent mark is the point Aristotle called the "reversal of the situation."[4] In Universal Grammar of Story this is known as the Midpoint Reversal of Fortunes.

This reversal makes a hairpin turnabout, changing the direction in which the story has been unfolding up to now. It usually consists of either a brutal test of the hero's commitment to the path chosen at the Point of No Return, or a momentary respite validating that path after a series of harsh defeats.

Aristotle also called for a scene of "recognition" coinciding with this point, where the hero has a profound realization about someone. In *Oedipus*, the fifty-percent point mark comes with the hero's devastating realization/recognition that he might be the murderer he has cursed: "O God, I think I have called curses upon myself in ignorance."[5]

In *Beowulf*, the halfway mark falls at the banquet celebrating Beowulf's triumph over Grendel. The banquet is a positive reversal of fortunes brought about by Beowulf's liberation of Hart after twelve years of terror, and his personal victory after nearly losing the most difficult battle of his life. Yet Beowulf holds a paradoxical doubling of reversals. At the celebration he sits subdued struggling with an inner defeat. Rather than restoring luster to his tarnished ego, fighting Grendel barehanded revealed the inescapable truth that he is not the man that his obnoxious bragging claims himself to be. He has suddenly moved from feeling great glory to feeling defeat.

This realization comes during the recitation of a poem as part of the evening's entertainment. Since the poem is not part of the plot, we can calculate the story proportion without it. However, when it is considered, it marks yet a third reversal of fortunes, albeit unrelated to the titular.

The poem tells the story of a woman taken from her people to become the wife of a rival king. During a war between her old and new kingdoms, her brother is killed on one side, and her son on the other. At the exact halfway point of the poem she unites her kingdoms in death by ordering the bodies of her son and brother burned on the same funeral pyre. For her, this is the brutal test. Since this is also the exact midpoint not only of the poem but also of Beowulf, we have in effect a three-way reversal of fortunes with, one for the queen in the poem, one for the community of Hart, and one for Beowulf who sits at the table listening to the poem.

In *Hamlet*, the Midpoint Reversal of Fortunes comes where Claudius runs from the room after seeing the play that exactly recreates the murder of Hamlet's father. Hamlet has proven that he is not just delusional, Claudius really did do the dirty deed. Hamlet has triumphed.

In *The Miracle Worker*, the Midpoint Reversal of Fortunes comes where Anne orders the family to leave the dining room, and commences a knockdown drag-out fight with Helen. Helen has now fallen deep into new territory where her tantrums have no power to help her get her way. From her perspective, her fortunes have shockingly, suddenly, and very badly turned.

In *Rainman*, the Midpoint Reversal of Fortunes comes when a small-town doctor demonstrates to Charlie that Raymond has a miraculous gift for numbers, one that will soon quite literally reverse their fortunes with card counting in Las Vegas.

Regardless of which way the fortunes turn at the fifty-percent mark, the next milestone will be the lowest of the lows when All Hope is Lost for the hero.

10.5: All Hope Is Lost

The next timing marker happens about two-thirds of the way into the story. Field noticed that in screenplays this occurs at about page eighty-five. He called this "Plot Point Two," and characterized it as a point where the story spins in a new direction.

Aristotle called this point, "the scene of suffering."[6] In Universal Grammar of Story it is known as *All Hope Is Lost*, and it carries the most profound moment of the story.

At The Challenge/Point of No Return heroes gamble everything on a bid to defeat their villain, but now by all measures it appears that utter defeat is at hand. With no way out of the dilemma brought on by the hero's own ego-centered choice, there comes a moment of psychological collapse—a necessary state for the sacrificial death of the ego in order for the soul to be made ready for transformation. In this moment nothing could be worse for the hero, who surrenders to grave despair.

Yet out of this very defeat will soon come a victory far greater than the one originally sought.

At this point in *Rainman,* Charlie learns that he was the reason Raymond was sent to an institution. Charlie collapses on the floor utterly distraught as his arrogance vanishes leaving him with nothing but regret.

Likewise, at this point in *The Miracle Worker* Helen collapses on the floor of the hunting cabin utterly despondent at the loss of her family and the hopelessness of being with Anne. For Anne, the moment comes when the family takes Helen away from the hunting cabin and she laments that the discipline she so painstakingly instilled in Helen will rapidly crumble with their indulgence.

In *Hamlet,* All Hope is Lost comes where Hamlet berates his mother against his father's command. The father's ghost suddenly appears, and Hamlet, recognizing he has failed, cowers and cries:

> Do you not come your tardy son to chide,
> That, lapsed in time and passion, lets go by
> The important acting of your dread command?
> O, say![7]

Up until this moment our heroes have been trying to use outdated and inappropriate tools from the old world. These tools worked before the Point of No Return but they will not work after. Up until this point Hamlet has used emotions to get his way: he broods, pouts, and feigns insanity. Now such behavior no longer works. He will have to change.

In *The Miracle Worker,* Helen has been using violent temper tantrums to get her way. At the point of All Hope is Lost she is alone in the cabin with Anne where her tantrums are useless.

Throughout *Rainman,* Charlie has bullied and manipulated people to get his way. Sitting on the floor in the bathroom, regretful, guilty, and distraught, he finds the tactics that have served him so well in the past are now worthless.

In *Beowulf,* All Hope is Lost arrives at the two-thirds mark when Grendel's mother comes to take revenge for the slow and brutal death of her son. She sneaks into Hart and kills Aeschere, King Hrothgar's beloved friend and advisor. It turns out that Beowulf has not saved the day after all. His bragging has led to this misery by leading him to fight Grendel barehanded. In doing so, he was barely able to kill the ogre, could not do it cleanly, has caused the death of Aeschere, and now must face Grendel's mother.

At the moment of All Hope is Lost the old-world strategies are nothing but dead weight so the hero must change in order to keep moving forward. Out of sheer habit the hero clung to the old tools until psychologically beaten bloody by them. Now, in despair, the hero surrenders old tools, but new ones are not yet grasped and so the hero exists in a state of purgatorial helplessness.

At this moment we witness a changing of the guard. The battle of the conflicting needs, which tore at the hero at the Point of No Return, now resolves. The hero surrenders the previously dominant self-centered need, for the weaker, typically nobler one. It is here that Hamlet's cowardice gives way to his need to be a loyal son.

Immediately after All Hope Is Lost comes The Climax (Chapter 9.4), in which the hero takes an action toward a third character signaling transformation. The Climax is the first step out of total despair and into the new realm.

10.6: The Miracle

Fate shines on those who humble themselves. As a reward for doing the right thing a miracle is granted. In Universal Grammar of Story this point is known as simply *The Miracle*. It comes on the heels of The Climax and is taken up in more detail in Part Four, which deals with mythology and philosophy. Presently, we are just marking the point where it occurs and briefly discussing its nature.

The Miracle is some unexpected gift with supernatural overtones, if not outright magical qualities in its character and/or means of arrival.

In *Oedipus,* The Miracle comes when Creon, the man Oedipus has so badly treated, withholds revenge and treats Oedipus with compassion, even letting him hold his daughters, the most precious thing left in his miserable life.

In *Beowulf,* The Miracle comes just after Beowulf humbles himself by admitting weakness. Unferth, who has been a harsh and jealous rival of Beowulf, softens and lends Beowulf the mighty sword, Hrunting, which has never failed anyone in battle.

In *Hamlet,* The Miracle comes when pirates take the ship and accept Hamlet as a hostage thus sparing him from certain death at the dock in England.

In *The Miracle Worker,* right after The Climax in which Helen pushes Percy away and reaches out her hand to learn, The Miracle unfolds with a chick pecking its way out of its shell in her hands.

In *Rainman,* The Miracle comes when Raymond's gift of card counting allows Charlie to resupply the money he has lost.

The remainder of the story serves to normalize the hero's transformation into the new way of being.

---

1. Sophocles 1954, translated by David Grene, lines 172-176.
2. *Beowulf,* translation by Heaney, 2000.
3. Ibid., lines, 220-225.
4. Butcher 1951, p, 278,
5. Sophocles 1954, lines 862-3.
6. Butcher, p. 43.
7. Shakespeare, *Hamlet*, Act III, scene 4, lines 106-109.

Conclusion of the Core Theories

THE PRECEDING CHAPTERS are meant as a guide to illuminate what every storyteller does by instinct. These theories capture the cadence of any journey, real or imagined. They work because they reflect the story of our own lived experience, be it in the small space of a day, over an entire lifetime, or over the centuries of an empire. The proportions of timing and sequence of events in Universal Grammar of Story pattern after the rhythm of real stories unfolding in our own lives.

We mature through transformation of perspective triggered by conflict. Because conflict is such an uncomfortable experience most of us generally, and unknowingly, try to avoid this rite of passage. Yet we cannot exist without it. It is how we grow, and how our relationships grow.

Now we turn away from logical and semi-logical theory to explore the realm of philosophy and mythology where the power and dynamics of human transformation are held in deeply intuitive and emotional states. Out of intuition rises our primal desire to seek stories in the first place.

©*Rick Denhart 2018*

PART FOUR

PHILOSOPHY AND MYTHOLOGY OF STORYTELLING

WITH A SOLID GRASP of the core narrative theories we can weave entertaining stories. But if we lack the capacity to wick spiritual philosophy into our art, the entertainments we crank out will remain momentary amusements, of little value to community survival, and soon forgotten. With the onset of modernity, Western literature has steadily lost its ability to nourish our spiritual nature with vicarious experience of mythical encounters.

Like a tourist curiously sampling opium, we began our cultural journey to this desperate point innocently enough. Then we plunged into a deep infatuation with logic, followed by a full-blown neurotic obsession that left us intolerant of anything mystical. Intoxicated by the righteousness of cold reason, the Western world began systematically destroying its mythological tradition with the efficacy of Islamic State radicals taking power tools to the great antiquities of Babylon. By the late nineteenth century, Friedrich Nietzsche declared the death of God, leaving only art to fill a horrible void in the human soul.

It took the Western world roughly 100 years to effectively kill off its own mythology built upon thousands of years of sacred traditions. Like sharpshooters from frontier trains, scientists took aim down the barrels of their microscopes and fired at everything moving in Western thought. Any idea unable to withstand the scrutiny of the scientific method was deemed worthless by a new "inquisition" of logic. By the middle of the twentieth century, the Abrahamic belief system was drained of its authority and evaporated under a hot rationalist gaze. The remaining residue was scraped off the slide, boxed up, labeled "anthropologically interesting," and shelved.

Joseph Campbell (1904-1987) writes:

> Wherever the poetry of myth is interpreted as biography, history, or science, it is killed. The living images become only remote facts of a distant time or sky. Furthermore, it is never difficult to demonstrate that as science and history mythology is absurd.[1]

Campbell urged writers to take up their roles as archetypal leaders in reconnecting humanity to its intuitive mind through encounter with the mythic realm. Campbell drew heavily on the work of Carl Jung (1875-1961), who a generation before had argued that the rise in the social importance of psychologists paralleled a reciprocal fall in the social importance of priests and other holy figures. Jung believed that much emotional illness in the Western world could be traced to the death of our mythic systems of belief and the subsequent, devastating blow to our self-image. It was a fast and hard fall from our station as beloved children of the mediaeval Heaven to that of meaningless cogs imprisoned in modern machines. Jung frequently treated patients in his psychiatric clinic by sending them back to their childhood faiths in search of redemption.

But Jung argued that we need more than just return to faiths that have been allowed to stagnate. Jung writes:

> Our myth has become mute, and gives no answers. The fault lies not in it as it is set down in the Scriptures, but solely in us who have not developed it further, who rather have suppressed any attempts.... We stand empty handed, bewildered, and perplexed, and cannot even get it into our heads that no myth will come to our aid although we have such urgent need of one.... What would these old storytellers have to say about Hiroshima?[2]

©Rick Denhart 2018
Carl Jung

Jung and Campbell urged writers to reclaim their archetypal role as leaders of culture by recognizing their daunting responsibility to nourish society's mythic and mystical needs, as did their literary ancestors.

The ancient Greeks deeply understood the sovereignty of the mystical realm as it moved through their stories. They wrote, produced, and attended plays as acts of prayer, as messages between the mundane and the mystical. In return, many of these plays were graced with immortality and continue to nurture us after thousands of years.

Stories from the ancient world demonstrate a quality that is largely missing from stories today, namely, *reverence for the audience*. We cling to ancient stories because they revere us, even as they nourish us. Indeed, ancient stories may well be the only source of reverence left for many of us.

The soul of a story, the essence giving it life, rises from acts of reverence which attract the mystical. We cannot capture, manipulate, will, summon, or bargain the spirit of a story into being. Nor can we copy or imitate its presence with a template, even using the most sophisticated of forgeries. Bringing the mystical into a story is like enticing a wild bird. We need to make an attractive and inviting place for it to come of its own accord. The spirit that graces a story with a life of its own, comes of its own free will.

We begin making such an attractive place by building a strong Unity of Opposites, a solid Proposition, and setting the story to the cadence of irresistible timing. Still, these elements alone are not yet enough to usher into it the life force inherent in great art.

We know when we are in the presence of great art and when we are not. We see it in Tolstoy's *Anna Karenina* but not the summer movie for teenagers. It stills our breath before Michelangelo's *David* but not the softball trophy on the mantel. It entrances us with Rachmaninov's Third Symphony but not radio jingles. In the presence of great art we feel *reverence*. That reverence allows us to penetrate the divine mystery that, in art, comes through some form of mythology.

Joseph Campbell devoted his life to understanding the role of mythology in stories. Drawing upon the wisdom of ancient and modern philosophers, Campbell developed a powerful theory of storytelling. In his immensely popular book *The Hero with a Thousand Faces*, Campbell observed that all stories repeat the same essential hero's journey, running through a gauntlet of alienation and despair on a quest for an ego-shattering encounter with the Divine. Every hero of every story repeats this journey and vicariously takes the audience along. Chapter Eleven explores Campbell's work with the essential structure of the mythic adventure.

For the more personal understanding of divine mystery, we turn in Chapter Twelve to Aldous Huxley (1894-1963) who attempts to explain the phenomenon of divine encounter.

Four years before Campbell published *The Hero with a Thousand Faces*, Huxley published *The Perennial Philosophy*, comparing the sacred writings of the world's great faiths and aligning the precise points at which they agree with one another. At these intersections we find the core, universal human experience of divine encounter.

In the golden eras of the past, humanity's storytellers responded naturally to the mythological call with stories of such rich form and substance that we grew fat on their bounty. But with modernity came a cataclysmic spiritual famine. The fat has long gone and our spiritual bones protrude.

Here follows a bounty of food for the soul.

---

1. Campbell 1968, p. 249.
2. Jung 1991, p. 173.

Chapter Eleven
Joseph Campbell's Hero's Journey

Every failure to cope with a life situation must be laid, in the end, to a restriction of consciousness. Wars and temper tantrums are the makeshifts of ignorance; regrets are illuminations come too late.

Joseph Campbell [1]

THROUGHOUT THE MODERN age, the study of mythology has been relegated to the social sciences. Well-intentioned scholars reason that our myth-urge serves a socio-psychological function by fulfilling our need for cultural cohesion and providing comfort against the specter of nature's horrifying shadow side.

In essence, such social scientists attempt to rationalize or explain away our deep need for mythic encounter and for connection with divine mystery. Carl Jung and Joseph Campbell flew in the face of this zeitgeist by arguing that the mythological drive is *an instinctive one,* hard-wired into human beings. Like baby ducks following after the mother, so all human beings follow after a set body of archetypes.

While this theory has gained traction in the century after Jung first proposed it, we nonetheless still live in an eminently logical era where scientists continue to ignore the idea as disturbingly unscientific. Studying the mythic drive in the manner that Jung proposed, would require recognizing intuition as a bona fide mode of human thought. The academy remains so vehemently opposed to such an approach that not even Berkley would consider going there on a scouting mission.

Drawing from Darwin's observation that instinct is as important to survival as are the physical structures of the body, Jung and Campbell boldly claimed that fulfilling the need for mythic encounter is vital to the healthy preservation of the species. They dedicated their lives to trying to awaken the world to that reality.

Joseph Campbell

Campbell's *Hero with a Thousand Faces* is an extraordinary achievement, one that can nevertheless be difficult to penetrate. Borrowing from James Joyce (1882-1942), Campbell seized upon the term *monomyth* as the essential definition of what makes a story a story: the repetition of a single, universal journey.

Well-intentioned interpreters of Campbell have tried to simplify his work by creating formulaic templates designed to help writers more easily engineer stories. Unfortunately, these templates all too often obliterate key concepts of Campbell's work by interpreting it too logically. Taking such a mechanical approach to Campbell yields not a *monomyth*, but rather a *monotone*—a flat, lifeless sequencing of events—giving us a new genre: the mediocrity of modernity. Film teams try to disguise such lackluster stories with sex, violence, shocking language, phenomenal special effects, and exotic movie stars. The box might sparkle, but the stuff inside is still as bland as milk-toast. It brings to mind Joseph Heller's Milo, a Kafkaesque entrepreneur in the novel *Catch-22*, who tries to make money off a glut of cotton in World War II Europe by dipping cotton balls in chocolate and selling them to the Army as food.

Around the turn of the millennium, the work of spicing up a dragging story has fallen ever more to the cinematographer whose job is to never let the camera hold still for a moment of meditative peace. In doing so, directors try to substitute camera movement for story movement. Undoubtedly, future satirists will spoof this era with exaggerated camera spin and the circling of the actors, ever faster, until the audience plunges into distracted dizziness and the cameraman flies off the boom. Increasingly, the more well-crafted the special effects, the less well-crafted the story, as if production teams have succumbed to their own distraction.

Regardless of how much technique or sophistication a story's presentation involves, the hero's journey will be exactly the same: be it a grand historical epic, a silly romantic-comedy, or a simple fairy tale. This journey makes a story a story, and we never tire of the perennial wonder it brings us.

Every hero ventures through three phases: Departure, Initiation, and Return.

11.1: Departure

All stories begin with Departure. *Oedipus, Beowulf, Hamlet, The Miracle Worker,* and *Rainman* share this same starting point.

The point of Departure arrives when life has lost its joy, and fear and disillusionment grip the world. In Universal Grammar of Story this is the destabilizing situation depicted in the State of Affairs (chapter 9.1). In simple stories, the hero might suffer a personal crisis. For example, in *Rainman* bankruptcy threatens Charlie's business. In stories about whole tribes, the entire society finds itself in desperate need of cosmic-level assistance; in *Oedipus* the kingdom of Thebes is threatened with extinction by a plague.

Out of the gloom comes a herald calling the hero to come forth and save the day through an adventure. This call is a metaphor for the awakening of the self and, as is with all symbols on the journey, reflects the reality of our own lived experience. One of the most profound real-life heralds comes at puberty when we first hear the call to take the psychological journey into adulthood.

In all great stories, the hero, like every pre-teen, at first refuses the call because accepting it means certain death to the ego. All hero-journeys end at the feet of the Divine before whom the ego is annihilated. Since the ego is the only point of reference for the unenlightened, the death of the ego means the death of the self therefore the vulnerable hero denies destiny's desire to destroy it.

Campbell argues that the refusal of the call is a metaphor for the infantile ego fearful of letting go of the parents. This metaphor is repeated in our everyday lives when, out of fear of the threat to our status quo, we forgo experiences that would allow us to evolve.

Campbell tells us that even after repeatedly hearing the call to adventure some heroes stubbornly refuse to step near the threshold. Ironically, an outright refusal can still act as a catalyst for Departure when a state of deep introversion drives one onto an inward journey. In Jack Kirkland's 1934 play *Tobacco Road*, based on Erskine Caldwell's novel of the same name, Jetter Lester unequivocally rejects the call to leave the horrid poverty of his Georgia backwater hovel for the promise of a job in Atlanta. Yet while Jetter remains, the world around him changes putting him on a journey toward utter destitution as he loses the family home and all that's left of the family's once glorious life. *Tobacco Road* remains the second longest running nonmusical play in the history of Broadway.

Whether through exodus or introversion, the call will eventually be accepted, for "destiny has summoned the hero and transferred his spiritual center of gravity from within the pale of his society to a zone unknown."[2]

At the crossing of the threshold to adventure, the ego-treasures of the old world are rendered useless and must be left behind. Marie Antoinette's crossing out of Austria offers an excellent, although purely symbolic example. She was forbidden to step one foot into the French world with anything whatsoever from her old life. Not only did she have to leave behind all her possessions, including her beloved little dog, but she was also stripped of every stitch of clothing.

Once across the border, the skills and knowledge having served the hero so well in the old world now vanish, just as treasures held in dream evaporate upon awakening. In *Rainman*, Charlie's gift of bullying is lost in the world with Raymond. In *The Miracle Worker*, Helen's powerful tantrums vanish into self-defeating liability in the world with Anne. Like the phantom sensations of an amputated limb, it takes some time for heroes to realize that they are fiercely clinging to something that is no longer there.

Emotionally unarmed and psychologically defenseless, in a state of ever growing weakness, the hero journeys into an utterly alien landscape where, Campbell tells us, cultures hold their devils and forbidden desires.

Filled with uncertainty, our hero prepares for violence or resistance. Instead, the first encounter will be with a benevolent, protective little figure, often a wise elder, who bears a gift from the supernatural for the hero to use against "dragon forces" waiting down the road. Certainly, not all stories have this exact character but they do nonetheless have its symbolic elements.

The symbol of "little elder" translates universally into that of a vulnerable person who knows the landscape. This "greeter" reflects the hero's vulnerability yet understands the new world and bears the amulets and knowledge that the hero needs to travel there. For example, in *Rainman*, the greeter is the frail, elderly lawyer who understands Charlie's misery, who explains the situation to him, and who gives Charlie the car which embodies his father.

The greeter for Oedipus is a priest who with loving kindness tries to remind Oedipus that he is a man, not a god. The priest invokes a supernatural presence by reminding Oedipus that he once received a miracle from the gods to solve the riddle of the Sphinx, which led to Oedipus becoming king. While this reminder is not a talisman or tangible gift, it nonetheless brings the supernatural into the greeting.

Beowulf is warmly greeted by the coast guard who, rather than turning him away as some banished wanderer seeking a new home, instead welcomes him with high compliments and even sets guards to watch over his boat.

Whatever the supernatural gift might be, it acts in some way to balance the loss of the old-world defenses left behind at the crossing. It also serves to remind the hero of the benevolent, omnipresent guardians of destiny who will appear if one can only remember and trust to call upon them. But of course, heroes, lost in vulnerability, do not remember. Nor do they realize that the vulnerability of the greeter reflects their own—but with one crucial distinction: greeters are at peace with their vulnerability whereas heroes are tormented by it. Through the hero's journey we realize that wisdom comes only through vulnerability and that while we can never be free of it, ultimately we do not want to be.

But it is a long, tortuous road to discovering that truth.

On any journey we take, real or imagined, we move away from the known world into the deeper territory of our banished thoughts. The descent is not so much into an actual landscape of some new world as it is into the phantasms of our own unconscious. In Campbell's analysis, this is a psychological and symbolic territory as much as a physical one. He reminds us of Columbus having to coax his sailors into the journey where at the edge of the world they had placed all the horrors of the mediaeval mind. Symbolically, Columbus' sailors were right.

The passage beyond the threshold into the new world brings not glory, but death. As Campbell tells us, "The hero, instead of conquering or conciliating the power of the threshold, is swallowed into the unknown."[3]

The magical greeting at the threshold soon weakens or vanishes, and the hero is swallowed into the belly of death.

So begins the next phase of the journey.

11.2: Initiation

After crossing the threshold to adventure and experiencing a bit of wonder in the new world, the hero begins a freefall and lands smack hard into hell. Here, in what Campbell calls the "Belly of the Whale," the netherworld attempts to burn away the hero's ego. The hero resists by clinging furiously to selfhood. But as the anguish grows ever more intense, it slowly dawns on the hero that the ego being clung to, is the very hell trying to be outrun. Near the end of the time in the Belly of the Whale, our hero realizes that the only escape from the hell of the self is to annihilate that very self into the divine essence. It is in this moment that Helen and Charlie cast off the armor they have forged through years of relentless suffering and let their ego-identity evaporate in the blazing furnace of divine purity.

This happens by the simple act of shifting one's thoughts from focusing on the *possession* and control of material things to embracing the *experience* of the transcendental world. Campbell saw this shift as symbolic of the child's psychological passage into adulthood. To successfully reach maturity we must transmute self-centered, materialistic childhood desires into acts of compassionate service for the good of the greater community. In other words, we move from being cared for, to taking care of others.

According to Universal Grammar of Story, this transformation begins when the hero enters the alien terrain of the antihero where strengths, once held with arrogant confidence in the old world, now whither. For example, Beowulf's bragging only weakens him before Hrothgar, who does not see him as a selfless brave hero, but as a child coming to repay the debt of his foolish father. In *The Miracle Worker*, Helen's violent temper tantrums have no sway in the world of the antihero, rather, they become ever more useless against Anne's superior physical brutality.

When the old ego-centered strengths dissolve, the hero is left with no other option except total surrender. With surrender comes emancipation from the ego-tyrant, bringing forth authentic enlightenment.

According to Campbell, enlightenment arrives in one of three modes: Meeting with the Goddess, Atonement with the Father, or Apotheosis.

In Campbell's world, Meeting with the Goddess means "boy-gets-girl." When the hero transcends beyond the child's petty mindset, he is mature enough for marriage and family. For this he is given the boon of mature love, becomes the master of his life, and is able to endure any challenge. For Campbell, Meeting with the Goddess advances the hero into the shoes of his father to rule as a good patriarch.

Although Campbell spoke strictly in terms of gender, what he refers to as Meeting with the Goddess is not a gender bound phenomenon, nor is it restricted to romantic love. Within Universal Grammar of Story, this mature love is known as the *Heavenly Union,* and may take the form of any nurturing, authentic, compassionate, *earthly love,* romantic or otherwise. Westerners frequently confuse this form of deep human bonding with sexual love. While this type of love can take a romantic or sexual form, such is a very narrow concept of it. Heavenly Union is the mature feminine aspect of love wherein two people nurture one another in equal support and symbiosis. Regardless of whether we are male or female biologically, all human beings possess masculine and feminine traits. Heavenly Union refers to our feminine ability to nurture one another. Reaching such a state comes first by attaining the maturity to respectfully and compassionately love and care for oneself. Only then can we find another with whom to share loving reverence.

We see the beginning of a Heavenly Union at the end of *The Miracle Worker* when Helen reaches a level of awareness and maturity to begin caring for herself. It is only then that she attains the capacity to genuinely love Anne, and in turn, wins Anne's love.

With Heavenly Union the journey comes to a "happily ever after" end with hope that such mature love will perpetuate the world.

Next, Campbell identified a second mode of transcendence which he termed: *Atonement with the Father.* Here, instead of the Heavenly Union, the hero seeks peace with the ruler of Heaven. In Campbell's view, when this state is achieved, the hero's perspective of the goddess radically changes. To the God-seeking hero, the goddess is revealed to be Maya: materialism, the antithesis of the father. Her flesh now feels tainted and our hero experiences a momentary revulsion for the acts of life and the organs creating it. Such is depicted in the naiveté of Oedipus where at first he treasured his beloved wife Jocasta above all else. But when he learns that she is actually his mother, he feels disgusted by his love for her. Thus, the goddess is demoted to devil. Campbell writes, "No longer can the hero rest in innocence with the goddess of the flesh; for she is become the queen of sin."[4] Her loving nature and prized beauty dissolves into an ugly specter. Campbell explains that the god seeking hero must move through physical temptation to reach heavenly paradise beyond.

Here, however, we must correct Campbell. He confuses *woman* as "sin-soaked temptation" for the greater truth that *any* relationship of the flesh will limit our reach for Heaven. Gender is an artifact of materialism but of itself has no bearing on the journey to Atonement. The limitation Campbell refers to is not *woman*; rather, it is the illusion that human love equates with divine love. The descent of the goddess into sin is but a metaphor for the dissolution of infatuation when the strain of an everyday relationship knocks the bloom from the rose. "Woman" or "lover," or even innocent "human love" are but metaphors for *anything* resident in the material plane, all of which at some point become disappointing. Instead of using our disappointment to motivate us to move into the transcendental plane, we tend to turn back to the earth looking for new infatuation. Love then becomes an anchor keeping us from sailing into enlightenment. Because the material world restricts the consciousness to the material plane, expansion of consciousness can only happen when the temptation of the flesh is denied.

But denying the flesh is just the first step. More difficulties must be traversed in reaching for the father. Just as the lover can be seen as an illusion of death, so the father of Heaven—at first sight—can be perceived as an ogre. Here the fantasized memory of the fearsome father from early childhood is projected into the present. After a first look at an ogre father, some heroes return back to the mother/female figure whose charms act to protect him from the "father's ego-shattering Initiation."[5] We see this in Hamlet where he shrinks in terror at his father's ghost who appears in his mother's chambers. However, once the ogre is successfully faced, its illusion disintegrates and the true loving aspect of the father is revealed.

The ogre aspect of the father and the sin-soaked experience of the lover or mother are metaphors for the Belly of the Whale, where a succession of seemingly endless, murderously painful events come to pass. These relentless trials form a kind of holy fire, burning away the remnants of the petty ego that imprison the hero in an infantile mind. After the death of the ego, the trials continue for a time, testing to affirm that the ego is gone.

Rainman, a classic story of Atonement with the Father, begins with a greedy, bitter son lusting for materialism. Through the Belly of the Whale, Charlie transforms, losing his lust for money and gaining a feeling of familial responsibility for Raymond. At the point of All Hope Is Lost, Charlie ends his trials in the Belly of the Whale with sudden understanding of his father. In that moment, the bully within Charlie vanishes with an entirely new understanding of Raymond, and of why their father abandoned Charlie. The vision of Charlie's father as an ogre dissolves with the realization that he, too, was capable of love. With this, Charlie experiences a complete Atonement with the Father.

The third and final mode of Initiation takes the form of *Apotheosis*. Such journeys are few and far between in the pantheon of human fables. Rather than win love or atone with the father, the hero triumphs over the ego to become a manifestation of the Divine. These are the stories of the saints.

Heroes reaching Apotheosis refuse such human distinctions as those of clan, race, nationality, or gender. This hero becomes a universal figure for all of humanity.

In journeys of Apotheosis, androgynous holy leaders integrate and balance the duality of male and female. They feel no disgust for flesh and direct no revulsion at the feminine or earthly forms of love. Neither do they differentiate between life and release-from-life, or life from death. In light of this paradox, we can only resolve life and death by dissolving the distinction between them. In this reality, Heaven and Earth share one existence. This is the story of the Buddha.

With Apotheosis comes the recognition that the power that fires life also directs creatures to kill for nourishment and survival. Apotheosis brings the understanding that life exists only through death. To withhold life would be to annihilate; yet to give life is also to annihilate.

The hero undergoing a journey toward Apotheosis does not abhor materialism as does the one undergoing a journey toward Atonement with the Father. Nor does this hero crave companionship, as does one seeking a sacred Heavenly Union. The hero of a journey toward Apotheosis can walk evenly through sin or sainthood without identifying with either. Here walks the saint seeking salvation for the world rather than the self.

Such heroes can disturb the status quo without feeling hatred or promoting it. While they are fierce forces of change, they harbor no animosity toward those they conquer but instead invite them compassionately back into society, as did Jesus to the unnamed prostitute whom he saved from stoning, and Muhammad to all he subdued in retaking Mecca. Modern day stories of apotheotic figures can be seen in the lives of such heroes as Gandhi, who showed respect and compassion to those opposing him as he led India to independence. We see it again in the life of Nelson Mandela, who after coming out of prison and into the power of the South African presidency, also showed respect and compassion to those who had brutally imprisoned him for nearly three decades.

While other venerable saint-like figures from history might come to mind, we can also spot such figures among more prosaic and playful fictions. For example, the hero of Ida Lupino's 1966 children's film *The Trouble with Angels,* is the hooligan school girl Mary Clancy who brings mischief and misery to a convent school until she attains apotheosis by surrendering her life to become a nun to serve the greater good.

Heroes on the path toward Apotheosis evolve into earthly parental figures whose love expands beyond the boundaries of tribe or station. This is boundless love for all of humanity.

Regardless of the path—whether toward Heavenly Union, Atonement with the Father, or Apotheosis—the phase of Initiation on the journey ends when the hero vanquishes the ego, overcomes doubt and fear, and finds joyful peace, be it with the lover, the family, or the world.

So concludes the phase of Initiation.

11.3: Return

Ironically, just as the hero refuses the first step of the journey at the Departure, so the last step is also refused. At the threshold of the Return, the hero must leave behind the bliss of paradise for the chaotic, gross ignorance of an unenlightened world. Campbell once characterized the Return as "a little like climbing back into a wet bathing suit."[6] Yet the life-restoring elixir, hard-won by the hero, is needed by a desperate world and can only be brought out of Heaven by human power. And so, heroes cannot stay long in the perfect joy of Nirvana.

Standing at Heaven's threshold, holding the elixir of life, the departing hero can ask the Divine for anything. While the greatest gift would be perfect illumination, most heroes ask for much less: romantic love, health, wealth, or a long life.

The hero arrives back in the material world still in a state of enlightenment that no one understands and bearing an ego-shattering elixir that nobody wants. Upon stepping off the threshold of Paradise and landing back into the everyday world, the hero is hit with a storm of confusion, resentment, and skepticism.

In *Rainman*, once Charlie finds peace and love with Raymond, he has to face a hearing with Raymond's guardian who is justifiably angry and skeptical of this egomaniac's reckless behavior.

Yet the hero's ultimate task is still to come. In our era, the hero must bring ethereal transcendence back to a world run by logic and empiricism. Campbell explains that just as our dreams seem glorious at night and silly upon awakening, so the boon of paradise seems impossible to share. The unenlightened masses—yearning for transcendence—nonetheless rationalize the elixir away. Campbell notes weaker heroes do not even try to return the elixir but instead seek refuge in monasteries or hermits' caves.

Other heroes become deluded into thinking they are excused from sin because they have seen God. This thinking damns the once-enlightened hero to tyranny, thus giving rise to a new villain requiring yet another hero to be dispatched to defend the world. Campbell writes that all tyrants began as heroes. Here, we see the movement of something sacred toward its opposite, arriving full circle, in accordance with the wisdom of Heraclitus.

When the hero brings back the elixir of Heaven, something new enters the world. Like a newborn baby or newfound idealism, this elixir carries a sense of the sacred. Nevertheless, as all things move toward their opposite in time, this sacred elixir will necessarily evolve into something profane, just as an innocent baby evolves—or devolves—into an adult who commits atrocious sins.

Like astronauts having just returned from the weightlessness of space, the hero has to survive the hard reentry into ordinary life. To live in peace the hero must be able to hold onto illumination while residing in an earthly mind and body. Personal ambitions have to be resisted and the hero willing to roll with the currents of life, living in contentment until the body disintegrates back to dust and the soul is freed once again.

Regardless of which path the hero takes—sacred marriage, atonement, or becoming a manifestation of the Divine—the core outcome is the same: the infant-tyrant ego is gone. With it goes the hunger for material gain. Just as the maturing child outgrows the need for the mother's breast, so the enlightened hero outgrows materialism. The hero no longer wants to *gather and control things* but instead cruises on the unfolding action of life's energy by enjoying *the experience of being present in the world*. In *Rainman*, Charlie gives up his pursuit of money to put his mind on visits with Raymond. He begins to experience life not as an accumulation of things but as the experience of constantly becoming.

In a state of enlightenment, in Nirvana with the godhead, the hero finds the elixir of life abundant and everywhere. Even so, only a few drops can be returned to the material world, and those drops quickly evaporate. Therefore, it takes a constant march of never ending hero journeys to keep a tiny but steady stream of unconditional love flowing into the world.

Conclusion of Joseph Campbell's Hero's Journey

In general, the sequence of events in Campbell's mythic hero's journey cannot be made to fit the proportions of timing in Universal Grammar of Story. Myth exists as an entity of its own that comes and goes as it pleases. Although myth follows a sequence of events, it might happen to match the timing of the Grammar, but then again it just as likely might not. For example, the hero's crossing of the threshold might happen at the Point of No Return but it also might happen at the Doldrums, the midpoint, or near the point of All Hope is Lost. No attempt to force alignment between the two systems will be successful. Mythology will not be constrained in the field of time, whereas the Grammar must be.

There is, however, one exception: The end of the Belly of the Whale will always fall at the same point as All Hope Is Lost, which is to say, near the two-thirds mark of the story. Up until the moment of transformation, all heroes view themselves as helplessly trapped by forces beyond their control. At the moment of awakening, they realize that no outward persecutor has been oppressing them. All along, it has been their own ego-ogre driving the misery.

According to Campbell, the Belly of the Whale is a metaphor for "the temple," where self-annihilation is carried out allowing rebirth in the Divine. This is not the death of life, but rather the death of ego-attachment, and ultimately, of fear. In that respect, the hero experiences the death of death.

The pain one encounters upon shattering personal psychological boundaries is the pain of spiritual growth. The journey of Atonement is a metaphor for our growth out of infancy and away from the mother's breast to face the world of adult action in the sphere of the father, who Campbell describes as an initiating priest through whom the young being passes into the larger world.

Having made this atonement, the hero receives a gift, a new identity in the world:

> If the god is a tribal, racial, national, or sectarian archetype, we are the warriors of his cause; but if he is a lord of the universe itself, we then go forth as knowers to whom all men are brothers. And in either case, the childhood parent images and ideas of "good" and "evil" have been surpassed. We no longer desire and fear; we are what was desired and feared.[7]

Thus, ends the cycle of the hero's journey.

---

1. Campbell 1968, p. 121.
2. Ibid., p. 58.
3. Ibid., p. 90.
4. Ibid., p.123.
5. Ibid., p. 130.
6. Campbell, from unknown audio recorded lecture, c. 1989.
7. Campbell 1968, p. 162.

Chapter Twelve
A Moment in Heaven with Aldous Huxley

You are one thought away from perfect happiness, and you are in control of that thought.
                                                    C. S. Black[1]

HEN WRITERS ARE in the zone of writing bliss, an easy incantation of pure thought casts characters into form and worlds into being without struggle. We resist the call from the mundane world for our return, just as we try but always fail to resist the summons of consciousness at the end of a nap.

The philosopher and theologian Henry Corbin[2] believed creativity to be a form of prayer, granting us moments of ultimate peace when we are in accord with it. When a story is gathered with humility, when the writer offers a sacrifice of will, time, and thought, the story receives a blessing to fulfill its potential in nurturing and sustaining humanity. We might liken such a writer to a toddler offering a scruffy bouquet of dandelions to a mother who in return grants everything the child needs for life. Just as the mother is elated at the humble gift, so the spirit of creativity is elated when artists achieve such a state of grace.

In Part One we dealt with the personal and social consequences of stories. Now we turn to the spiritual ones. Without doubt, the most immediate and profound spiritual consequence for writers, is being taken by the zone of writing bliss. Sages and mystics explain such trance as a form of divine encounter.

In his 1945 book *The Perennial Philosophy*, Aldous Huxley (1894-1963) begins by explaining that divine encounter cannot be explained. Still, Huxley gets as close as humanly possible to understanding the subject in a logical world.

Huxley studied sacred writings from the world's great faiths in search of shared ideas about the existential phenomenon we call the Divine. In part, his work was driven by an attempt to reckon with the horrible devastation of World War II, which ended the same year the book was published. The world was frightened, shattered, and desperately seeking unity.

Huxley combed through religious and spiritual treatises in search of the logos—or the reality of the Divine at the core of everything. And he found it. Sadly, the world was not ready for such revelation. Huxley wrote in the dense nomenclature of academia as did Campbell who published four years later. Yet Campbell's work would soar in popularity a half-century on, while Huxley's sifted deeply beneath a sediment of obscurity awaiting a brave new world of thinkers confident enough in their intellectualism to plumb the internal world of intuition. Reading Huxley requires the seeker to disrobe completely from logic and take a forbidden skinny-dip in the clear turquoise waters of the spirit.

Campbell shows us the steps of the journey to the feet of the Divine using heroes from stories as proxy. Huxley, on the other hand, brings us as close as we can get through language to understanding what it feels like to be there ourselves.

©Rick Denhart 2018
Aldous Huxley

Huxley found twenty-seven points of agreement among scriptures, which provide a roadmap of sorts to divine experience. He reminds us that no map, however carefully drawn or intimately studied, will ever come close to the reality of traveling to that place and experiencing it firsthand. That journey can begin by reading scriptures of other faiths in the quest to better understand our own. In doing so, we will discover familiar points of our own cherished ideals in alien places. The surprise of finding the familiar in the foreign will reawaken the power of messages that have grown dull by repetition. Huxley explains:

> Familiarity with traditionally hallowed writings tends to breed, not indeed contempt, but something which, for practical purposes, is almost as bad—namely a kind of reverential insensibility, a stupor of the spirit, an inward deafness to the meaning of the sacred words.[3]

Huxley attempts to revive the power of our scriptures by aligning them with those unknown to us.

In stories, the hero's acceptance of any of the twenty-seven points signals the moment of transformation. This is the movement from ignorance to enlightenment that confers divine grace. It happens at the point of All Hope is Lost occurring in the Belly of the Whale when we witness the convergence of the hero and the villain.

Here follows a brief review of twelve out of Huxley's twenty-seven findings. The reader is cautioned that I have reinterpreted, simplified, and renumbered these twelve points. A serious study requires reading all of Huxley in the original. Even then, Huxley would argue that fully grasping the universal message of divine grace takes more than a chapter, or a book, or even volumes of books. Indeed, all the volumes of all of the sacred books of all time hold but a fragment of the logos. As the Qur'an states:

> If all the trees in the world were pens and all of the oceans, and seven oceans more, were ink, it would still not be enough to hold all the words of the Divine.[4]

And yet the logos is so powerful that a single word of it can sustain and power a lifetime.

12.1: The Divine Is Everywhere

Just as certain industries develop to satisfy our need for food, so certain industries arise to satisfy our need for philosophies, stories, and artifacts to quench our hunger for the Divine. The marketplace entices us to buy material items to meet a nonmaterial need. While sacred artifacts can and do help us focus on our heavenly pursuit, we need them no more than we need alarm clocks to remind us to eat. The material world deludes us into thinking that we are separate from spirit, so we go about looking for Heaven/Paradise/Nirvana in the external world. The sacred scriptures tell us that we will never find the divine-presence outside of ourselves. We can only know it by turning inward. That can be a scary place. At first glance we see only our own ego, a gargoyle guarding paradise, yelling at us to leave well enough alone. That ego must be slain before we can reach the "Devir,"[5] the holiest of holies, where the entire universe unfolds in magnificent glory. Unfortunately, the horrifying sight of our ego-gargoyle generally drives most of us back to the outside world, adding currency to the delusion that God will be found there.

Those turning inward to go the distance manage to move beyond language—the symbol of thought—reaching for pure thought itself.

Just as we do not cure disease by uttering the word "medicine," so Huxley reminds us that we cannot achieve spiritual deliverance out of materialism by repeating God's name to the outside world. Rather, we must achieve deliverance by direct experience in a realm far beyond language.

Paradoxically, in the outer world, although we go to holy places in search of the Divine, we are actually bringing the Divine with us to those places.

One story tells of a pilgrim in search of divine experience who traveled thousands of miles to visit a famous woman guru. For an entire month the disciple followed the guru walking first over the holy grounds of the ashram and then up through the nearby mountains where ascetics meditated in caves. At each place the pilgrim asked, "is God here?" The guru shook her head. After a month, the exasperated pilgrim packed up her suitcase and said goodbye to the guru.

"Finally! You found the Divine!" cried the guru jubilantly.

"Where?" the pilgrim asked.

"In your suitcase. You brought God with you."

The simple moral: We take the Divine wherever we go.

In keeping with the principle of *The Divine is Everywhere*, a story's hero finds redemption in the realization that salvation is a state of mind that cannot be achieved by anything material. Burning away material desire in the Belly of the Whale frees one to see joy everywhere for the taking.

A hero's choice of humility triggers death in the ego, to leave us with a happy ending. In *Rainman*, Charlie begins the story lusting after money which he believes will insulate him from emotional pain. After he falls into the Belly of the Whale and his fortunes are lost, he comes to see the icons of wealth as dead weight. At the moment of All Hope is Lost, Charlie releases himself from material sway by realizing that the comfort he seeks is found in loving his brother and tending to the poverty of his own soul.

On this point, Huxley quotes an anonymous Sufi aphorism, "When the heart weeps for what it has lost, the spirit laughs for what it has found."[6]

Even stories ending in tragedy can grant their heroes moments of rapture. Such moments allow the hero to see the full face of their own ego-ogre and then beyond it in a lightning strike of illumination. In tragedies the moment is fleeting. The horrified hero rejects the truth, falls back into ego-darkness, morbidly grieves the loss of the stakes, and blames the consequent despair on others. In doing so, a new villain is born. While *Hamlet* appears to end in tragedy, with bodies littered on the floor, including the hero's, it is not a spiritual tragedy. Hamlet dies a noble death as an illuminated soul having seen his limitations and transcended them. By contrast, *Oedipus* is a true tragedy because his ego-ogre is not fully slain but rises in the end to continue its love of attack. He turns the attack on himself instead of others, but it is an ego attack nonetheless. Oedipus leaves his story not with nobility but with idiocy.

12.2: The Divine Cannot Be Described

The experience of divine encounter is far greater than even our ability to describe it. We can share the beauty of sacred scriptures with one another, but only alone can we experience the life-altering encounter with divine ecstasy. Those who have been to the mountaintop of enlightenment look knowingly, silently into each other's eyes with no attempt to use the flawed medium of language. Having made the journey to the summit of the Holy and been forever altered by its grace, the devotee can never really tell anyone about the experience because it is impossible to convey.

In stories, the hero returns as an ecstatic pilgrim to an unenlightened world that casts the hero's transcendence as crazy. This is George Baily's story in Frank Capra's 1946 film *It's a Wonderful Life*. At the beginning of his journey, in desperate financial circumstances, George thinks the only way he can save his family and community is to kill himself for life insurance money. He jumps from a bridge during a snowstorm but is pulled from the icy water by a guardian angel, Clarence. George's encounter with Heaven frees him from the chains of materialism and brings him utter joy, but when he returns home he cannot communicate his experience to anyone. The same is seen in *Rainman* with Charlie's failed attempt to convey to Raymond's legal guardians the divine rapture he found in caring for Raymond.

Not only are enlightened souls unable to explain what has happened, but they also return carrying that ego-incinerating elixir that everyone needs but nobody wants. In Mary Chase's 1944 play *Harvey*,[7] the ordinary world attempts to give an anti-elixir elixir to the blissfully happy character Elwood who finds joyful peace in the company of a púca, which in this case takes the form of a six-foot, three-and-a-half inch tall invisible rabbit, the titular Harvey. The anti-elixir—a serum the doctor aims to give Elwood—promises to snap him out of his joyful delirium and make him miserable like everyone else. This is a story of society's struggle to deal with one among us who holds the terrifying elixir of peace and happiness.

It's bad enough that the divine experience cannot be explained, but in fact, we can hardly bear to look upon those who have seen its light.

12.3: All Saints Have the Same Personality

Humans have a wide variety of personality traits settling along continuums of: introversion/extroversion, warmth/aloofness, diplomacy/frankness, logical/emotional, and egotistical/humble, among other qualities. When it comes to the saintly personalities the sacred texts of the world teach that there is only one type, embodying the uncompromising traits of: humbleness, gentleness, peacefulness, joyfulness, sereneness, dynamism, magnetism, and androgyny. There are no macho or sissy saints; for they maintain a perfect balance between being independent and nurturing.

Nevertheless, the journey to sainthood demands an overthrow of deep self-doubt and personal resistance before the fated role can be accepted. We see this in the dread of Jesus as he contemplates the brutality awaiting him with his execution. His words, "Let this cup pass from me," express his resistance. We see this again in the anguish of Muhammad, who trembles in fear and confusion as he seeks comfort in the arms of his beloved wife Khadijah, when Allah chose him to receive the Holy Qur'an. Both of these men developed immense emotional strength and physical courage in the face of unbelievable terror. Yet they developed and maintained a divine-level of mercy and forgiveness for those who mistreated them. In the last moments of his life, Jesus asks God to forgive his tormentors and executioners. When Muhammad returned and took control of Mecca after years of harsh exile, he opened his arms and welcomed everyone back—including his most hated enemies whom he allowed to retain their diplomatic positions and whom he showered with gifts. With total power in his hands, Muhammad chooses beneficence by returning Jews, Christians, and Pagans back to their homes in the sacred city to earn their livelihoods and practice their faiths in peace.

Modern day heroes such as Nelson Mandela and Gandhi also demonstrate saintly personalities. After being imprisoned for twenty-seven years by the oligarchs of the South African apartheid government, Mandela ascended to the presidency where he chose to rule with compassion over those who had severely mistreated him and his people. Likewise, Gandhi led India out of Britain's austere rule and into independence with the guiding hand of respect and compassion for the departing oppressors. Perhaps even more illustrative of Gandhi's saintly nature was his final act: forgiving the assassin who had just shot him.

Mundane stories with the theme *All Saints Have the Same Personality* might depict arrogant characters who do not realize that the strange one standing before them is a saint. Such is the story of Henry King's 1943 film *The Song of Bernadette*, in which a harsh mother superior brutalizes a serene young nun without realizing the girl is actually a saint.

12.4: Good Deeds Do Not Bring Salvation

In the year 1040, Rabbi Bachye warned us:

> The man who does good works is more likely to be overtaken by pride in them than by any other moral mischance; and its effect on conduct is injurious in the extreme. Therefore, among the most necessary of virtues is that one which banishes pride; and this is humility.[8]

According to an old saying; "the road to Hell is paved with good intentions." To this, the perennial philosophy adds "good deeds" as well. Only selfless good works grant entry to Paradise. When we do good works pridefully in order to feel good about ourselves, we feed something that instead should be starved out of existence. The painful irony is that one person might slip into Hell after years of living a monastic life of celibacy, fasting, and prayer; while another might find enlightenment drinking whiskey in a whorehouse. Certainly, many a devout nun having committed her life to the godly work of educating children, forever burns in Hell in the memory of those former students she egotistically mistreated. Good acts can be dangerous to the soul that is not fully awakened.

Heroes in stories of this genre point to their good acts to justify their indulgence in pleasures of flesh, power, or other materialism. Such is the story of Oedipus, the oh-so-righteous king who kills his father and marries his mother. Because Oedipus commits incest unknowingly, this is not his sin. Rather, his bloated ego is what brings about his damnation.

Truly selfless good deeds arise out of altruism which comes about only after the death of the ego. A scoundrel can turn out to be a saint and a source of enlightenment for others, like Mary Clancy in *The Trouble with Angels*.

The pursuit of selflessness is also at the heart of Robert Duvall's 1997 film *The Apostle*, in which the righteous evangelist Sonny Dewey kills a rival in a fit of jealous rage and sets off on a fugitive journey of "good deeding." Sonny tries against all odds to triumph over his steely ego-ogre, begging God for peace as he continues a life of evangelizing while on the run. Those many good deeds do not bring about his salvation, nor do they cause the audience to forgive him. Rather, it is when Sonny slays his ego dragon through humility that he finds salvation—on a prison chain gang—and the audience forgives him. Although in the end he lives in what many would consider a worldly hell, it doesn't touch him because his mind resides in an other-worldly heaven. Like Apostle Paul, who experiences divine joy in the horrors of a Roman prison, so Sonny discovers, "for when I am weak, then I am strong."[9]

When the ego truly dies, bad deeds die with it.

12.5: Destruction Follows Arrogance

Nemesis follows hubris. From Proverbs 16:18, the Christian world knows: "Pride goeth before destruction and a haughty spirit before the fall." Few temptations are as seductive as the intoxication of arrogance. Be it an ever so subtle slip of the tongue, or a bombastic, relationship-destroying rampage, even a momentary indulgence can bring about catastrophe.

Rudyard Kipling's 1888 short story *The Man Who Would Be King*, which John Huston adapted into a 1975 film of the same name, tells of the dire consequences of arrogance. Danny Dravot rises from a low life at the bottom of the British army in India to rule over a remote Afghan community that mistakes him for a god. As he ascends to the throne, Danny grows ever more prideful and arrogant. Finally, he crosses a fatal line by commanding a beautiful young woman marry him. At the wedding ceremony, in terror at the idea of marrying a god, the bride bites Danny. Blood pouring from his arm reveals him to be neither god nor devil, but an ordinary man. The community turns on him in vengeance. Unable to outrun the angry mob, Danny bids farewell to the world on a rope bridge over a deep ravine. As it is cut loose he literally demonstrates that pride goes before the fall.

Huxley warns that our destruction of nature is a form of arrogance that will in turn bring about a fatal fall. Richard Fleischer offered and early cinematic story of environmental arrogance in his 1974 *Soylent Green*. The theme laid relatively low until the turn of the millennium when it took on more box office interest with works such as Roland Emmerich's 2004 *The Day After Tomorrow*, and Christopher Nolan's 2014 *Interstellar*.

12.6: Creativity Yields Both Good and Bad

According to the perennial philosophy, every act of creativity has both good and bad consequences. Huxley notes the example of airplanes which bring good in that we can fly great distances much more quickly than we can drive. But this comes at the terrible price of planes dropping bombs making it easy to kill multitudes in war.

Another example comes from a tale of the Egyptian god Thoth's invention of writing. When he asked King Thamus for an honest opinion of his creation, Thoth got it. Thamus agreed that without doubt writing was good and would spread knowledge. He also saw the bad side: that writing would make people lazy because reliance on the written word would cause them to lose the discipline of memory. Thamus feared that without dependence on oral tradition, people would squander the direct connection to what came before them.

The idea that creativity has both positive and negative consequences lies at the heart of science fiction. We see it in early modernity in Mary Shelley's *Frankenstein*. We see it again a century and a half later in Stanley Kubrick's 1968 film *2001: A Space Odyssey*, which adapted Arthur C. Clarke's novel of the same name and brought to the viewer's imagination the frighteningly calm, ever so polite, disembodied voice of the tyrannical computer, Hal, who brings evil to a whole new level by triggering a new genre of robotic malevolence.

These stories prepare us to manage the inevitable misery accompanying the excitement of our achievements. They also help us to recognize some of the limits of human accomplishment. At its core, this genre reminds us not to worship new inventions or our own ingenuity, but to balance the good and the bad of it.

In the current era driven as it is by logic, one of the great dangers of our fixation with science and technology is the fanatical belief that it is always good to pursue it. We hold innovative science to be so sacred that anyone daring to speak against it is cast as ridiculous. In the full glory of postmodernity we will topple this intolerance as we work to legitimize other equally useful ways of understanding the world to live in healthier balance.

12.7: Self-Punishment Is Easier than Ego Release

Denying hunger cravings in order to lose weight can prove extraordinarily difficult. Even with a disciplined mind bolstered by the expectation of renewed health and buoyant energy, we struggle against the dictates of the body, preferring the evil we know: the self-inflicted punishment of excess weight that restrains our freedom of movement. Toiling with excess weight seems easier than resisting the tyranny of craving.

Even more difficult than resisting food is restraining the tongue in moments of bitterness when we are tempted to use words that diminish others. Time and again we regret causing another person injury, yet our remorse is never strong enough to prevent the next cruel slip. Instinctively we know there will be unpleasant consequences for injuring another. Yet so difficult is it to discipline the ego that we prefer karma's punishment to simple restraint.

Upon realizing that he is the criminal he seeks, Oedipus has a fleeting moment of genuine humility. Here is his chance to humble himself, acknowledge his wrong, and walk away. If he will do so, Apollo has assured Oedipus's freedom and promised him forgiveness. Instead, Oedipus turns his rage inward, takes Jocasta's pins and plunges them into his eyes until he is blinded. Then he compounds his punishment by asking Creon to banish him from the kingdom he loves. Doing this, Oedipus seizes upon a grandiose martyrdom that traumatizes not just himself but everyone around him. His punishment for the egotistical act of killing his father in a fit of road rage is to turn that same rage on himself. Thus, the punishment for one act of egotism is another act of egotism.

Beowulf also acquiesces to his ego by unnecessarily fighting Grendel barehanded, an act that leaves Beowulf nearly defeated, and worse, places Hrothgar in an even more vulnerable position.

Likewise, Hamlet sulks through his story under the weight of a self-imposed penalty of heavy doubt and such pouting that it makes everyone around him unhappy. In *The Miracle Worker*, Helen keeps herself locked in the horrible dungeon of ignorance rather than surrender her ego and therefore avail herself of the glory of knowledge. And in *Rainman*, Charlie chooses a life of isolation by bullying the people around him rather than softening and opening to a world waiting to love him.

12.8: Power Knows No Restraint

In 1888, John Dalberg-Acton warned, "power tends to corrupt and absolute power corrupts absolutely." This insight into the corrosive influence of power is deeply rooted in lessons from sacred scriptures. They teach that the human capacity for power knows no corporal limits and can continue to amass uncontrollably in the mind of the powerful. Other indulgences have limits: the glutton gets full, the drunkard passes out, and the Casanova reaches an end of the body's capacity to perform. No such physical limit prevents us from exercising still more power. Resistance to it must come from the outer world, which at some point will tire of the despot, gather into a collective and destroy the tyrant.

Power, however, is of no use beyond the bounded material realm. Worldly power has no spiritual capacity. In fact, for the person on a spiritual quest it amounts to a liability. While no internal physical limit to power exists, nonetheless, all power-mad souls eventually self-destruct, triggering by their own hands conflict with the outer world. This is the story of Danny in Kipling's *The Man Who Would Be King*, as well as the real-life story of innumerable tyrants who drunk on power, sober up to the hangman.

The constant rise and fall of tyrants guarantee that our world will always be subject to the terror of their personal egotism. Tragedies of this variety always end in the death or exile of the tyrant.

12.9: Cleverness Becomes the Enemy

Kierkegaard lamented the present era's obsession with cleverness, which continues into the present with our investment of vast amounts of time and resources into developing ever more ingenious ways of distracting ourselves. Unbeknownst to us, no matter how much intelligence we amass, it will not yield a trifle of wisdom.

Through the ages, the perennial philosophy has taught that cleverness soon becomes a root source of spiritual blindness, moral evil, and social disaster. Huxley believed that at no previous time has intellectual vision and spirituality been less valued than in these days as we stand before the specter of cleverness that we worship so highly.

Stories following the theme of clever folly give us characters who mesmerize and dazzle outwardly but have no internal peace. As a result, they visit their anxiety and restlessness upon others. This is especially important in the present era where our lives are ensnared by clever technological devices driving us to suffer ever-increasing busyness. We hunger for stillness and the peace that comes when we can share silence with another.

Like many grandparents, I feel alienated from my descendants. Their world revolves around social media technology that I have not been able to embrace. I thought this was an artifact of life in the Western world until I spent two years in Saudi Arabia living and working among both urban and Bedouin women. At wedding parties, again and again I witnessed the heartbreaking scene of young women gathered around their devices showing each other screens, their faces bathed in blue light, while their elderly grandmothers looked on with bewildered, grieving faces. These elderly women possessed a mass of wisdom from a vanishing life that few have recorded.

We have spent trillions on technology that effectively channels away the vis-à-vis wisdom of our elderly. Once it is gone, no amount of clever invention will replace that soul invigorating wisdom we receive when we look into the dancing eyes of old people as they tell us their stories.

12.10: Three Faces of Grace

We achieve a state of grace when we live in accord with the energies of life. Such grace comes in three forms: animal, human, and spiritual.

We achieve *animal grace* when we find the means to live in accord with our own body regardless of its state. Heroes in stories on this theme come to terms with physical challenge. For example, James Marsh's 2014 film *The Theory of Everything*, tells the true-life story of

Stephen Hawking who attained a joyously successful life despite utter physical disability. By contrast, Clint Eastwood's 2004 film *Million Dollar Baby* tells the fictional story of a female boxer, Maggie, who denies animal grace after her neck is broken in a fight that leaves her quadriplegic. Maggie chooses death for the animal body in which she dwells and in doing so denies the audience its experience of vicarious animal grace. Her suicide advances a socially dangerous stereotype that only physical integrity matters in life. This theme is further romanticized in Thea Sharrock's 2014 film *Me Before You.*

The experience of paraplegics such as Franklin Roosevelt and quadriplegics such as Christopher Reeves attest to the fact that it is the human mind and not the body determining life's successes, joys, and worthiness to be endured. To think that Maggie should kill herself because her body fails her is as foolish as thinking Stephen Hawking should have done the same. Living in accord with our animal body grants sanctuary for our mind. And it is that mind, the human mind, which we celebrate as the highest biological manifestation in the world. It is, after all, what differentiates us from the animal kingdom. Yet the mind must reside in an animal body, wherein animal grace provides for its manifestation and evolution.

Huxley further warned of the dangers of our attempting to mechanize grace, which he believed was an act of brutality and one of the great evils of the industrial revolution. For example, since the time of Descartes we have been using a "machine" metaphor to describe the human body, with a "computer" metaphor for the mind. We see this in advertisements hawking muscle-building foods called "fuel" for the body machine, and in the sale of new methods to advance our intelligence by "rewiring" the brain with scientifically based programs. This way of thinking denies our animal grace and the reality that the body and mind together exist as more of a delicate rainforest than they do in the scientific fantasy of a computer driven machine.

The real-life stories of Helen Keller and Stephen Hawking outwardly celebrate animal grace, as does that of the Nobel Prize winning economist John Nash, whose struggle with schizophrenia is depicted in Ron Howard's 2001 film, *A Beautiful Mind.* This theme is also presented in Scott Hicks' 1996 film *Shine*, about pianist David Helfgott's struggle with another nonstandard way of thinking. Keller, Hawking, Nash and Helfgott are giants in the cause of human advancement in the face of social intolerance for their biological way of being.

The second form of grace, *human grace*, brings forth stories of heroes who find the capacity to live in *social* accord. For example, in *Rainman*, Charlie achieves human grace by finding the means to love Raymond, and thus rebuild his family.

Mechanistic, digitized systems cannot facilitate human grace which requires an organic process of sharing emotions face to face. Human grace comes when we survive conflict with one another, experience regret and attain relief from it, together. In *The Miracle Worker*, Helen achieves both animal and human grace when she lets go of the wild animal dominating her life and aligns herself with others through language. We see human grace whenever two or more people find harmony in their relationship however tenuous or arduous.

The final form of grace, *spiritual grace,* comes when we are in accord with our own soul, recognizing our divine nature. Spiritual grace exists only through the complete defeat of the ego. Just as matter and antimatter cannot exist in the same place at the same time, so ego and spiritual grace are utterly incompatible. We can feel spiritual grace in moments, but it is difficult to attain and nearly impossible to maintain. This is the state of the saints who never become deluded by the illusion of the material realm.

12.11: Evil Is Anything Not Moving Toward God

The wisdom of the perennial philosophy teaches that every act taken for the self, pivots us away from enlightenment toward evil. Acts of humility serve others and in doing so, evidence a soul moving along the path toward its heaven. Such acts are hard to attain because the ego taunts us with easy temptation to serve ourselves instead. The Christian Bible calls out these temptations as the seven deadly sins of the self: envy, pride, greed, lust, wrath, gluttony, and sloth. Gandhi offered seven more for the modern world: wealth without work, pleasure without conscience, knowledge without character, commerce without morality, science without humanity, religion without sacrifice, and politics without principle. Indulgence in any of these, moves us away from the Divine.

Stories about heroes who transform from self-service to divine-service are about selflessness, not religion. In *Rainman*, Charlie's transformation comes when he gives up his pursuit of money to care for Raymond. In *The Miracle Worker*, the devil in Helen gives way when she realizes her love for Anne. Beowulf at last gives up his bragging, finds peace with Unferth, and humbly declines the second celebration in his honor by choosing instead to quietly return home. Hamlet gives up his self-loathing and play-acting to carry out his duty to his family. He will die for his choice, but not by his own hand. Thus, he has a moment of peace before dying.

However, Oedipus fails in this regard. The toppling of his ego is only momentary. He soon clutches it back to his breast and gives it life by choosing to punish himself so egregiously and unnecessarily.

12.12: None May Suffer in Place of Another

We can pay another person's debt, repair the damage that person has wrought on the world, or take the fall for a crime someone else committed. But we cannot *suffer* for another. While we might make the mistake of enabling another to postpone suffering by aiding them in avoiding their culpability, ultimately, we cannot stop that person from suffering or take that suffering on ourselves.

Healthy suffering is a vital and necessary part of life. We must distinguish it from *needless suffering* brought on by hubris. *Healthy suffering* is another matter altogether. It provides the catalyst for evolution, and for maturity without which life ends. A common early experience of suffering comes with a child's displacement in the birth order when a new child takes mother's breast and her attention. The displaced child must grieve the loss of position and let the heartbreak pass. Then comes the realization that this newcomer is no adversary but rather the means of social advancement—a promotion to big brother or sister.

On the journey through life we will experience many disappointments, heartbreaks and deep bouts of grieving. Fortunately, as we move through the anguish, if we can accomplish it selflessly, we will find a new understanding of the nature of life that lets us plumb ever further into its extraordinary beauty.

Though we don't often see healthy grieving modeled for us, I once watched a wonderful exchange in which a young mother helped her daughter through it. I had taken my children on our annual Christmas visit to the state's largest department store which dedicated an entire floor to a children's wonderland. Along the perimeter at the ceiling, a monorail train for children moved through magical exhibits of winter fairylands. At the entrance to the ride was an archway, four feet high: the maximum height for any rider. One whose head so much as scraped the arch was turned away. My little ladies scampered through. Just behind them came a girl who had gained more than just a few inches in the past year. Like my girls, she ran full force to the archway along with her little brother who passed through with ease. But the entrance rejected the girl as she struck her head on the arch which hurtled her back to the ground and forever away from this childhood joy. Of course, the girl began to cry. The mother waived the brother onto the train, helped her daughter to her feet, and led her to a bench. However, instead of trying to bargain away the pain and disappointment with a consolation gift, which is typical of American parents, this mother embraced the child and let her weep for a few minutes in silence. Then the mother spoke: "Yes, it hurts. It's really disappointing. It's time to say goodbye to the train. It's a good time to cry."

The girl cried for a while longer, then rose and awkwardly walked around the waiting area. She returned to the arch a few more times, checking to be certain there had been no mistake. When the incontrovertible truth finally settled on her, she nodded and sighed. Then to my surprise, instead of succumbing to defeat, she brightened, gasped, and raced back to her mother. Though her face was still puffy from tears, she smiled and cried out with excitement, "This means I'm big! I'm really big! I will be able to go in the pool myself!" And she set about making plans for the coming summer. Instead of interfering with the process, this mother facilitated her child in working out her own grief with loving support.

Healthy suffering is a form of release. If we do not go through the process by ourselves we never attain that release. All beings must suffer through release on their own. Deny a creature healthy suffering and you deny it life. If we try to help the butterfly out of its cocoon it will die. The same is true with the little chick—it needs the struggle to live. Through suffering, we evolve.

In stories, at the moment of All Hope is Lost, the hero experiences the worst suffering possible just before the cocoon falls away and the wings emerge. A new being is born of the old.

We need today's writers to develop strong models for us to recognize and tolerate healthy suffering so that we too might cast away the cocoon and fly.

Conclusion of A Moment in Heaven with Aldous Huxley

In the last few months of his life, my elderly father visited me. "I've brought you something," he said. "This is everything you will ever need for the rest of your life." Then, with eyes dancing, he recited Rudyard Kipling's 1910 poem, *If*.

I can think of no better way to summarize the perennial philosophy:

IF

If you can keep your head when all about you
Are losing theirs and blaming it on you;
If you can trust yourself when all men doubt you,
But make allowance for their doubting too;
If you can wait and not be tired by waiting,
Or being lied about, don't deal in lies,
Or being hated don't give way to hating,
And yet don't look too good, nor talk too wise;
If you can dream—and not make dreams your master;
If you can think—and not make thoughts your aim,
If you can meet with Triumph and Disaster
And treat those two impostors just the same;
If you can bear to hear the truth you've spoken
Twisted by knaves to make a trap for fools,
Or watch the things you gave your life to, broken,
And stoop and build 'em up with worn-out tools;
If you can make one heap of all your winnings
And risk it on one turn of pitch-and-toss,
And lose, and start again at your beginnings
And never breathe a word about your loss;
If you can force your heart and nerve and sinew
To serve your turn long after they are gone,
And so hold on when there is nothing in you
Except the Will which says to them: 'Hold on!'
If you can talk with crowds and keep your virtue,
Or walk with Kings—nor lose the common touch,
If neither foes nor loving friends can hurt you,
If all men count with you, but none too much;
If you can fill the unforgiving minute
With sixty seconds' worth of distance run,

Yours is the Earth and everything that's in it,
And—which is more—you'll be a Man, my son!

Getty Images

1. My mother.
2. Corbin brought mystical Islam to the west. His thoughts on creativity and prayer are available free at www.archive.org. Also see Corbin 1998.
3. Huxley 1945, p. x.
4. The Holy Qur'an, Luqman 31:27.
5. The inner most sacred room in the ancient temple of Solomon, built in Jerusalem in the tenth century BCE.
6. Huxley, p. 106.
7. For the film version see: Koster 1950.
8. Bachye, 1904, p. 32.
9. The words of Apostle Paul in The Holy Bible, II Corinthians 12:10, NIV.

CONCLUSION

A Confession, A Concession, and A Beg Your Pardon

OR THOSE NEW to *Beowulf*, I must make a confession. For those scholars who know the text and have persisted to this point, I thank you for your open-mindedness and patience. Surely, I will have ruffled the feathers of some academic priests of expertise, so I must take a moment to settle them down.

While nothing in the structure of *Beowulf* is changed, and while all the elements of Universal Grammar of Story draw exclusively from the original form, I have set the story down here as it is evolving through interpretation in the wider culture, rather than from the exact word for word form that resides at the British Library. In the original text, Grendel's mother is smaller and weaker than her child. However, in the popular mind, as I have heard the story repeated, the mother is bigger and more terrible than her baby. I hear something along the lines of, "Beowulf kills Grendel and then finds out he was only the baby. Now momma's coming." The sense is, mother is far scarier. Also, in the original story, Aeschere does not appear until he is killed. His death brings great distress to Hrothgar, but since we have not encountered Aeschere before, we are not so sympathetic. I bring Aeschere into the story at the first, having him greet Beowulf, instead of the servant of Hrothgar. In this way, I have captured the story as it seems to be growing. These changes have no bearing on the benchmarks of timing or the elements of theory. The grammar remains the same without them. The changes help the story better connect with the contemporary audience than does the original form. Since the tenth century, the story has remained in a form that Heraclitus might call "blasphemously stagnant," which could explain why it faded from public memory for so many centuries. Before it was set to parchment, it was evolving by taking on Christian themes that would not have been present in the oral versions before Christianity came to the world of the Germanic tribes.

I have hope, however, that if my trespass on the exactness of the old text manages to perk readers' interest in *Beowulf* leading to greater library check out rates, then perhaps the guardians of the academy will forgive me. They might even allow me back on campus to buy a paper cup of coffee from the vending machine and sit on a bench outside to enjoy the beautiful landscaping and drink in the glory of intellectual pursuit.

In an organic human environment all fables evolve over time.

Kirtlan, who inspired Tolkien's generation in the forward to his 1914 translation of *Beowulf*, urged the coming generation of writers to be bold in shaping the next era of fables. It was a mystery to him that no competent writer had taken up the story of King Alfred or King Arthur to develop a hero for the English people who seemed to have none of their own. Kirklan writes, "Both Alfred and Arthur are waiting for the sympathetic voice that will tell forth to the world the immortal splendor of their personalities."[1]

Twenty years later, T.H. White reintroduced King Arthur and Merlin to the world in his 1938 novel *The Sword in the Stone*. Before that, King Arthur had not been in the social consciousness at all. So successfully did White's revival of the legend integrate into the modern Western psyche that we use the word "Camelot" to characterize the American presidency of John F. Kennedy.

King Alfred still awaits his writer.

From great tales come the seeds of other fables. Kirtlan translated *Beowulf* knowing the English people had no proper national hero and he hoped a competent writer would pick up the epic and advance its spirit. Indeed, J.R.R. Tolkien did just that in 1938 with *The Hobbit*, a tale heavily influenced by *Beowulf*.

Though *Beowulf*'s only manuscript was saved from the fire, translated, and pressed into eternity with movable type, it would have been essentially lost without Tolkien's adaptation of its ideas. There remain other great stories of antiquity that we have outgrown, abandoned and left to calcify. Yet their healing magic is still there waiting for a "competent singer" to adapt them so we might use those powerful ancient incantations against the unprecedented hallucinations of our time. Doing so requires us to free our legends to evolve by moving past our present-day obsession with perfect repetition. The time has come to balance the extremes between our knowledge gluttony and the wrenching reality of our philosophical famine. To do so, we must free our legends to evolve.

Of course, our great myths should never be changed haphazardly.

Fortunately, they are guarded by powerful archetypal forces making it difficult for foolishness to penetrate them with any success. When artists alter archetypal stories beyond a comfortable limit, these stories are greeted with apathy and soon forgotten.

Universal Grammar of Story provides a compass for writers, so they might take up the mantle of their literary ancestors, develop the great archetypes of the past, and use them to guide humanity along the frightening, uncharted edges of the social terrain.

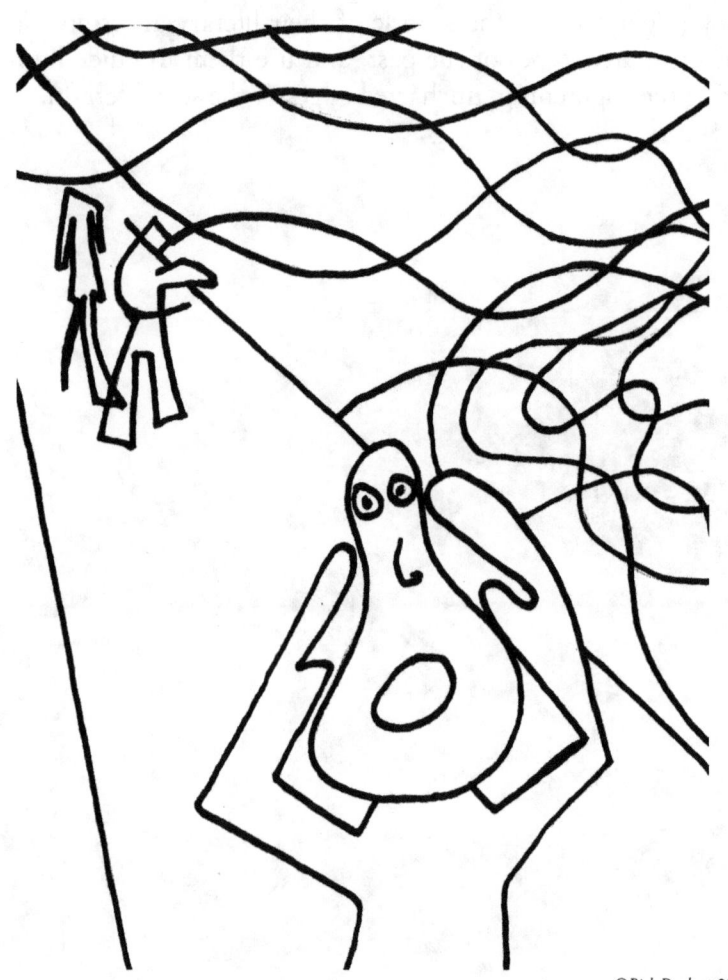

Casting the Logos

ERACLITUS COINED THE term *logos,* meaning *the word that orders the world.* Storytellers make sense of the chaos around us by ordering the world into meaningful tales. Unfortunately, in modernity, writers have forgotten their duty to serve humanity. We find ourselves on the eve of the extinction of our folk mythology—and perhaps of the species. Never in human history has ancestral wisdom been more necessary and yet less valued than now. Our native, pedestrian mythology holds the key to our human identity and graces us with the life-sustaining elixir of the gods, yet even as writers we ignore it, and the culture is on the point of losing it altogether.

When we distill the meanings of the world's great stories and spiritual texts, they all fundamentally point to the same thing: the human ego at the root of all our individual and social problems. Ego drives the misery of the world and great stories are the ballast to it.

In these strange times the most common person among us possesses a pocket super-computer, yet without such devices even well-educated individuals are unable to name a single living philosopher, recall the culture's basic folk tales, or even a single line of sacred text or epic poetry. Young adults enter college preparing to become nuclear physicists who do not know the story of Little Red Riding Hood or why they even should.

Present-day writers will have to pull out all the stops to rehabilitate storytelling and return it to its once-respected position as a means of forming discipline, building ethos, and ensuring our survival.

The role of writer has never been an easy one. True storytellers face down their own demons, marshal the power of the logos, and cast it forth to benefit the world. When writers can do this with courage and dignity they give rise to legendary characters who tell stories that guide the rest of us in purging personal evil.

This is the hope of the future.

And now dear reader, it's time to transform into a writer. It is all there within you. Everything you will ever write is already completed in your unconscious. All you need do is sit by the window and daydream like you did as a kid in school.

Listen. The bell is tolling. Now is the time to face the blank page, gather a few words, and write for the soul of the world.

Getty Images

---

1. Kirtlan 1914, p. 8.

APPENDICES

Core Story Summaries

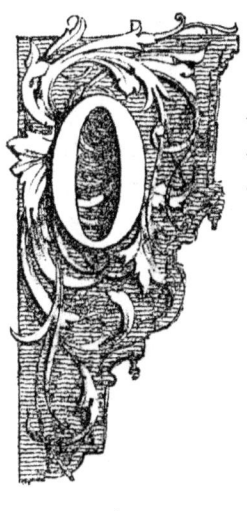*EDIPUS, BEOWULF, AND HAMLET* once held their audiences rapt with potent and irresistible heroes. When they were cast into print, the context of their societies slowly began to freeze in time while the rest of human society moved on into the future. The stories eventually petrified into archaic language and bizarre custom lost beneath a thick sediment of time. Still, at their core, these old stories are every bit as timely, relevant, and riveting as the most expensive, high-tech, whiz-bang-blockbuster-crowd-pleaser out of Hollywood today.

Like Indiana Jones, all we need do is lift them from the obscurity of time for their magic to be unleashed again.

Oedipus, Beowulf, and *Hamlet* are simplified and summarized here to aid the reader in recognizing the key milestones in Universal Grammar of Story. These summaries are not intended as a substitute for the texts proper. The reader still needs to tackle—in their entirety—*Oedipus* and *Beowulf* in scholarly translation, and *Hamlet* in Shakespeare's original Elizabethan form. Theoretically, we modern English readers can still navigate the Elizabethan form but that will not be the case for long. With each generation Shakespeare becomes more difficult to understand. Very soon Hamlet's native tongue will have vanished into the blurry margins of incomprehensibility joining Beowulf's Old English as an utterly foreign language that must be translated to be understood.

Appendix One
Summary of Oedipus

SOPHOCLES (c. 497–405 BCE) composed *Oedipus* as a devotional act for communal worship during the Festival of Dionysus in 429 BCE. The play germinated in the richness of the Greek Golden Age and remains with us as foundational to Western culture. So integrated is it in our present era that a derivative of its hero's name is familiar to most everyone. Men who partner with older women are said to have an *oedipal complex,* a term coined by Sigmund Freud after he saw a performance of *Oedipus* in the 1890s. Freud used the term to describe a child who shows affection for the parent of the opposite gender while demonstrating dissatisfaction with the one of the same gender. Freud viewed the complex as openly apparent in *Oedipus,* whereas, it was present but repressed in *Hamlet.*

©Rick Denhart 2018
Sophocles

In spite of Freud's usage, *Oedipus* is not the story of a man lusting for his mother. Nor is it based on the moral that "no one escapes their fate," as many philosophers and literary critics argue. The idea that we are trapped by fate belongs more to the Christian Protestant Reformation than to the Greek Golden Age. Oedipus is no passive agent damned by predestination like some sixteenth-century Presbyterian. Rather, he is an active agent in his own downfall, playing out the universal and incontrovertible spiritual law that *arrogance leads to its own destruction,* or, *pride goeth before the fall.* Oedipus could have certainly escaped his fate had he chosen to discipline his ego.

Oedipus, the King of Thebes,[1] begins his story by stepping out onto his palace veranda and into the bright, warm glory of his pride.

His beleaguered subjects are gathered at his palace altar, burning sacred incense and fervently praying with holy artifacts in hand.

OEDIPUS: What is this crying and lamenting? I, your world-renowned king, love you more than any other. You know that I do everything possible to take care of you. There is nothing I would not do for you. I will answer your prayers. Tell me, what is ailing you?

Oedipus appoints a priest in the crowd to speak. The priest steps forward but is cautious. The situation is delicate because Oedipus is subtly behaving like a god: he appears in response to prayers, declares his intention to answer those prayers, and uses a priest for an intermediary with the people. The priest tells of a terrible plague on the city that has left everything barren: the fields, livestock, and wives. Before he asks Oedipus for help, the priest cautions:

PRIEST: Even though we pray at your altar, we do not think of you as a new god but as a favorite of the gods in their gift-giving and visiting.

Only then does the priest continue, offering the requisite praise to Oedipus:

PRIEST: When you first arrived in Thebes, our king was dead, and we were ruled by the brutal Sphinx who terrorized us night and day. She would not free us until someone could answer the riddle: "What walks on four legs in morning, two legs in afternoon, and three legs in the evening?" In desperation we offered the throne and the hand of our widowed queen to anyone who could answer.

OEDIPUS: I answered.

PRIEST: You alone could save us.

OEDIPUS: "Man" was the answer. Man walks on four legs as a baby, two legs as a man, and uses a cane in old age. The Sphinx was so distraught by my perfect answer that she jumped to her death from a cliff into the ocean. I became your rightful king, and you gave me the most wonderful woman on the earth, my beloved wife Jocasta. No man could be happier than me.

PRIEST: You are the savior of Thebes. Now, the people need your help again. We don't know how you got the answer to the riddle. Maybe it was luck, intelligence, or help from the gods. Whatever it was, we need it again now. Great King Oedipus, we plead for you to help us.

OEDIPUS: This situation hurts me more than anyone. I hurt for myself, but I also hurt for every one of you. Have no worries. I will save you. I alone can save you. You see, I already know of this plague and have sent my wife's brother to the oracle of Apollo for guidance.

PRIEST: I see him coming.

Creon arrives, appearing jubilant.

CREON: I have good news amid the woe. We know why Apollo brought the plague.

OEDIPUS: Tell us.

CREON: In public? Or should I follow you inside to tell you privately?

OEDIPUS: The message from the oracle is more for these subjects than it is for me. Tell it for them to hear.

CREON: Very well. Before you became king, our king was Laius.

OEDIPUS: I know the name. But I never met him.

CREON: Apollo tells us that he was murdered and that the killers still roam this kingdom. They must be removed, whoever they are, either by death or banishment. Their presence pollutes the kingdom. That is the source of the plague.

OEDIPUS: How in the world can we find the perpetrators of a crime committed before my grown children were even born? What traces could possibly be left?

CREON: The god said, "Who that seeks will find, who that sits with folded hands, or sleeps instead, is blind."

OEDIPUS: Was Laius traveling or at his palace here when he was killed?

CREON: He was on the road to the oracle of Delphi on holy business. But he never returned.

OEDIPUS: Any witnesses?

CREON: One. A servant of Laius' managed to run for his life and lived to tell the story. He testified that it was not a single killer but a group of bandits.

OEDIPUS: Tell me, Creon, why were the killers not sought before?

CREON: It happened in the time of the Sphinx. All of our effort went into being rid of her terror. When that crisis passed, time dulled our passion for vengeance. We let it slip.

OEDIPUS: I will start the investigation from a clean slate. I will bring the light over this darkness and find the culprit. This serves the city, but it serves me also because someone who would kill the last king might come after the present one. My unhappy children rise up from your praying and feel hope. Your prayers are about to be answered.

Oedipus pauses to consider his strategy.

OEDIPUS: I didn't know of the crime before now.... I never knew Laius...and the evidence is long gone. I think it best to offer amnesty. Let it be known that if the killer is a citizen, he will suffer no worse than banishment. If it is a foreigner you reveal to me, then you will have no punishment for keeping the secret. I will give you my thanks and a reward. But if any of you keeps silent of the deed there will be no mercy; no one in this land will speak to you, pray with you allow you sex, food, or a place of rest. I carry out this noble cause for King Laius as if he were my own father. I govern from his throne, love his gracious wife, and have raised the children he would have raised had he lived. Even without this plague on the land, such guilt cannot go unpunished! Now, upon the vile soul of this disgusting murderer I lay a curse: let him live in complete and utter wretchedness! And as for me, if the monstrous killer somehow gets into my palace, then let the curse I lay upon him fall just the same on me.[2]

The chorus, representing the consciousness of the people, steps forward, singing to Oedipus.

CHORUS: The gods should tell us who has done this.

OEDIPUS: No man can make the gods speak if they want to be silent.

CHORUS: The next best thing is to call on the blind prophet, Teiresias, who can see more than any sighted man. He is famed for truthfulness and the ability to discern any mystery. Teiresias can decipher and unravel all.

OEDIPUS: Creon has already told me, and twice I have called for the blind prophet but still he has not come.

CHORUS: There, he comes, led by a boy.

Teiresias enters the scene.

OEDIPUS: Teiresias, the one who knows of wisdom and veiled mysteries. Through your blind eyes you see things the rest of us can never know. Tell me, where is the source of the plague devouring our city? You are our only medicine against it. A word from you and the killers of Laius, along with this pestilence, will be driven from our land. Save yourself, save your country, and save your king.

TEIRESIAS: It is miserable to be wise when no good will come from it.

OEDIPUS: What's troubling you, my good man? Why are you so melancholy?

TEIRESIAS: Just let me go home. I will bear my burden and you bear yours.

In a flash, Oedipus' niceties morph into rage:

OEDIPUS: You are a disgrace! No loyal patriot would deny the word of prophecy to his dying people![3]

TEIRESIAS: Your words, O king, are way off the mark.

OEDIPUS: My words?! You possess the cure for this dying land and will not speak!? Are you seriously a traitor? Would you destroy this state?

TEIRESIAS: I am not going to distress myself or you, sir. You are asking to hear something that you will refuse to listen to.

OEDIPUS: You become the Sphinx with your riddles! Your silence brings a new terror. What will compel you to speak? Will nothing give you compassion?

TEIRESIAS: Easy to blame me, but not yourself. What will come, will come regardless of whether or not I speak.

OEDIPUS: Then you have nothing to lose by telling me. It is your duty. Speak.

TEIRESIAS: I have nothing to say. Rage all you like.

OEDIPUS: It must be you. You are the leader of the band of killers. That's why you refuse to speak. If you weren't blind, you probably would have killed Laius with your own hands.

TEIRESIAS: Now you force me to defend myself. And so, I will.

OEDIPUS: Speak!

TEIRESIAS: You, sir, are the man you seek.

OEDIPUS: What? You make no sense.

TEIRESIAS: You are the killer who has cursed this land.

OEDIPUS: Filthy liar! You have the audacity to taunt me and think you can just freely walk away?

TEIRESIAS: Yes. I am free. "I am strong in the strength of truth."[4]

OEDIPUS: Tell me what you know.

TEIRESIAS: I have. And you refuse to listen to it.

OEDIPUS: Tell me again. I missed it.

TEIRESIAS: I said you are the killer that you look for. Do you want me to keep telling you, and you keep denying it? This is only enraging you more and more.

OEDIPUS: Say all you want, but it's a waste of breath.

TEIRESIAS: You are a producer of incest and are blind to your shame.

OEDIPUS: Why do you slander me!? I am a good man! I am not ambitious. I never sought this throne. I never asked for it, never even dreamed of it. It was given to me for saving you. I am a good man! (*Long pause*). I know what's happening here—this is a plot of Creon. Yes, he's jealous of my rule and wants to take the throne from me. And you are one of the bandits helping him. Creon doesn't like for "simple" Oedipus to have the rule. And you...tell me old man, if you are such a great prophet why didn't you defeat the Sphinx? Maybe you are no prophet after all. Get out. Leave me alone.

TEIRESIAS: (*turning to leave*) Soon, you will be blind and driven from this city. Your real parents would understand the truth of this prophecy.

OEDIPUS: Wait. Come back. What do you know about my parents?

At first Teiresias mumbles incoherently, then he turns and speaks:

TEIRESIAS: The vile killer of Laius walks in this city, passing as a foreigner. Soon he will be proven a native Theban. This will bring him no happiness, for he will leave to live like a foreigner, blind and in rags. He will learn that his children are his own siblings and the woman who bore them, bore him also. Think on that for a while. And if you find I'm wrong, then declare to the world that I am no prophet.

Later, Creon learns that Oedipus accuses him of conspiring to take the throne. He comes to the palace courtyard amid a crowd of citizens to confront Oedipus.

OEDIPUS: Here he comes, my murderer. How dare you come to my door? Are these the robbers who've come to help you take my crown?

CREON: Listen to me first.

OEDIPUS: Oh yes, the silver tongue of my brother-in-law. But you can't hide from the truth that I know you hate me.

CREON: It's not true.

OEDIPUS: Tell me it is not true that you are a scoundrel.

CREON: Your stubborn persistence of nothing destroys your reasoning.

OEDIPUS: Is that so? Tell me then, why did you advise me to call the blind prophet?

CREON: He knows how to save the city.

OEDIPUS: Why did he not come forward with this before?

CREON: I don't know.

OEDIPUS: He never said a word until you put him up to it. If he knew this, why is it that over the decades he has not so much as given me a suspecting glance?

CREON: I have no answer.

OEDIPUS: I do. You want the rule.

CREON: I have the rule. When you married my sister, she and I gave you an equal share of the triple rule.

OEDIPUS: Why did you plot against me? Was it because you see cowardice or ignorance in me? Or, just that I came as a foreigner, a simple traveler? Do you feel shame knowing that someone like me rules beside you?[5]

CREON: I never wanted the forward position. I am happy in the background, having my quiet life and freedom to come and go as I please. You relish the turbulence of the public face. I wanted it no other way.

Queen Jocasta enters.

CREON: Your husband wants me banished from our land or put to death as a felon. He accuses me of the murder of Laius.

OEDIPUS: It is true. Your brother is plotting to overthrow me and take the crown. (*to Creon*) You will be banished or die for treason.

CREON: If I have done wrong, then let the gods curse me. I will openly receive their punishment. But I will not let you destroy my name. I swear to heaven I have done no wrong. This is madness.

JOCASTA: Believe him, Oedipus. He swears to the gods. I know him. You know him. The people know he would not do this. For the sake of your people, for the sake of our kingdom that is dying…for my sake…Oedipus, believe him.

The choir steps forward and pleads for Oedipus to respect Creon's sworn oath and to remember that he is friend and kin. They beg Oedipus to not disgrace Creon with banishment. At length Oedipus relents, but he screams to the choir and to the crowd:

OEDIPUS: If you want Creon to go free, then you are wanting me to be banished or dead.

CHOIR: Never! We love you, mighty Oedipus. We would rather die a slow, painful death than to think such a thing. But, we are sickened that the land is dying, and the heart of the people is dying, and still our great king is willing to stoop to such poverty of reason, such pettiness that he would add this misery on top of the plague already killing the city.

OEDIPUS: If this is what you want, then let him go. Even if it means that I will be disgraced and driven from Thebes forever. Creon may go, but my hate follows him.

CREON: You are slow and saddened to concede. But you are fast and brutal to rage. Justice will be served, and perfectly, because people like you always push too far and end up bringing the worst of their cruelty onto themselves.[6]

OEDIPUS: Get out! Leave me be.

CREON: You have never been so completely wrong. And everyone here knows it.

Creon and the crowd exit, leaving Jocasta and Oedipus alone.

JOCASTA: What has possessed you?

OEDIPUS: Your brother accuses me of murdering your first husband.

JOCASTA: On what evidence?

OEDIPUS: The word of the blind old prophet.

JOCASTA: Have no worries. Prophets can be wrong. One told Laius long ago that he would be killed by his own son, a child borne by me. But that cannot be. Laius was on his way to the oracle at Delphi when he was killed. He was in a foreign place where three roads meet and the only Theban natives with him were his servants. As for the son who was prophesied to kill him, the poor baby was put to death at three days old. Laius had his ankles pierced and pinned together, then cast the child away on a mountain side at the edge of the dense woods.

OEDIPUS: I feel a creeping dread coming at me.[7] When was Laius killed?

JOCASTA: In the days of the Sphinx. Just before you came to save us.

OEDIPUS: What did Laius look like?

JOCASTA: He looked like you. Swarthy, with greying temples and beard.

OEDIPUS: Oh god! I may have laid that curse on myself.

JOCASTA: No, there was a witness. One of Laius' servants escaped the scene. When he came back, he asked to be sent into the mountains. He never wanted to set eyes on Thebes again.

OEDIPUS: I heard a similar prophecy. Long before I came to Thebes, I was at a banquet with my parents when a drunk blurted out that I was not really their child. My parents ignored the man, but it sparked rumors, and bothered me enough that I secretly went to Delphi to ask Apollo the truth of my parentage. The god replied with the horrible prophecy that I would kill my father, marry my mother, and father my own siblings. On the way back from the oracle I came to where three roads meet, just like you described. An old man's chariot blocked the way and I got angry. The driver threatened to run me off the road. I was quick to rage and struck him. Then the old man raised his staff to hit me, but I knocked him from his chariot. He died in the fall. Then, I killed the others in his retinue. But this servant you speak of…he said that Laius was slain by robbers and not by a single robber? If so, then I am safe. But if he says there was only one…then I'm guilty.

JOCASTA: He testified in public that it was many, not one. He cannot very well un-say what all have heard. So, you see, the oracle is not unfolding. That baby I birthed could not fulfill the prophecy, because the poor thing was killed. So much for prophecy.

OEDIPUS: Your reasoning is sound. But we must hear this witness.

As Oedipus and Jocasta leave the scene, the chorus steps forward singing of hypocrisy. They tell of one who claims he is leading with innocent righteousness but who betrays his evil through irreverent speech and action. They sing of the age-old lesson that tyrants are filled to the bursting point with disrespect, and while such tyrants can scale to the height of the throne, they will always topple over and lie at its base among the ruins. One who sins in excess pride cannot heed justice or grant reverence. Jocasta returns alone to the palace altar, carrying incense and holy wreaths.

JOCASTA: Gracious Lord Apollo, I beg you. Oedipus is panic stricken. Free him from this fear. We need our captain to guide us out of this black storm.

An elderly messenger arrives from Oedipus' former kingdom. He tells Jocasta that Oedipus' father, Polybus, has died. The kingdom of his birthright asks that Oedipus return to rule in his father's place. Instead of being humble and gracious when he learns of this, Oedipus becomes irreverent and then blasphemous.

OEDIPUS: Ha! Apollo's oracle said I would kill my father. But my father is dead, and I am here. So, it was not me. The only way I could have killed him was if he died from missing me. We have the proof. The oracles are nothing more than lifeless dust, ashes…like my father's corpse.

Oedipus paces. Then his mood abruptly changes.

OEDIPUS: But, my mother… she still lives.

JOCASTA: It is a common thing for men to dream of sex with their mothers. Every man knows such dreams are but ridiculous fantasies of sleep. So, this comes to you by dream of day instead of by night. Give it no regard. Brush it aside. It is a phantom.

OEDIPUS: I cannot rest in this as long as my mother lives.

The messenger, who has been listening to Oedipus worrying about the prophecy, now speaks.

MESSENGER: You are safe from this prophecy because I knew your parents. Before becoming a messenger, I was a shepherd. I found you in the deep woods and brought you as a gift to King Polybus who had no son. Your ankles were pinned together, and I removed the pin. This is how you were named: "Oedipus," meaning "swollen foot."

OEDIPUS: Who pinned my ankles?

MESSENGER: I don't know. I was not the first to find you. Another herdsman found you and gave you to me. He is the servant who witnessed the murder of Laius. You have already sent for him. Queen Jocasta will know this man. She is the one who sent him into the mountains when he came back to

Thebes just after the murder.

JOCASTA: (*anxiously*) Let this matter drop, Oedipus. It's time to forget this whole affair. Look no further, please…for me, no further.

OEDIPUS: Why? Are you afraid you are going to find out I am nothing more than a foundling, an unwanted shepherd's castoff? Creon doesn't think I am fit to rule, and now you? Will you not want me if my parents were lowly shepherds?

JOCASTA: It isn't that at all. Please, I beg you, Oedipus, stop this quest.

OEDIPUS: Even if I am from the bottom of the barrel, it doesn't matter. I am the favorite of the gods.

The herdsman enters, claiming to know nothing. However, in a long exchange between the messenger and the shepherd it is revealed that decades ago, the two men spent many months together with their sheep. The herdsman tries to stop the messenger from telling the story of how the herdsman found a baby in the deep forest and gave it to the messenger. The herdsman accuses the messenger of talking nonsense. But it is too late and Oedipus flies into a rage.

OEDIPUS: Tell me!

HERDSMAN: For Apollo's sake, please ask no more.

OEDIPUS: If I have to ask you again, you'll leave here in chains.

HERDSMAN: I did find the babe. It was from Laius' house.

OEDIPUS: A slave? Or a member of the royal family?

HERDSMAN: Answering this will doom me.

OEDIPUS: Hearing it will doom me. But I must hear it.[8]

HERDSMAN: It was the son of Laius. But your queen knows better than I.

OEDIPUS: Did she give you this baby?

HERDSMAN: She did.

OEDIPUS: Why?

HERDSMAN: To return it to the gods.

OEDIPUS: Was she the mother?

HERDSMAN: Yes, just as the prophecy ordained.

OEDIPUS: Prophecy?

HERDSMAN: A prophecy that the child would kill his father.

OEDIPUS: Why did you give it life then?

HERDSMAN: I could hardly let the tiny thing die.

Oedipus is now undone. Jocasta runs inside the palace and locks herself in her room. Oedipus goes after her, but by the time he crashes through the door she has hung herself. He lowers her lifeless body to the floor, then takes the broaches holding her robes in place and plunges them into his eyes, over and over, blinding himself. Never again will he have to look upon the horrible world. The chorus enters and sings of the impossibility for any human to find happiness. Earthly life gives us only the illusion of happiness which quickly vanishes amid constant struggle. Blind Oedipus feels his way out of the palace, now radically changed from the arrogant and disrespectful tyrant to the humiliated beggar.[9]

CHORUS: What demon made you blind yourself?

OEDIPUS: Apollo! It was Apollo that brought this pain, this suffering to me. But alas, no. He did nothing to me. I have damned myself.[10] I don't want to see when the world is filled with nothing but ugliness. I treated Creon so wrongly and now I must face him. He will have nothing but fire to pour over me.

Creon enters.

OEDIPUS: I beg you, my lord, banish me to the hills where my parents sent me to die as an infant. Death is too kind a punishment. Force me to grovel in wretched misery all the days of my life.

CREON: I have already ordained it, Oedipus. I grant you your desire.

Oedipus' daughters enter the scene and step to their father who embraces them with a moment of joy.

CREON: I know your daughters bring you delight, as they always have.

Oedipus responds to his daughters with joy. He pleads with Creon to shelter and respect them despite his misdeeds. Then he asks:

OEDIPUS: Let me keep them.

CREON: You are in no position to ask for anything.

Then comes Oedipus' final line:

OEDIPUS: Of course, my lord.

He accepts Creon as king. The play closes with Creon's final line,

CREON: Resist the craving for power and authority. For the power that sends you soaring will be the very same that sends you crashing into humiliation and despair.

****

Oedipus teaches that our downfall is driven by ego. We can see here that Oedipus is no innocent victim of fate, but rather someone who sealed his own destiny with self-delusion. He sees himself as too good to do evil, yet he kills his father in a foolish act of road rage. His refusal to listen with compassion and his obsession to blame others is what brings complete calamity crashing over him.

Oedipus succumbs to humiliation, yet his transformation is incomplete because the self-mutilation is still a grand egomaniacal act. Not satisfied with blinding himself, he further orders himself to live out his days in groveling misery. The ego lives on by transferring to himself what he did to others.

Yet a glimmer of salvation comes with acceptance that he damned himself; and in his final line honoring and respecting Creon—whom he had so mistreated before. In return, Oedipus is given his daughters to hold when all hope was lost of his ever touching them again.

Oedipus ends the tragedy transformed from arrogance to humiliation, but the question of his salvation is unresolved.

---

1. These quotes are largely derived from my own rude translation of the original Greek, triangulated by a synthesis of numerous scholarly translations in English.
2. This claim of an overly confident ego exhibits the same excess as Beowulf's claim to be able to fight Grendel barehanded.
3. Oedipus instantly flies into a rage, becoming disrespectful and cruel when his ego-centered vision is questioned. Teiresias does not flatter him with speech of near-worship as others do; and Oedipus cannot bear to feel that he might be

less than perfect. This is the first clue we have that he might not survive his ego transformation intact.
4. From the translation by F. Storr. See Sophocles 1912.
5. The ego shows itself. He is insecure about his power, intelligence, and social standing.
6. The moral of the story and the premonition of the ending.
7. Rather than reject the idea as he did before, Oedipus opens his mind to the possibility that he might not be so great after all. He is becoming more vulnerable here and we hold the possibility that he might humble himself for transformation.
8. He moves to the threshold of salvation where hope emerges that he might transform.
9. This is an exterior change, from king to beggar. But it is the interior change that matters. The ego is hurt, but is it dead?
10. Sophocles 1970, translation by Berkowitz and Brunner.

Appendix Two
Summary of Beowulf

First Page of the Surviving Beowulf Manuscript

HE JUMBLE OF Old English words unspooling from the speaker felt deeply familiar, even primal in its rhythm. *Beowulf* lulled me with its spell of passionate, incomprehensible syllables from my mother's-mother's-mother's mother tongue, some thirty generations gone.

The modern English translation held no such sway over me, especially when I learned that *Beowulf* is not about the medieval English but rather the Germanic tribes. My disappointment, however, was short-lived when I came to understand that the Germanic tribes were the ancestors of my English ancestors.

At some point between the seventh and tenth centuries,[1] the telling of *Beowulf* had become a popular evening entertainment in England. It was a means for the medieval English to preserve the memory of their nearly forgotten ancient Saxon ancestors. Now, the medieval English have themselves become nearly forgotten ancestors. In essence, *Beowulf* is the story about nearly forgotten ancestors told by those who are now nearly forgotten ancestors. This fragile thread of cultural continuity bridges a span of time so vast it can no longer be exactly measured.

Beowulf was set to parchment not long before the Battle of Hastings in 1066. That proved a wise move, for the story would be abandoned within the next few generations. The children and grandchildren of the generation which secured *Beowulf* in print, would have been part of a new hip culture born out of the milieu of conquering French and subjugated Anglo-Saxons and Celts. From that point on, *Beowulf*'s wise lesson on human emotional survival would be lost for many generations.

After the cataclysmic change of culture in the English lands, *Beowulf* went missing from the collective memory for hundreds of years. During those centuries there existed only a single copy of the manuscript, lost in an archive. In 1731 that copy was badly damaged in a fire, but its near-destruction triggered enough renewed interest to generate more copies of the surviving lines. It took another seventy-five years before the first partial translation of *Beowulf* was made into modern English by Sharon Turner in 1805. It is quite possible that a long span of great English authors ranging from Chaucer to Shakespeare to those into the nineteenth century, may well have had no idea *Beowulf* existed.[2]

It took yet another century before serious interest was turned to the work. At the onset of World War I, Ernest Kirtlan offered a new translation of *Beowulf* in 1914. With it he issued a challenge for a new generation of writers to awaken to their ancestry and breathe it back into the world:

> 'Beowulf' may rightly be pronounced the great national epic of the Anglo-Saxon race. Not that it exalts the race so much as that it presents the spirit of the Anglo-Saxon peoples, the ideals and aims, the manners and customs, of our ancestors, and that it does so in setting before us a great national hero. Beowulf himself was not an Anglo-Saxon. He was a Geat-Dane; but he belonged to that confraternity of nations that composed the Teutonic people. He lived in an heroic age, when the songs of the wandering singers were of the great deeds of outstanding men. The absolute epic of the English people has yet to be written.

Twenty more years passed before Kirtlan's challenge of *Beowulf* was met.

In 1936, an Oxford scholar, deeply and irrevocably influenced by the legendary epic, unleashed the old spirit with a single lecture: "Beowulf: The Monsters and the Critics." That scholar—J.R.R. Tolkien—then altered the course of English literature by opening a wholly new genre of stories: the modern epic fantasy. Tolkien's novels *The Hobbit* and *The Lord of the Rings* spawned from the very soul of *Beowulf*.[3]

Beowulf's spirit continues to powerfully shape stories, even in postmodernity, as witnessed in the landmark tales of J.K. Rowling's Harry Potter books, as well as George R.R. Martin's *A Game of Thrones* and its popular television spinoffs.

Its resurgence brings us a lesson which is as relevant and vital today as it was a millennium ago, and it will remain so long after we will have faded into the obscuration of time.

We owe a great debt to *Beowulf* for coming to our aid against the modern monster of the industrial machine.

Worrying that I might damage the immortal tale with my interpretation, I took comfort in Alexander Green's 1916 insistence that "a good interpretation should speak for itself," avoiding "a patchwork of capricious alterations" while providing new opinions with an open mind in the interpretation of the old work:

> The more the literature of the subject is delved into, the less room and ground there seem to be for new opinions. When

Justinian began his codification, there could be found no library spacious enough to hold the Roman Law. When he ended his work, the libraries were practically of no use, for the law became the matter of a single book.⁴

Beowulf is an epic poem totaling 3,182 lines, telling of three mythic battles fought by a Geat Dane with the title name, Beowulf. As a single story it is difficult to navigate, but when approached as a trilogy it becomes much more accessible. The first two stories narrate connected battles taking place when Beowulf is a strong, young warrior. The first depicts Beowulf's fight with the monster, Grendel, while the second tells of his battle with Grendel's mother who comes to avenge the death of her child. By contrast, the third story takes place fifty years later when in old age Beowulf fights a dragon.

My interpretation of *Beowulf* involves only the first two battles, covering lines 1–2,192.⁵

Kirtlan provides a context for the time in which it was written by reminding us that a thousand years ago, the Anglo-Saxons held a:

> ...somber view of life that is characteristic of the Teutonic peoples. There is none of that passionate joy in beauty and in love that we find in the Celtic literature. Life is a serious thing in *Beowulf* and with us of the Anglo-Saxon race. The scenery of *Beowulf* is massive and threatening and mist-encircled. Angry seas are boiling and surging and breaking at the foot of lofty and precipitous cliffs. Above the edge of the cliffs stretch mysterious and gloomy moorlands, and treacherous bogs and dense forests inhabited by malignant and powerful spirits, the foes of humanity. In a land like this there is no time for love-making. Eating, drinking, sleeping, fighting there make up the business of life. It is to the Celtic inflow that we owe the addition of love in our modern literature. The composer of *Beowulf* could not

©Rick Denhart 2018

Grendel

have conceived the Arthur Saga or the Tristram love-legend. These things belong to a later age when Celtic and Teutonic elements were fused in the Anglo-Norman race. But we still find in our literature the sombre hues. And, after all, it is in the forest of sorrow and pain that we discover the most beautiful flowers and the subtlest perfumes.

Having set the context, let us begin.

"Hwæt wē, Gār-Dena in geār-dagum…" The translation: "Listen we have, of the Javelin-Danes in years past…"

Once upon a time, a boat drifted onto the shore of Denmark. It was laden with treasure and carrying the cradle of a foundling baby. The child was named "Shield" and he rightly earned that name by growing into a powerful king and great protector of the Danes. He was feared by all and collected tribute from every land within reach of his warships. Shield's son and grandson likewise grew into good kings. But it was the great-grandson, Hrothgar, who became a warrior king with no equal. Hrothgar built a great army from the throngs of young men who eagerly flocked to join and obey him. He loved his warriors and they loved him. And so it was that "The fortunes of war favored Hrothgar."[6] To reward their service, he built for them the most magnificent mead hall the world had ever seen using the best craftsmen he could find.

He named the great hall "Hart."[7] In Old English, a hart is a mature stag of at least five years—at the height of its power and agility. Over the entrance Hrothgar bestowed a crown of royalty with massive antlers built of wood.

All lived together within the walls of Hart where nobility and subjects ate together at table and sung rowdy ballads to strumming harps. At night the benches were pushed aside making way for straw mats where they slept comfortably side by side, king and soldier, in an atmosphere of fraternity and love.

But the joy of Hart was brief.

The noise of the humans tormented an ogre named Grendel who lived at the bottom of the lake edging the forest near Hart. When Grendel could stand no more, he climbed from his watery home, stalked through the forest, and tore the doors of Hart from their hinges. Once inside, he grabbed thirty warriors in one massive embrace and dragged them back to his liar, eating them one by one and tossing their bones aside along the way.

From then on, Grendel returned to terrorize anyone who remained in Hart after sunset. Night after night, the Danes defied the monster and stayed in Hart after dark. They lost every fight. Finally, Hrothgar had to abandon the great hall for huts. Grendel was satisfied and never bothered the Danes in humble dwellings.

Twelve years passed before word of Hrothgar's plight reached across the sea to Geatland (southern Sweden). The Great Geat Warrior Beowulf was stunned that Hrothgar's massive army, so feared by all in the known world, could be this easily and completely defeated.

Declaring that he alone could drive away the ogre, Beowulf set sail with fourteen men outfitted with the best armory. Not a single one in Geatland tried to stop him, not even the elders who loved him dearly and had the power to stand in his way.

But he was met with resistance from the Danes whose coast guard did not take kindly to the unannounced arrival of armed strangers. Beowulf made things difficult by breaking with protocol and disembarking with his army without first seeking permission. Such was an act of the kind of men who had been banished from their own land and seeking another.

The gleam of Beowulf's exquisite armor made the officer of the day reconsider. The officer realized he was in the presence of nobility when he noticed that all fourteen soldiers were likewise adorned in gold-trimmed armor and bearing swords of the finest smithing.

But, still, there was protocol to observe and the officer respectfully shouted, "None comes ashore without permission."

"You want permission?" Beowulf asked with a smile of humor.

"Your business?"

"To serve Hrothgar. We come to rid him of the Ogre," Beowulf said. "I alone can save the Danes."

"I have never seen such a fine army," said the officer. "Come, then. I'll set a guard to watch your ship."

In shining clinking armor Beowulf and his men made their way to the magnificent, antler-crowned doors of Hart. They stopped at the våkenhus (weapon-house) on the porch to leave their swords and shields as was the custom in all such places at the time.[8]

Aeschere, a tall elegant man sitting next to the king, rose and moved gracefully across the great hall to greet Beowulf and lead him back to Hrothgar.[9]

As he reached the throne Beowulf cried out with a voice so fierce it seemed as if he was trying to scare the monster away with it: "I am Beowulf!" He looked to Aeschere whose eyes crinkled slightly, and then to the king who remained expressionless. In a calmer tone, Beowulf said, "I have come to put out the life of the ogre." Placing a hand on his chest he declared, "I alone can do it."

Aeschere raised an eyebrow. Hrothgar remained expressionless, motionless.

Beowulf pressed on. "My people have sent me to you. They have seen me soaked in the blood of their enemies. I subdued *five* monsters, killed sea-monsters at night, and endured great suffering to bring my people peace. But I didn't start any of those battles. I only came forward to defend the helpless." He carried on like this at some length before he finally tired of his own voice and fell silent.

Hrothgar touched Aeschere's shoulder, pointed to Beowulf and said, "I knew him when he was a child. Now I hear he has the strength of thirty men in one grip."

"It's true!" Beowulf declared. "And I can defeat Grendel without weapons. He uses none, so I will fight him as an equal and kill him with my bare hands."[10]

Hrothgar addressed Beowulf directly: "God almighty has sent you to aid us. For that I am grateful." But something in the king's voice conveyed he was not impressed by Beowulf's bluster.

"I come to restore your honor and your life," Beowulf said, squaring his shoulders. "I could not resist coming to your aid, great king, when I heard that the great hall of Hart stands empty each night. I come to end the humiliation of your men."

"You are not the first of your kinsmen to come here," Hrothgar said. "I knew your father. And I was with your own king, your uncle, when he arranged the marriage of his sister, your mother, to your father.

Beowulf shifted his weight, as if to prepare for an unpleasant burden.

The king continued, "Your father started a fight with a nobleman in a rival kingdom. He needlessly killed that nobleman and very nearly brought Geatland to war. Your people sent your father here to shelter with me hoping to preserve the peace. I was a young king at the time, barely having assumed the throne. I gave your father shelter and one of my first acts as king was to buy peace for your country with blood money to the offended tribe. That settled the matter. In return, your father pledged his loyalty to me. Your presence here pays the debt your father incurred by a foolish act of youth. You, lad, are here to honor the oath of loyalty your father pledged to me."

"I am the man you need," Beowulf said.[11]

Hrothgar nodded and cracked an approving smile. Then he ordered a bench to be readied for the Geats and cups of sparkling mead set for them.

Before taking his glass in hand the king said, "It pains me to tell anyone what Grendel has done. He killed the best of my men, those who refused the humiliation of leaving after dark. They stayed on drinking their beer until the ogre came and used their bodies for his own cup. He drank their blood and shattered the empty vessels on the rock mantle. Those warriors went to their graves as honorable men." At last Hrothgar raised his glass and said, "Now take your place at the table and relish the triumph of heroes to your heart's content."[12]

Beowulf and his troop lifted their steins. Before Beowulf could sip, he was interrupted by a squat, stout man who had just settled at the foot of the king. Aeschere made the introduction: "This is Unferth."[13]

"Are you the 'mighty' Beowulf who lost the battle with Breca?" Unferth asked.

"Unferth does not like those who might best him," Aeschere explained.

Unferth laughed, pointed to Beowulf and said, "He isn't one of them." Then Unferth gulped a great mouthful of beer, wiped his mouth and turned back to Beowulf. "It is said that no one could persuade you to give up the stupid idea of swimming for seven nights in the deep sea. You were reckless, and for what? It served nothing. You lost. You expect to defeat Grendel when you act like a child who cannot even win a swimming contest?"

Beowulf replied, unruffled, "My dear friend Unferth.... You are full of beer and short on truth. In fact, I was the stronger swimmer against the massive sea waves. I could have easily left him, but because he was weaker and needed looking after, I stayed with him. Breca has been my friend since childhood. As children we agreed to have the swimming contest, and yes, the foolish idea of children was carried out by men, who were *upholding their word*. We swam five nights, not seven, and in full armor with each man having a bare sword against sea monsters. Then came a storm separating us and riling awake the greater monsters of the deep. One dragged me under. But I killed it with my sword at the bottom of the sea. On my return to the surface, nine more attacked and I killed them all. Today the sea is safe for sailors because the vermin are gone. I was washed ashore on the coast of Finland, too tired and weak to stand. But I survived." Beowulf paused to sip his sparkling brew. Then he turned on Unferth. "If you were so much better than me, Unferth, then Grendel could never have brutalized your king like this. Grendel does whatever he pleases to Danes: humiliates your king, murders Danish warriors to his heart's delight—and with no dread of punishment from the likes of you. It will be different with me when he learns of the Geats' skill in the art of killing."

Hrothgar burst into hearty laughter. "I see I can count on you, young Beowulf," he said. "I take heart in your confidence as well as your word." His tone conveyed a sense that Beowulf might well be more entertainment than resolution. The king's laughter spread quickly among the men in the room.

It was just then that the Queen entered adorned in her gold and carrying the ritual mead cup. She offered the first cup to her king and the next to Aeschere, his mentor and closest companion. One by one she next visited the king's faithful warriors. Lastly, she came to Beowulf's bench.

"Beautiful Queen," Beowulf said gently. She was not convinced of him as either gentle or entertaining. To her, as to most others, he was a dangerous man who thrived on battle. Seeing her apprehension, he said, "For you, I will kill the beast or die honorably trying." His tactic worked, and the words melted her fears away. She suddenly beamed with delight as she took the cup back from him and then returned to sit beside her king.

Before the sun had completely gone, Hrothgar rose and bid good evening to all. Before leaving he did something he had never done before. He handed leadership of Hart over to another—to Beowulf. Then Hrothgar and his queen left in somber quiet with Aeschere as their guard.

That night for the first time in twelve years, the sun set upon Hart filled with men and hope. They sang songs inspired by the excitement of war to come. Their voices grew louder and louder. It was as in the old days.

After a time the benches were pushed away and straw sleeping mats were brought forth. The men took their armaments from the våkenhus and clutching them, took to their beds wearing armor for bedclothes.

But Beowulf prepared for battle in the opposite way. Rather than adjusting his armor to secure it mas did his men, he removed it. He took off the helmet first, then the chainmail breastplate guarding his heart.

"Grendel is my equal," he declared loudly. "I need no sword or armor to conquer him."

By midnight's approach all but one had fallen into his cradle of warm sleep. But no measure of rest would come to Beowulf who was so eager to fight he could hardly wait for his worthy adversary.

His wait was short. The unhappy creature whose life held no dreams or aspirations, came stalking. The talons on the end of Grendel's fingers dug into the heavy doors, tore them from their iron hinges and tossed them away like cards. Pausing in the entryway, he greedily looked at the warriors stirring on the floor and selected his first course. He picked up a dazed warrior and bit into him, tearing away chunks of warm meat and swallowing it down with a few fresh bones. Grendel tossed the lifeless remainder aside and strode to another. Beowulf feigned sleep as Grendel came to stand over him, raised a massive hand and swept steely talons toward the soft neck of his prey. This one would be no easy meal. Beowulf rolled to his side and grasped the ogre with his mighty hand. Grendel pulled his arm sharply away, but the hand of his adversary clenched ever tighter holding like an iron shackle over the ogre's scaly limb. Grendel twisted his body hard and shoved with all his might, but he could not fling the human away. Beowulf knocked the monster off balance and the two tumbled over the scattered warriors who were still dazed from sleep. Beowulf's strength proved itself with Grendel's failed attempts to toss the warrior away. The ogre cried out in rising panic as the fury dragged on with neither lacking for strength. The only thing giving out were the massive benches with their iron straps twisting and snapping in the brawl. Beowulf's men, now alert and armed, worked as they could to defend their lord, but not one blade would pierce the ogre's scales. The swords fell away as useless as raindrops.

Never had Grendel thought a human could defeat him, but now he sought to give up the fight. He looked to the door for escape but could not free himself from Beowulf's powerful arms. At length, Grendel howled a terrifying shriek that seemed to have come out of the heart of Hell itself.

In a moment of feverish determination, Beowulf jerked on Grendel's arm, then pulled and pulled again until there came a "crack," followed by the sound of ripping flesh. Grendel's arm slowly slipped from its socket and then gave way, sending Beowulf flying across the room still clutching it. The monster looked down at his shoulder where muscle and sinew fingered the air for its missing part. Grendel announced the price of his freedom with a scream of anguish, bolted through the open door and ran through the forest to the lake's edge. There he plunged into the cold scum and swam to his cave, where he took mournful rest in his deathbed. Steam rose from his mangled bloody body, a dragon's flame finally extinguished.

Back in the warm lighted hall of Hart, Beowulf raised the trophy arm and his men gave out a great "Hurrah!"

At daybreak jubilation rolled across the land with resounding joy that none could restrain, as years of fear and grieving gave way to euphoria.

Hrothgar retook command of Hart, called for repairs to be made, and the hall readied for a legendary celebration. Grendel's massive arm was hung over the entry door above the antlers.

As the day came toward its close, the doors were rehung, benches were repaired and put back in place, and a feast was set. Lavish gifts were brought forth to Beowulf: treasure, horses, saddles, bridles trimmed in gold, and armaments of the highest quality. Most of this he would tender back to his king in Geatland, but so bountiful were these gifts that what was left for him would still be enough to honor a king.

Yet amid the robust clatter of happiness, Beowulf was far calmer than expected. Gone was his boasting and arrogant spirit. His countenance was edged with somberness.

Hrothgar looked into Beowulf's eyes for an explanation.

"It was not a clean kill," Beowulf confessed. "I hadn't the strength to finish him hand to hand."

"Dead is dead, and that's all we asked of you," Hrothgar replied.

"The prey did not die in my hands. He died without witnesses, in his lair," Beowulf said.

"Witnessed by God!" bellowed Hrothgar. "Now drink!" Beowulf

©Rick Denhart 2018

Grendel's Mother

nodded and emptied his mead cup.

The celebration carried on long into the night with loud song rumbling against the great beams of Hart. Hrothgar's queen came with the ceremonial cup. This time Beowulf accepted it with a humble spirit. The queen then gave him two golden bangles fashioned with such intricate detail that they captured his eyes for a long while. When he looked up, the men were waiting with raised cups for the toast. The mighty Geat nodded, then sipped. With that, the crowd let loose another "Hurrah!" and the formal drinking commenced.

Beowulf savored the rich, sparkling mead to his heart's content and with each cup he grew less and less in awe of the ever more magnificent gifts brought before him. By the end of the night he had drunk so much that this great defeater of Grendel teetered like a baby. His men happily accompanied him to bid good night at the door of a special chamber that had been set aside for him in Hrothgar's own sleeping lodge.

So it was that the Danes and their Geat liberators settled down on fresh straw mats for a peaceful night's rest. The great hall, so long forbidden, was free and breathing once again with the snoring of men.

But the peace would not last for long.

Vengeance sparked and began to burn in the dark, under the lake waters, in the ogre's cave. The body of Grendel lay lifeless, beneath his kneeling, grieving, raging mother.

Her child had sought only quiet from the tormenting noise of the humans. This mother had no taste for the bodies of men, but her hunger for justice was ravenous. She stepped from her cave, swam to the surface, and slithered from the water to stand upright on the sand.

From the door of Hart, in the flickering moonlight, her yellow flashing eyes watched the men sleeping. A drop of blood from her child's arm slipped down her forehead and nose. She looked up at the trophy above, then climbed the timbers and retrieved it.

She could hold her fury not a second longer. Bursting through the doorway, she grabbed a man from the floor. In an instant, the others roused and were grabbing for their swords. She panicked when they rose all at once and ran carrying her two prizes, the man and the arm, back to the lake.

Beowulf was rattled from his sleep. When he stepped into the hall, Hrothgar was already at his chair, head in hand, grieving. "Aeschere," he said. "The Hell Dame took Aeschere."

"We will seek revenge," Beowulf replied.

"There were tales of a mother to the monster," said Unferth.

"She came to avenge the death of her child," said Beowulf. He turned to Hrothgar who was still in the spell of misery. "Aeschere was everything to me," Hrothgar cried. "No two men could be closer."

"My lord," Beowulf said gently. "Turn your grief to vengeance."

"Aeschere was my right hand. My teacher. My wisdom. My heart," Hrothgar cried.

"Come back to your strength, good king," said Beowulf. He stared silently into Hrothgar's eyes for a time. At last he said, "Return to the man I need you to be."

Hrothgar sent his grief away with a deep, sharp scream, then squared his shoulders.

"I will find her and end her," Beowulf said.

"Whatever you need I will put into your hands," Hrothgar said.

"I need the strength of God this time," Beowulf replied somberly. He wondered to himself how he could succeed. He was barely able to fight Grendel, who, it now turns out, had been a child.

There was little time to dwell on it. Beowulf and the men, both Geats and Danes readied their horses and charged for the lake. Hrothgar led the army and it was he who first saw Aeschere's head bobbing at the shoreline.

Beowulf's men helped him with his armor. When the catches were secured and the helmet strapped, the mighty Geat reached for his sword. Unferth's hand stopped him.

"I have another," said Unferth, as he took from a scabbard an ancient and beautifully jeweled sword. "It is called Hrunting. It has seen many heroic feats as terrible as this one and in all the centuries it has never failed the hand wielding it in battle." Unferth placed Hrunting in Beowulf's hand then clasped the back of his fist.

Beowulf pondered how different he and Unferth suddenly were. There was no doubting one another now. It hardly seemed possible that they could be the same boastful braggarts they were just a few days ago. Beowulf looked at the sacred sword and turned to Hrothgar. "Should I perish at the hands of Grendel's mother, see that the treasure of my king reaches him in Geatland. And what is left to me, give here to gentle Unferth. With Hrunting, I will win or die honorably."

Beowulf bid farewell and stepped into the gory water in search of Grendel's cave.

He had not swum long before the brutal clutch of Grendel's mother held him firm. She pinned his arms against his side so he could not draw Hrunting. If it were not for the chainmail shielding his body, the she-monster would have easily crushed him.

By the light of her fire inside the cave he saw her horrid claws with talons like daggers. She threw Beowulf to the ground like prey and swiped into his chest. Again, the chainmail spared him and he rolled to his feet. He drew Hrunting and jabbed toward her. She stood boldly still as he plunged the sacred shaft to her heart. But it bounced away without even grazing her. For the first time in the centuries since it was forged, this mightiest of swords failed.

Grendel's mother stepped near her fire to take up a knife. Beowulf moved backwards, lost his footing and fell.

"We all die," he said to her. "Life is nothing more than the waiting for death. And so it comes for me."

She gestured to a small chamber where the armless body of Grendel lay.

"He only wanted quiet," she roared back at him. "And now he has it." For a moment, the mother was again lost to her grieving.

As Beowulf turned to escape toward the entry way he saw a relic far older than Hrunting, leaning against the wall near the fire. It was a sword of the giants, forged when they roamed the earth before the rise of man. It seemed as if it had been waiting for him, for just this very moment. No weaker man than Beowulf would have had the strength to lift it. He took it in hand and raised it just as Grendel's mother pounced. Bringing it down in the soft of her neck it carried through to the bone. She fell choking on blood that gushed out and then strangely back into her body. Her demonic yellow eyes flamed brightly for a moment, then faded with the life pouring out of her. A moment later she joined her son.

Beowulf sat on the cave floor resting by her body for a moment. It was then that he realized the cave was laden with treasure. He would take none of it. The treasure he sought was in Grendel's chamber. There, Beowulf raised the giant's sword and severed Grendel's head. The sword then melted to the hilt into gory streams from the ogres' toxic blood.

On the shore of the lake, the men saw the mass of blood bubbling up to the surface. They cried out, believing that their beloved hero was dead. The Danes then mounted their horses for the sad return to Hart, while the Geats steadfastly remained. Hardly had the Danes departed when Beowulf rose out of the water.

It took four men to hoist Grendel's head, which was carried back to Hart and placed above the antlers.

Beowulf declined the offer of a second celebration, even though he surely had earned this one. He wanted a quiet night and an early morning departure for his homeland. And so, the first night of freedom from the ogres passed quietly in Hart.

When the hour of leaving came with the dawn, Hrothgar placed his hand on Beowulf's shoulder.

"You are the hart among harts, the mighty stag in the flower of glory. Be careful of pride young man. It comes easier than anything else in life and taints all that it touches. Pride speaks to but a passing moment of your life. Weakness will come to you sooner or later as it has to me. Yet you can be mighty forever if you give over your pride and choose what outlasts it. Do not measure yourself by things that are envied but by wisdom that all others desire to be near. Enjoy your strength today but cultivate your wisdom eternally and you will find peace."

The gift of Hrothgar's wisdom outlasted all of the other trophies that followed Beowulf home to Geatland. It was that wisdom which made Beowulf the most loved of all kings when he ascended his uncle's throne to live a long and respected life.

---

1. Heaney 2000.
2. Ibid.
3. Carpenter & Tolkien 1977.
4. Green 1916, "The Opening of the Episode of Finn in Beowulf," p. 797.
5. Readers seeking a purer understanding of the ancient text are referred to the translations of Kirtlan or Heaney, as well as the recently published (and very long-awaited) translation by Tolkien from 1926.
6. Heaney 2000, line 64.
7. The Old English word is "Heort," which Heaney and Tolkien both translate as "Heorot," meaning male deer in the more general sense. Kirtlan translates the word as "Hart," meaning a fully mature stag, five years or older—a powerful, fierce, and wild force of nature that sustains human life.
8. Harrison and Sharp 1883, *I. Beówulf.*
9. In the original manuscript, it is another who greets Beowulf. I place Aeschere here because he plays a prominent role later, but is not introduced until very late

in the original. His introduction does not change any elements of the Grammar from the original. And it grants the listener a chance to meet him earlier, which then delivers a more powerful emotional impact when he is killed.
10. This gratuitous claim reflects Oedipus's curse laid upon the murderer. It is a statement of a dangerously over-confident ego that summons fate to undercut it.
11. Notice that Beowulf does not fly into a rage at being put in his place. Instead, he focuses on the task at hand. By contrast, Oedipus instantly turns disrespectful and vicious when Teiresias brings him into reality. This is our first clue that Beowulf will triumph over his pride.
12. Heaney 2000, lines 489–490.
13. Tolkien explains, "Unferth means Unpeace, Quarrel." See Tolkien & Tolkien 2014, *Beowulf: A Translation and Commentary*, p. 218.

Appendix Three
Summary of Hamlet

AMLET IS ONE of the most influential works of world literature. Composed between 1599 and 1602, *Hamlet* was Shakespeare's longest play and the most popular during his lifetime. Hundreds of years later it remains one of the most frequently performed plays in the world today.

Hamlet opens his story as a depressed, pouting, immature man who faces an excruciatingly difficult situation. His father, the king, has just died. Within only a few weeks of the funeral, his mother marries his father's brother—who has assumed the throne. Hamlet is so crippled by grief that he can barely function. Uncle King Claudius characterizes this grieving as obstinate and stubborn, telling Hamlet, " 'tis unmanly grief."[1]

Things get worse. Along comes Hamlet's friend Horatio with some unusual news: he has seen the ghost of Hamlet's father walking around the palace. Horatio takes Hamlet to the ghost who explains that he is stuck in purgatory because he was not cleansed of his sins before dying. Worse, the ghost says he was murdered by his own brother who took his throne, and much beloved wife. Hamlet is stunned to learn that his uncle killed his father and seduced his mother.

The ghost commands Hamlet:
Revenge his foul and most unnatural murder.[2]
But the ghost warns Hamlet:
Taint not thy mind, nor let thy soul contrive
Against thy mother aught: leave her to heaven.[3]

©*Rick Denhart 2018*

Our Pouting Hamlet

In these three lines, we have the plot: Hamlet must avenge his father's murder without taking vengeance on his mother for her incestuous marriage to her brother-in-law. This will be a difficult journey for little Hamlet, who lacks the maturity and courage to carry it out. Hamlet was born into nobility, but nobility has not yet been born into him. He comes into the story as a childish man who is lost in a deluge of emotional pain.

Not surprisingly, Hamlet sets off in completely the wrong direction. Instead of moving toward maturity he chooses a child's path of pretending to be insane. In his first act of lunacy he frightens the woman he loves, the fair Ophelia, by appearing in her room unannounced and disheveled. Ophelia details to her father that Hamlet's clothes were falling off and that he was pale white and shaking:

> My lord, as I was sewing in my closet,
> Lord Hamlet, with his doublet all unbraced;
> No hat upon his head, his stockings foul'd,
> Ungarter'd and down-gyved to his ancle;
> Pale as his shirt, his knees knocking each other,
> And with a look so piteous in purport
> As if he had been loosed out of hell
> To speak of horrors, he comes before me[4]

Ophelia then says that Hamlet got a bit rough with her, stared strangely at her, and then let loose a bone-shattering cry;

> He took me by the wrist and held me hard;
> Then goes he to the length of all his arm;
> And with his other hand thus o'er his brow,
> He falls to such perusal of my face
> As he would draw it. Long stay'd he so;
> At last, a little shaking of mine arm,
> And thrice his head thus waving up and down,
> He raised a sigh so piteous and profound
> As it did seem to shatter all his bulk
> And end his being: that done, he lets me go.[5]

Hamlet not only horrifies Ophelia, but his behavior raises Claudius' suspicions enough that he sends Hamlet's school chums to spy on him.

These chums/spies know Hamlet loves theatre and they invite a troupe of actors to come to the palace to soothe him. Indeed, Hamlet himself is a natural actor, so while he is playacting in the role of madman, he enjoys himself enough to momentarily move beyond his grief. He is also clever enough at his craft to fool everyone in the court into thinking he is crazy—even the audience begins to wonder if his insanity is just an act.

When the actors arrive, Hamlet experiences a burst of excitement and joins them in reciting lines from a play about Hecuba—who faced a similar situation to his own. Hamlet knows the play so well that he recites his lines from memory, stepping into the role with complete abandon in a mesmerizing performance.

When Hamlet steps away from the actors, the weight of reality hits him with brutal self-doubts. He despises himself for so eagerly and willingly taking a stand for the fictional Hecuba when he has taken no stand for the far more dramatic reality of his father's murder and the moral destruction of his mother.

Hamlet's most ardent adversary is himself, with whom he sets to emotional combat. Alone, he cries out:

> O, what a rogue and peasant slave am I!
> Is it not monstrous that this player here,
> But in a fiction, in a dream of passion,
> Could force his soul so to his own conceit...
> ...and all for nothing!...
> For Hecuba!
> What's Hecuba to him, or he to Hecuba,
> That he should weep for her?...
> ...Yet I,
> A dull and muddy-mettled rascal, peak,
> Like John-a-dreams, unpregnant of my cause,
> And can say nothing; no, not for a king,
> Upon whose property and most dear life
> A damn'd defeat was made. Am I a coward?
> Who calls me villain?...
> But I am pigeon-liver'd and lack gall...
> O, vengeance!
> Why, what an ass am I! This is most brave,
> That I, the son of a dear father murder'd,
> Prompted to my revenge by heaven and hell,
> Must, like a whore, unpack my heart with words....[6]

Yet out of this self-battle Hamlet seizes on a plan of action to use his love of theatre in the service of reality. Before he can act on his father's murder he must have hard proof of it. To get that proof he will use the actors:

> I'll have these players
> Play something like the murder of my father
> Before mine uncle: I'll observe his looks.[7]

Hamlet then writes a scene to add to the beginning of the actors' play that recreates the murder exactly as told by the ghost.

Before the performance, Hamlet visits Ophelia again. Before entering her room, he lapses into another self-battle presented in a long soliloquy. This scene comes near the forty-percent mark of the play, at the dreaded coordinates of writers' doldrums where slackening creative winds generally threaten fatal writer's block. Yet it is here that Shakespeare gambles on continuing a sequence that might easily kill any other story. In doing so, St. Shakespeare unleashes his perfect genius with the most famous lines of English theatre:

> To be, or not to be: that is the question:
> Whether 'tis nobler in the mind to suffer
> The slings and arrows of outrageous fortune,
> Or to take arms against a sea of troubles,
> And by opposing end them? To die: to sleep;
> No more; and by a sleep to say we end
> The heart-ache and the thousand natural shocks
> That flesh is heir to, 'tis a consummation
> Devoutly to be wish'd. To die, to sleep;
> To sleep: perchance to dream.[8]

Hamlet, still trapped in the mind of a recalcitrant child, contemplates suicide as a means of getting out of grown-up duty. He presses on with his foolish plan of acting insane. Knowing the king is eavesdropping, Hamlet again uses Ophelia, the love of his life, to rattle the king. Hamlet launches a vicious attack on her, telling her never to marry because husband and children will turn her evil. Five times he pleads with her to

> Get thee to a nunnery![9]

After Hamlet leaves her, the king steps out from eavesdropping and makes plans to send his lunatic nephew-come-stepson to England, where he'll either recover from his insanity or no one will care.

As the court gathers to watch the play, Hamlet appears strangely playful with Ophelia, even though he has just emotionally brutalized her. Now, he teases her, and lays his head in her lap to watch the play.

When the murder scene unfolds, King Claudius jumps up from his seat and runs out of the room—thus proving his guilt to Hamlet. The young prince has no choice now but to kill Claudius.

Hamlet's opportunity comes in the next scene, when he comes upon Claudius kneeling in prayer. It would be easy for Hamlet to plunge a dagger in his back. However, in contemplating the moment, Hamlet realizes that if Claudius dies while praying, he will gain entry to Heaven. This means Hamlet's father's ghost would languish in Purgatory while Claudius would go scot-free to paradise.

Thus, Hamlet passes up the opportunity and instead goes to confront his mother in her room. Unbeknownst to Hamlet, they will not be alone. Ophelia's father Polonius hides behind a curtain there. Just before entering the room, Hamlet steadies himself, reminding himself not to go crazy and kill his mother in a rage of vengeance:

> Soft! now to my mother.
> O heart, lose not thy nature; let not ever
> The soul of Nero enter this firm bosom:
> Let me be cruel, not unnatural:
> I will speak daggers to her, but use none,[10]

Indeed, once inside the room he does speak daggers to her.

> You are the queen, your husband's brother's wife;
> And—would it were not so!—you are my mother.

Then,

> Nay, but to live
> In the rank sweat of an enseamed bed,
> Stew'd in corruption, honeying and making love
> Over the nasty sty,— [11]

The queen, unable to bear the harsh words any longer, cries for help. Polonius cries back from behind the curtain. Hamlet, mistaking Polonius for Claudius, loses his head in a moment of rage, and drives his sword through the curtain, killing Polonius. Yet, Hamlet shows no remorse at the sight of the lifeless body of Ophelia's father now lying at his feet. He returns to the disrespectful and violent screaming at his mother.

Suddenly, the ghost of Hamlet's father appears. But only Hamlet can see him. His mother trembles in fear at the bizarre one-sided conversation.

Having failed to carry out his father's directive: by not avenging his murder, and by now taking vengeance on his mother in defiance of his father's command, Hamlet crumbles into a sniveling mass, crying out before the ghost:

> Do you not come your tardy son to chide,
> That, lapsed in time and passion, lets go by
> The important acting of your dread command?
> O, say![12]

The unhappy Ghost replies:

> Do not forget: this visitation
> Is but to whet thy almost blunted purpose.[13]

The ghost reminds Hamlet of his mission to save his mother, not disrespect her:

> But look, amazement on thy mother sits:
> O, step between her and her fighting soul:
> Conceit in weakest bodies strongest works:
> Speak to her, Hamlet.[14]

In this moment we understand that the throne was not the highest prize bringing discord between the two king-brothers. *It was the queen they most highly desired*, whom they both deeply loved, and for whom one killed the other.

Irrespective of her mistakes, Hamlet's mother still needs a leader and it is Hamlet's duty to rise to that station. A noble man is one who moves beyond his rage, bears his injuries with dignity, and, with grace, leads the very ones who injured him. Regardless of how badly Hamlet's mother behaved or how deeply she wounded him, she still needs a noble leader. This is a transcendental moment, when nobility is born into Hamlet and he matures into the leader she needs him to be.

> For the first time, he speaks softly and gently to his mother, asking,
> How is it with you, lady?[15]

He has overcome his tantrum and begins respectful leadership by telling her the truth: that he is not mad but only acting so to prove the murder of his father. She is shocked at the news and turns to him, now as the first subject in his new realm, allowing him to direct her on what to do next. But for poor Ophelia, it is too late. She falls into madness with the news of her father's death.

Claudius banishes Hamlet to England (on the basis of his madness), although he orders the young prince to be assassinated at the dock upon his arrival.

Fate intervenes on the voyage when pirates overtake the ship and accept Hamlet as a prisoner for ransom. Horatio (the friend at the beginning who sees the ghost with Hamlet), arranges for the ransom to return Hamlet to Denmark. Hamlet arrives during the funeral for Ophelia, who has drowned herself. He jumps onto her coffin after it is lowered in the grave, that he might be near her one last time. Ophelia's brother, seeking vengeance for Hamlet killing their father which led to Ophelia's suicide, jumps into the grave to fight with Hamlet. The fight stops and the two agree to a duel.

When Claudius learns that Hamlet is back, he arranges to make it certain he is killed in the duel by poisoning the sword of Hamlet's opponent as well as Hamlet's drinking chalice.

In the duel, Hamlet is scraped by the poison sword. The fight then turns chaotic, both swords are dropped, and each man unwittingly takes up the sword of the other. Hamlet takes revenge for the earlier scrape by cutting his opponent. Just then, Hamlet's mother accidently drinks from the poison chalice and dies. Next, Ophelia's brother succumbs to the poison of the sword cut and dies. Hamlet then turns and runs his sword into Claudius, who collapses and dies. At last, Hamlet succumbs to his own fatal poisoning.

With no one left to defend Denmark, it is invaded and taken over by a foreign power at the hands of Fortinbras, a prince like Hamlet, but one who chose duty over emotion.

Curtain.

---

1. Shakespeare, *Hamlet*, act I, scene II, line 94.
2. Ibid., scene V, line 25.

3. Ibid., lines 84–86.
4. Shakespeare, act II, scene I, lines 77–84.
5. Ibid., lines 88–96.
6. Shakespeare, act II, scene II, lines 523–561.
7. Ibid., lines 570–572.
8. Shakespeare, act III, scene I, lines 56–64.
9. Ibid. line 121.
10. Shakespeare, act III, scene II, lines 375–379.
11. Ibid., scene IV, lines 91–93.
12. Ibid., lines 106–109.
13. Ibid., lines 110–111.
14. Ibid., lines 112–114.
15. Ibid., line 115.

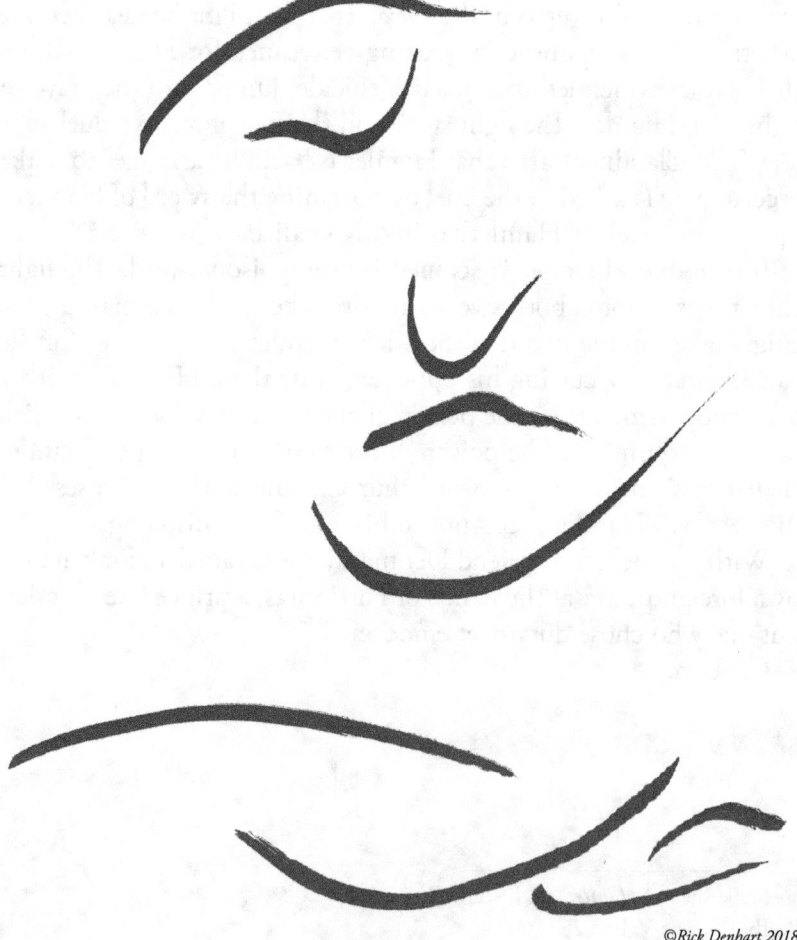

©Rick Denhart 2018

ACKNOWLEDGMENTS

Great appreciation is given to Jessica Peterson for her excellent interior design, bringing this book to an amazing level. Heartfelt gratitude is bestowed to Akiala I. for delightful and energetic developmental editing and creative insight. And a special thank you to Amanda Cassingham-Bardwell for her remarkable knowledge and skill in collaborating with Rick Denhart on the cover design.

Photography and Art Credits

Cover: *The Call to Write*, Rick Denhart, 2018; an adaptation of Rossetti's *Venus* with permission from the Russell-Cotes Museum.
P. vii: *Chokmah of Wedding Day*, Rick Denhart, 2018.
P. ix *Binah of Wedding Day*, Rick Denhart, 2018.
P. 4: *Hod of Wedding Day*, Rick Denhart, 2018.
P. 6: *Hazel and Grandmother on Wedding Day*, Hazel Denhart, 1973.
P. 8: *Member of Mara-18 Gang*, Guatemala, Getty Images.
P. 10: *An Echo in Briah*, Rick Denhart, 2018.
P. 12: *An Echo in Yitzerah*, Rick Denhart, 2018.
P. 14: *The Echo*, Rick Denhart, 2018; an interpretation of Munch's 1893 *The Scream*.
P. 15: *Charlie Chaplin, 1936* in *Modern Times* © Roy Export S.A.S.
P. 16: *Pruitt-Igoe Housing Development Demolition*, U.S. Department of Housing and Urban Development, 1972.
P. 17: *A Blob of Time*, Rick Denhart, 2018; an interpretation of Salvador Dali's *The Persistence of Memory*.
P. 19: *The Fall of Modernity*, Rick Denhart, 2018.
P. 20: *A Monkey in Harlow's Study*, reprinted in the public domain from Harlow, H., 1958. "The Nature of Love." *American Psychologist* (13: 673–685).
P. 22: *Grandmother 1926, Welcomed for Thanksgiving as a Baby in the Arms of Her Mother*. Reprinted in the public domain from family archives. Name withheld upon request.
P. 23: *The Wire Mesh Momma*, Rick Denhart, 2018.
P. 26: *Ruins of the Theatre of Dionysus*, courtesy of Jorge Lascar.
P. 28: *The Rising Dust of Postmodernity*, Rick Denhart, 2018.
P. 31: *The Strictly Logical Mother*, Rick Denhart, 2018.

P. 34: *Jung Descending*, Rick Denhart, 2018.
P. 35: *A Blob of Synchronicity*, Rick Denhart, 2018.
P. 37: *God's Good Idea of Jung*, Rick Denhart, 2018.
P. 41: *Jung's Good Idea of God*, Rick Denhart, 2018.
P. 52: *Heraclitus Hearing*, Rick Denhart, 2018.
P. 61: *Heraclitus Forming*, Rick Denhart, 2018.
P. 69: *Heraclitus Arriving*, Rick Denhart, 2018.
P. 72: *Crying for the Soul of the World*, Rick Denhart, 2018; an interpretation of Johannes Morseele's *Heraclitus*.
P. 76: *Lajos Egri*, Rick Denhart, 2018.
P. 89: *Helen Keller and Anne Sullivan, c. 1888*, courtesy of Perkins School for the Blind.
P. 91: *Bernard Grebanier*, Rick Denhart, 2018.
P. 92: *Aristotle*, Rick Denhart, 2018.
P. 125: *Sense-able Machine*, Rick Denhart, 2018.
P. 130: *Jung Pretending*, Rick Denhart, 2018.
P. 134: *Joseph Campbell*, Rick Denhart, 2018.
P. 148: *Aldous Huxley*, Rick Denhart, 2018.
P. 164: Walking through the Heather, Getty Images.
P. 170: *An Echo Somewhere in Assiah*, Rick Denhart, 2018.
P. 172: *History lies in within these pages*, Getty Images.
P. 177: *Sophocles*, Rick Denhart, 2018.
P. 193: First page of the surviving Beowulf manuscript, courtesy of the British Library, *Cotton MS Vitellius A XV* (ff 94r–209v).
P. 196: *Grendel*, Rick Denhart, 2018.
P. 203: *Grendel's Mother*, Rick Denhart, 2018.
P. 209: *Our Pouting Hamlet*, Rick Denhart, 2018.
P. 216: *The Timeless Guardian*, Rick Denhart, 2018.
P. 233: *The Prince and the Sun*, Getty Images.

Every effort has been made to locate the owners of copyright materials appearing in this book to secure permissions as required and provide acknowledgement in the references and endnotes. Should it become known that any material has been used without permission, please contact the publisher.

ART SERIES ABSTRACTIONS

The series abstractions by Rick Denhart are meant to be seen together and so are provided here to enhance the viewer's perspective.

Wedding Day Series by Rick Denhart (2018).

| Original Wedding Photo © Hazel Denhart 1973 P. 6 | Hod of Wedding Day P. 4 | Binah of Wedding Day P. ix | Chokmah of Wedding Day P. vii |

The Echo Series by Rick Denhart (2018); an interpretation of Edward Munch's *The Scream* (1888).

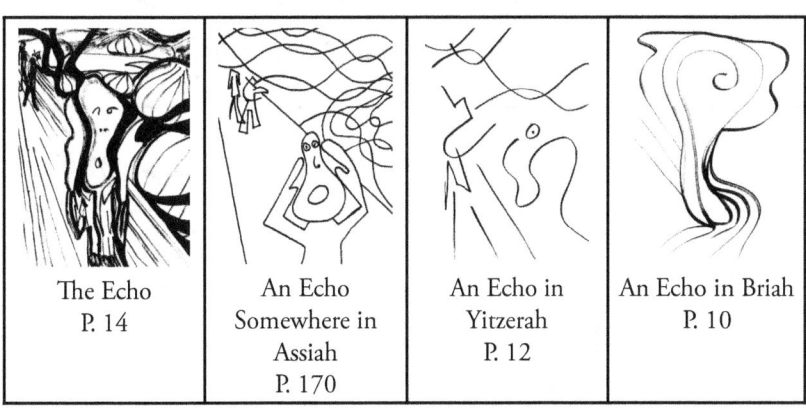

| The Echo P. 14 | An Echo Somewhere in Assiah P. 170 | An Echo in Yitzerah P. 12 | An Echo in Briah P. 10 |

Interpretations of *The Persistence of Memory* by Rick Denhart (2018).

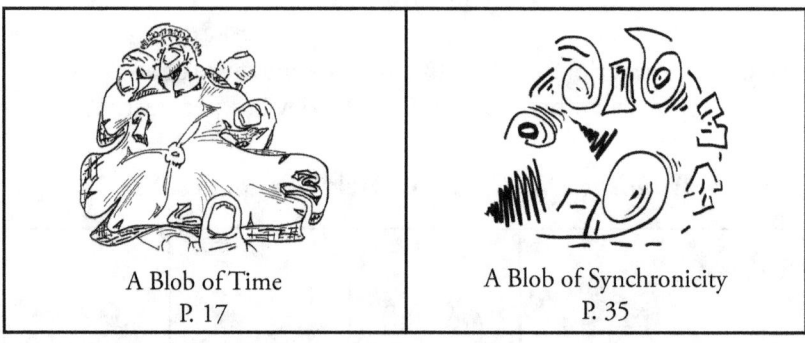

The Pruitt-Igoe Demolition Abstractions by Rick Denhart (2018).

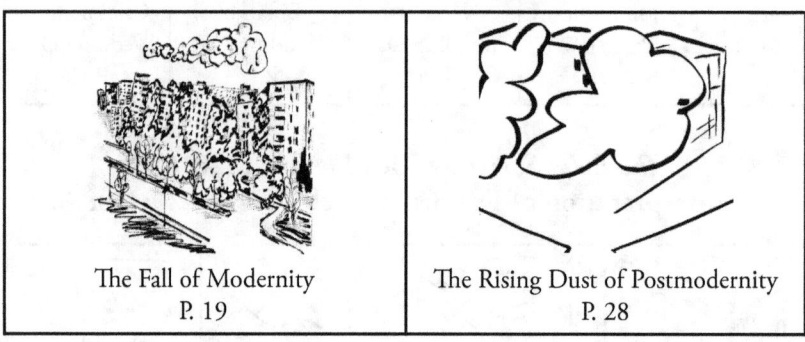

The Wire Mesh Momma Series by Rick Denhart (2018).

ART SERIES ABSTRACTIONS • 221

Jung Series by Rick Denhart (2018).

| Jung Pretending P. 130 | Jung's Good Idea of God P. 41 | God's Good Idea of Jung P. 37 | Jung Descending P. 34 |

Heraclitus Series by Rick Denhart (2018).

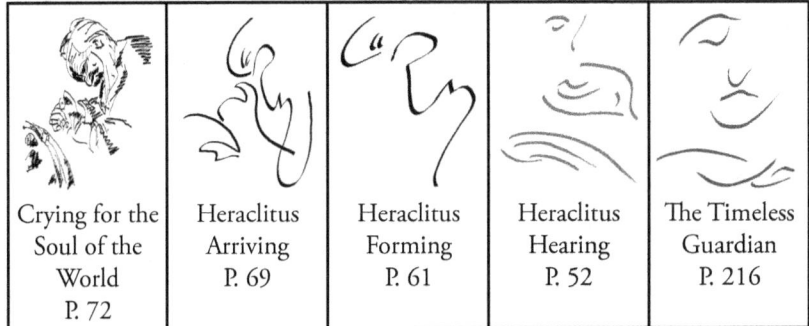

| Crying for the Soul of the World P. 72 | Heraclitus Arriving P. 69 | Heraclitus Forming P. 61 | Heraclitus Hearing P. 52 | The Timeless Guardian P. 216 |

BIBLIOGRAPHY

Abbott, Edwin. *Flatland: a Romance of Many Dimensions.* Boston: Roberts Brothers, 1885.

Armstrong, Karen. *Jerusalem: One City, Three Faiths.* New York: Ballantine Books, 2005.

Associated Press. "Spain Grants Citizenship to 4,300 Descendants of Sephardic Jews." Haaretz (October 2, 2015).

Bachye, ibn Pekuda. *Duties of the Heart.* Translated by Edwin Collins. Wisdom of the East. E. P. Dutton and Company, 1904.

Baker, Sydney. "The Theory of Silences." Journal of General Psychology 53 (1955): 145–67.

Banham, Reyner. *The New Brutalism.* New York: Architectural Press, 1966.

British Broadcasting Corporation. *Hamlet: The Actor's View.* May 16, 1954.

British Broadcasting Corporation. *The Race for Everest.* May 27, 2003.

Bly, Robert. *The Sibling Society.* First ed. Reading, MA: Addison-Wesley, 1996.

Burnet, John. *Greek Philosophy.* London: Macmillan and Co., 1914.

Butcher, S. H. *Aristotle's Theory of Poetry and Fine Art.* Fourth ed., New York: Dover, 1951.

Campbell, Joseph. *The Hero with a Thousand Faces.* New York: Bolligen Foundation Inc., 1949.

Capra, Frank. *It's a Wonderful Life.* United States: RKO Radio Pictures, National Celebrity Video, 1946.

Carpenter, Humphrey. *J. R. R. Tolkien: A Biography.* London: G. Allen & Unwin, 1977.

Chaplin, Charlie. *Modern Times.* US: United Artists, 1936.

Chase, Mary. *Harvey, a Comedy* (1944). Dramatists Play Service, New York, 1971.

Clark, William George, and William Aldis, eds. *The Works of William Shakespeare.* Vol. VIII. Cambridge, MA: MacMillian and Co., 1866.

Corbin, Henry. *Alone with the Alone: Creative Imagination in the Sūfism of Ibn 'Arabī.* Princeton, New Jersey: Princeton University Press, 1998.

Dalberg-Acton, John Emerich Edward. "Letter to Mandell Creighton (5 April 1887)." Chapter appendix in *Historical Essays and Studies*. Edited by John Neville Figgis and Reginald Vere Laurence. Macmillan and Co., 1908.

Dali, Salvador. *The Persistence of Memory*. Museum of Modern Art, New York, 1931.

Denhart, Hazel. *Baikal*. Directed by David Demke, 35 minutes. Portland, Oregon: Interstate Firehouse Cultural Center, 1991.

———. *Bite Your Tongue*. Directed by Daniel Brunnet, 45 minutes. Berlin, Germany: Twelfth Internationales Literaturfestival Berlin: Shakespeare and Sons Books, 2012.

———. *The Frailing*. Directed by Angela Wheeler, 35 minutes. Portland, Oregon: Portland Community College, Little Theater, 1985.

———. *To Walk in the Sun*. Portland, Oregon: Dramatists Resource Center, 1990.

Duvall, Robert. *The Apostle*. USA: October Films, 1997.

Eastwood, Clint. *Million Dollar Baby*. USA: Warner Bros. Pictures, 2004.

———. Sully. USA: Warner Bros. Pictures, 2016.

Egri, Lajos. *The Art of Dramatic Writing: Its Basis in the Creative Interpretation of Human Motives*. Rev. ed. New York: Simon and Schuster, 1960.

———. *How to Write a Play: The Principles of Play Construction Applied to Creative Writing and to the Understanding of Human Motives*. New York: Simon and Schuster, 1942.

Emmerich, Roland. *The Day After Tomorrow*. USA: Twentieth Century Fox, 2004.

Epstein, Jason. *Book Business: Publishing Past, Present, and Future*. New York: W. W. Norton & Company, 2001.

Fan, Lixin. *The Last Train Home*. China: Zeitgeist Films, 2009.

Field, Syd. *Screenplay*. New York: Dell, 1982.

Fleischer, Richard. *Soylent Green*. USA: Metro-Goldwyn-Mayer, 1973.

Gardner, Howard. *Multiple Intelligences: The Theory in Practice*. New York: Basic Books, 1983.

Gibson, William. *The Miracle Worker: A Play for Television*. First ed. New York: Knopf, 1957.

———. *The Miracle Worker*. USA: United Artists Corp., 1962.

Graham, Daniel. "Heraclitus." Stanford Encyclopedia of Philosophy, 2015. Accessed July 14, 2017. https://plato.stanford.edu/archives/

fall2015/entries/heraclitus/.

———. "Heraclitus (fl. c. 500 B.C.E.)." Internet Encyclopedia of Philosophy. Accessed July 14, 2017. https://www.iep.utm.edu/heraclit/.

Grebanier, Bernard. *Playwriting: How to Write for the Theatre.* New York: Harper & Row, 1961.

Green, Alexander. "The Opening of the Episode of Finn in Beowulf." Modern Language Association Papers 31, no. 4 (1916): 759–97.

Guthrie, W. K. C. *The Greek Philosophers from Thales to Aristotle.* London: Routledge, 1968.

———. *A History of Greek Philosophy.* Vol. I. Cambridge: University Press, 1962–1981.

Harlow, Harry. "The Nature of Love." American Psychologist 13 (1958): 673–85.

Harrison, James Albert, and Robert Sharp. *I. Beówulf: An Anglo-Saxon Poem—II. The Fight at Finnsburh: A Fragment.* Boston, MA: Ginn, Heath, & Co., 1883.

Harrison, Jane Ellen. *Ancient Art and Ritual.* London: Williams and Norgate, 1913.

Heaney, Seamus. *Beowulf: A New Verse Translation.* First bilingual ed. New York: Farrar, Straus, and Giroux, 2000.

Hegel, Georg Wilhelm Friedrich. *Hegel's Science of Logic.* Muirhead Library of Philosophy. London, New York: Allen & Unwin, 1969.

———. *The Science of Logic.* Translated and edited by George di Giovanni. Cambridge Hegel Translations. Cambridge, MA: Cambridge University Press, 2010.

Heller, Joseph. *Catch-22.* New York: Simon and Schuster, 1961.

Hicks, Scott. *Shine.* USA: Fine Line Features, 1996.

Huston, John. *The Man Who Would Be King.* USA: Allied Artists Pictures Corporation/ Non-USA: Columbia Pictures, 1975.

Huxley, Aldous. *The Perennial Philosophy.* New York: Harper, 1945.

Ibsen, Henrik. *The Doll's House.* Copenhagen, Denmark: Royal Theatre, 1879.

Ibsen, Henrik, and Alyssa Harad. *Four Great Plays.* Enriched Classics ed. New York: Pocket Books, 2005.

Jaworski, A. The Power of Silence: Social and Pragmatic Perspectives (Language and Language Behavior). Newberry Park, CA: Sage Publications, 1993.

Jencks, Charles. *The New Paradigm in Architecture: The Language of Post-Modern Architecture.* Seventh ed. New Haven: Yale University Press, 2002.

Jensen, Derrick. *Walking on Water: Reading, Writing, and Revolution.*

White River Junction, VT: Chelsea Green Publishing, 2004.
Joyce, James. *Finnegans Wake*. London: Faber and Faber, 1939.
Jung, Carl G. *Letters, Vols 1-2*. Bollingen series. Princeton, New Jersey: Princeton University Press, 1973.

———. *The Portable Jung* (Portable Library). Translated by R. F. C. Hull. New York: Penguin Classics, 1976. First published 1971.

———. "The Problem of Evil Today." Chapter 35 in *Meeting the Shadow: The Hidden Power in the Dark Side of Human Nature*. Edited by Connie Zweig and Jeremiah Abrams, 170–73. Los Angeles, CA: Jeremy P. Tarcher, 1991.

Jung, Carl G., and Marie-Louise von Franz. *Man and His Symbols*. Garden City, New York: Doubleday, 1964.
Kafka, Franz. *In Der Strafkolonie* [in German]. Leipzig: Kurt Wolff Verlag, 1919.

———. "The Penal Colony." Partisan Review (March/April 1941): 46–58, 98–107.

Kierkegaard, Søren. *The Present Age*. Translated by Alexander Dru. New York: Harper Torchbooks, 1962.
King, Henry. *The Song of Bernadette*. USA: Twentieth Century Fox, 1943.
Kipling, Rudyard. "The Man Who Would Be King." In *The Phantom 'Rickshaw and other Eerie Tales,* 114. Allahabad, Uttar Pradesh, India: A. H. Wheeler & Co., 1888.

———. "If." *In Rewards and Fairies*. Garden City, New York: Doubleday, Page & Company, 1910.

Kirkland, Jack, and Erskine Caldwell. *Tobacco Road: A Three Act Play*. New York: The Viking Press, 1934.
Kirtlan, Ernest J. B. *The Story of Beowulf: Translated from Anglo-Saxon into Modern English Prose*. New York: Thomas Y. Crowell, 1914.
Koster, Henry. *Harvey*. USA: Universal Pictures, 1950.
Krey, August C. *The First Crusade*. Princeton: Princeton University Press, 1921.
LaFrance, E. D. B. The gifted/dyslexic child: Characterizing and addressing strengths and weaknesses. Annals of Dyslexia, 47, 163-182, 1997.
Lao-Tse. "Tao Te Ching, or the Tao and Its Characteristics." Translated by James Legge. *In Sacred Books of the East*. Oxford: Oxford University Press, 1891.
Lax, Eric. *Woody Allen: A Biography*. New Edition ed. Cambridge, MA: Da Capo Press, 2000.
Levinson, Barry. *Rainman*. USA: United Artists, 1988.

Lloyd, C. A. *We Who Speak English and Our Ignorance of Our Mother Tongue.* New York: Thomas Y. Crowell, 1938.
Lupino, Ida. *The Trouble with Angels.* USA: Columbia Pictures, 1966.
Mann, Michael. *Ali.* USA: Columbia Pictures, 2001.
Marsh, James. *The Theory of Everything.* United Kingdom: Focus Features, 2014.
May, Rollo. The Courage to Create. New York: Norton, 1975. First ed.
Mendes, Sam. *Skyfall.* United Kingdom: Metro-Goldwyn-Mayer (MGM) and Columbia Pictures, 2012.
Munch, Edward. *The Scream.* National Gallery of Oslo, Norway. 1893.
Nietzsche, Friedrich. *Die fröhliche Wissenschaft.* Chemnitz, New York: Ernst Schmeitzner; E. Steige, 1882.
Nolan, Christopher. *Interstellar.* USA: Paramount Pictures, 2014.
Ostafin, B., and K. Kassman, "Stepping Out of History: Mindfulness Improves Insight Problem Solving." Consciousness and Cognition 21, no. 12 (June 21, 2012): 1031–6.
Plato; Jowett, Benjamin; and Campbell, Lewis. *Plato's Republic: The Greek Text.* Three vols. Oxford: Clarendon Press, 1894.
Polti, Georges. *The 36 Dramatic Situations.* Cincinnati, OH: James Knapp Reeve, 1921.
Price, W.T., *The Analysis of Play Construction and Dramatic Principle.* New York: W.T. Price, Publisher, 1908.
Robertsone, O.; Robinson, J. and Stephens, R. "Swearing as a Response to Pain: A Cross-Cultural Comparison of British and Japanese Participants." Scandinavian Journal of Pain 17, no. 1 (October 2017): 267–272.
Rodis, P., Garrod, A., & Boscardin, M. L. *Learning Disabilities and Life stories.* New York: Allyn & Bacon, 2001.
Rowe, Kenneth Thorpe. *Write That Play.* New York and London: Funk & Wagnalls Company, 1939.
Saks, Gene. *The Odd Couple.* USA: Paramount Pictures, 1965.
Sandelands, Lloyd. "The Sense of Society." Journal for the Theory of Social Behaviour 4, no. 24 (1995): 305–38.
Shakespeare, William. *The Works of William Shakespeare.* Edited by William George Clark, William Aldis Wright, John Glover, and John Mounteney Jephson. London and Cambridge: Macmillan and Co., 1866.
Sharrock, Thea. *Me Before You.* UK: Warner Bros. Pictures, 2014.
Shelley, Mary. *Frankenstein*, or the Modern Prometheus. First ed. London: Lackington, Hughes, Harding, Mavor and Jones. Published anonymously in London, 1818.

Sophocles. *Oedipus*. Translated by David Grene. Chicago, IL: University of Chicago Press, 1954.

———. *Oedipus King of Thebes*. Translated by Francis Storr. London: George Allen & Unwin Ltd., 1912.

———. *Sophocles: The Three Theban Plays*. Translated by Robert Fagles. New York: Viking Penguin, 1982.

———. Oedipus Tyrannus. Translated by Luci Berkowitz and Theodore F. Brunner. In *World's Masterpieces*, edited by Maynard Mack, 343–72. New York: W. W. Norton, 1970.

Spielberg, Steven. *Saving Private Ryan*. USA: DreamWorks Pictures, 1998.

Stephens, Richard, J. Atkins, and A. Kingston. "Swearing as a Response to Pain." Neuroreport 10, no. 12 (2009): 1056-60.

Sunnafrank, Michael, and Artemio Rameriz Jr. "At First Sight: Persistent Relational Effects of Get-Acquainted Conversations." Journal of Social and Personal Relationships 1, no. 23 (June 2004): 361–79.

Tokuhama-Espinosa, Tracey. *Mind, Brain, and Education Science*. New York: W. W. Norton, 2010.

Tolkien, J. R. R., and Christopher Tolkien. *Beowulf: A Translation and Commentary, Together with Sellic Spell [and the Lay of Beowulf]*. First US edition. Boston: Houghton Mifflin Harcourt, 2014.

Twain, Mark. *The Wit and Wisdom of Mark Twain: A Book of Quotations*. Dover Thrift Editions. Mineola, NY: Dover Publications, 1999.

van der Kolk, Bessel A. *The Body Keeps the Score: Brain, Mind, and Body in the Healing of Trauma*. Reprint ed. New York: Penguin Group, 2015.

West, Thomas. *In the Mind's Eye*. Buffalo, N.Y.: Prometheus, 1997.

Willis, Janine, and Alexander Todorov. "First impressions: making up your mind after a 100-ms exposure to a face." Psychological Science 17, no. 7 (July 2006): 592–98.

Wilson, August. *Fences*. New York: Plume, 1986.

Wong, Kate. "The 1 Percent Difference: Genome Comparisons Reveal the DNA That Distinguishes Homo sapiens from Its Kin." Scientific American 311, no. 3 (September 2014): 100.

Index

2001, A Space Odyssey, 155
A Beautiful Mind, 159
Abrahamic golden age, 39
adjectives, defining iv
    for hero/antihero, 77-78
    in unity of opposites, 78-81, 83
African American Vernacular English (AAVE), 12, 78
Ali, 82
all hope is lost, 86, 120-122, 140, 144, 149, 150, 162
Anglo-Saxon;
    culture, 195-196;
      language, 47, 55, 59, 195-196
antihero, 67, 76-89, chs 7-9, 138 see also villain and villainy
The Apostle, 154
apotheosis, 138, 141-142
archetypes, iii, vi, 40, 133, 169
Aristotle, vii, 72, 91-92, 100, 119, 120
Arrested Development, 23
art in society, 11, 14-15, 36-39, 131
atonement, 138-145
audience block, 11
Baikal, 5, 6, 9, 11, 23, 71, 74, 77, 78, 103
Bachye, ibn Pekuda, 153
Battle of Hastings, 55, 194
belly of the whale, 138, 140, 144, 149, 150, see also all hope is lost
Beowulf, 59, 66, 69, 76, 82-83, 84, 88, 102, 103, 114, 115, 118-123, 135, 137-138, 156, 161, 167-168, 175, 190 fn, appendix 2
Berlin Wall, 16
Bhagavad Gita, viii
Bite Your Tongue, 12-13, 71, 74, 78, 79, 103

Bloodlines, 7, 11, 23
Bly, Robert, 8
Buddha, 141
call to adventure, 135
call to write, 217
Campbell, Joseph, vi, 26, 40, 129-131, 148, ch 11
Catch-22, 134
cause of the action, 93-94
the challenge, 94, 100-106, 108-111, 114-117, 120
character block, iv
Chang, C.C., 9
Chaplin, Charlie, 15
the climax, 94, 106-111, 122-123
Corbin, Henry, 147
Coleridge, Samuel Taylor, 117
Confucius, viii
core narrative theories, 63-125
Dalberg-Acton, John, 157
Dali, Salvador, 14-15, 17
Dark Ages/Middle Ages, v, 17, 49, 74, see also Medieval era
The Day After Tomorrow, 155
departure, 134-137, 142
destabilizing event/situation, 95, 97-99, 114-116, 135
dialectics, see unity of opposites
Dionysus, 25-26, 177
divine grace, 149, 151, 160
doldrums, 117-119, 144, 212
A Doll's House, see Ibsen
dramatic question, 94, 103-110, 117, see also plot situation
dramatic situation, 67, 69, 80
dyslexia/dyslexics, vii, 30, 32, 33, 48, 51
earthly love, 139
Egri, Lajos, vii, 65, 75-78, 89 fn, 218, 224 also see ch. 8.1
Einstein, Albert, 32, 35-36
elderly/elders, 18, 20-22, 53, 136, 158

elixir of life, 142, 144
emotional thinking/intelligence, 3, 8, 9, 17-19, 26, 29-33, 37-38, 54, 56, 59, 130
Epstein, Jason, 26
façade of character, 84, 65, 78
Field, Syd, vii, 113-115, 116, 120
filler words, 54-57, 59
Flatland, 35
four pillars of the grammar, iv
The Frailling, 48
Frankenstein, 14, 155
Freud, viii
Friends, 22
Gandhi, 141, 152, 153, 160
Gnostic Gospels, viii
Goldberg, Natalie, vii
Grebanier, Bernard, 91-95
Greek, see language
Greeks, Ancient, iv-v, vii, 25-26, 39, 47, 73, 82, 130, 177
Grendel, 82, 102, 103, 115, 118, 119, 121, 122, 156, 167, 190 fn, appendix 2
guardians, mythological, 137, 151
Hamlet, 10, 66, 69, 77, 83, 84, 87, 88, 95-97, 103, 106-108, 110, 115-116, 118, 120-123, 135, 140, 151, 157, 161, 175, 177, appendix 3
Harlow, Harry, 20
Hegel, viii, 49
Harvey, 151, 152
heavenly union, 138-139, 141-142
Heraclitus, 40, 65, 71-76, 83, 143, 167
hero, adjective choice for, iv, 87-91,
  façade of, 65, 78,
  in postmodernity, 23
  in plot situation, 68-69
  internal conflict of, 96-99
  labels for, 77
  transformation of, 82-84
hero-villain theory of convergence, 82-84

Hillary, Edmund, 27-28
Hrothgar, 102, 103, 121, 138, 156, 167, 197-199
Huxley, Aldous, 36, 131, ch. 12
Ibsen, Henrik, 17-19, 87
Information Age, see postmodernity
initiation, 134, 137-142, internal conflict of, 96-99
Interstellar, 155
intuition/intuitive thinking, 3, 8, 15, 17, 29-30, 33-38, 74, 83, 125, 133, 148
It's a Wonderful Life, 151
Jesus, 141, 152
Jung, C.G., iii, vii-viii, 3, 11, 26, 35-36, 40, 71, 88 fn, 130, 133
Kafka, Franz, 14-15
Kentucky, 6, 18, 19, 53, 91
Kierkegaard, Søren, viii, 39-40, 157
King Arthur, 168
Kipling, Rudyard, 154, 157, 163
Lamont, Anne, vii
language, chs 5-6
  Anglo-Saxon, 47, 55, 59, 195-196
  English, written form, 47-48, 50,
  filler words, 54-57, 59
  Greek, 47
  Latin, 47, 55, 89 fn
  Middle English, 59
  nonverbal/paralanguage, 45, 54, 56, 57
  parasite words, 56
  profanity, 53-56, 59
Last Train Home, 18
Latin, see language
learning disability, see dyslexia
logic/logical/rationalism, 3, 8-9, 13-15, 17, 29-33, 36-39, 40, 55, 59, 72-73, 91-93, 129, 133-134, 143, 147-148, 156
logos, 73, 148, 149, 171
Lupino, Ida, 142
The Man Who Would Be King, 154, 157

Mandela, Nelson, 78, 142, 152-153
masque, 81, 85-87
May, Rollo, 11, 36
Me Before You, 159
Middle Ages/Medieval era, v, 13, 15, 25, 130, 137, see also Dark Ages
meeting with the goddess, see heavenly union
Middle English, see language
midpoint reversal of fortunes, 119-120
Million Dollar Baby, 159
the miracle, 122-123
The Miracle Worker, 66, 69, 77, 81-82, 84-85, 87-88, 98-99, 101, 105, 107, 109-110, 120-122, 135-136, 138-139, 157, 160-161
Modern Times, 15
modernity, 13-19, 26, 129, 132, 134, 155, 171
Muhammad, 141, 152
Munch, Edward, see *The Scream*
mystical realm, 28, 130
mythological call, 25-28, 131-132
mythology, iv, 40, 122, 125, 129, 131, 133, 171, see ch. 11 and 12
mythopoetic, iv
Nietzsche, Friedrich, 129
nonverbal, 45, 56, 57
Norgay, Tenzing, 27-28
The Odd Couple, 76, 79
Oedipus, 10, 66, 76, 79, 83-84, 88, 102, 114-115, 118-119, 122, 135-137, 139, 151, 153, 156, 161, 175, appendix 1, 208 fn
Old English, see Language, Anglo-Saxon
paralanguage, 54, 56, 57
parasite words, 56
Perennial Philosophy, 131, 147-164
The Persistence of Memory, 14, 17
personal call, iii, 3-11, 13, 26, 83, 117-118
philosophy, 38-39, 71-75, 104, 122, 125, 129-131, see also Perennial Philosophy
Plato, 72
plot points, 113, 116, 120
plot situation/dramatic situation, 65, 67-70, 80
point of no return, 116-117, 119-122, 144
Polti, Georges, 65, 67
postmodernity, 13, 15-23, 26, 96, 156, 195
premise (Aristotle), 92-93
Price, Edward T., vii, 66, 91, 93-96
Price-Grebanier Proposition, 95
profanity, see language
proposition, 91, 93-95, 101, 104, 105, 108-111, 131
Pruitt-Igoe project, 16-17
pseudo tribes, 22
psychology, 3, 37
Race For Everest, 27
Rainman, 66, 69, 77, 79, 82, 84, 88, 97, 98, 100, 104-105, 107-109, 114, 120-121, 123, 135-136, 140, 143, 150-151, 157, 160
rationalism, see logic
Renaissance, 39
resolution, 97- 99
Rico, Gabriele Lussar, vii
return, 142-144
reversal of fortune, see midpoint reversal of fortunes
May, Rollo, 11, 36
Romeo and Juliet, 93, 94
Saving Private Ryan, 79, 87
The Scream, 14
Seinfeld, 22
setup, 113
Shakespeare, 10, 39, 51, 52, 59, 95, 97, 110, 118, 123, 175, 194, 209, 212, 215 fn- 216 fn,
Shine, 159

Skyfall, 22
social call, xi, 3, ch 2, 26
Socrates, 27, 38, 85, 92
The Song of Bernadette, 153
Sophocles, 10, 38, 114, 177, 191, 218
Soylent Green, 155
Spinoza, viii
the stakes, 97-99, 115
state of affairs, 94-101, 104-106, 114-117, 135
stereotypes, 84, 88
story chemistry, 91-111
Sully, 17
syllogism, 91-93
synchronicity, 35-36
Tao Te Ching, viii
technology, 15, 18, 34, 156, 158
ten-percent mark, 114-115
Tevin, 6-9, 11, 23
The Theory of Everything, 158
third character, 78, 82, 106-108, 122
timing, v, 113-123
To Walk in the Sun, 34
Tobacco Road, 135
Tolkien, 168, 195, 207-208 fn
Transparent, 23
Trouble with Angels, 142, 154
unity of opposites, ch 8, 71-90, 95-99, 104, 110, 114-115, 131
villain/villainy, 7, 8-10, 65, 76, 82-88, 96, 110, 120, 143, 149, 151
William the Conqueror, 55
Wilson, August, 12
writer's block, 7, 11, 103, 212
Yamasaki, Minoru, 17

©Getty Images

www.ingramcontent.com/pod-product-compliance
Lightning Source LLC
Chambersburg PA
CBHW052053110526
44591CB00013B/2198